SEXUAL RIGHTS IN AMERICA

PAUL R. ABRAMSON
STEVEN D. PINKERTON
MARK HUPPIN

SEXUAL RIGHTS
IN AMERICA

*The Ninth Amendment
and the Pursuit of Happiness*

New York University Press • *New York and London*

NEW YORK UNIVERSITY PRESS
New York and London

Library of Congress Cataloging-in-Publication Data
Abramson, Paul R.
Sexual rights in America : the Ninth Amendment and the pursuit of happiness / Paul R.
Abramson, Steven D. Pinkerton, and Mark Huppin.
p. cm.
Includes bibliographical references.
ISBN 0-8147-0692-4 (cloth : alk. paper)
1. Sex and law—United States.   2. United States. Constitution. 9th Amendment.   I.
Pinkerton, Steven D.   II. Huppin, Mark.   III. Title.
KF9325.A93   2003
342.73'085—dc21   2003000531

New York University Press books are printed on acid-free paper,
and their binding materials are chosen for strength and durability.

Manufactured in the United States of America

10   9   8   7   6   5   4   3   2   1

Contents

I

Sex and the Constitution

THE FREEDOMS OF SPEECH AND PRESS are trumpeted through-out the land. These rights are fundamental, we are told, because they form the foundations of democracy. They are so important, in fact, that they are guaranteed by the First Amendment to the United States Constitution.

But what about other forms of expression, such as sexual intimacy? Are Americans free to express themselves sexually? Specifically, are sexual rights protected by the Constitution?

If sexual freedoms do exist in the Constitution, they certainly are not explicit. Perhaps this was intentional—as though sex didn't belong in such rarefied company as the freedoms of speech and the press, or protection against self-incrimination.

Yet, without sex, the human race cannot endure. The survival of the United States, in particular, depends upon sex. Thus, in the grand scheme of things, sex matters—certainly as much as speech and press. Moreover, ours is a nation conceived upon the "self-evident" truth that all men (and women) have a fundamental right to the pursuit of happiness. The pursuit of sexual fulfillment, we will argue, is integral to the overall happiness and well-being of the American populace.

But if sex is so important, why can't we locate it in the Constitution? The problem, we believe, is not that sex is absent from the Constitution, but rather that it is hidden away, subsumed by the most misunderstood of the ten amendments that make up the Bill of Rights—namely, the Ninth Amendment.

The purpose of this book is to establish a vital and functional constitutional foundation for sexual rights in America, based on the Ninth Amendment. This historically neglected amendment states that "The enumeration in the Constitution, of certain rights, shall not be construed to deny or disparage others retained by the people."

The first eight amendments of the Bill of Rights, appended to the newly fashioned Constitution in 1791, guarantee all Americans specific rights, such as the freedom of speech, the right to assemble, religious freedoms, and the right to a speedy and impartial trial by jury in criminal prosecutions. Recognizing the incompleteness of this enumeration, the framers of the Constitution crafted the Ninth Amendment to protect those rights—whether potential or extant—not captured by the delineation of the first eight amendments.[1] The Ninth Amendment is thus an explicit acknowledgment that the Bill of Rights does not, and cannot, comprehensively encompass all foreseeable fundamental rights.

The Bill of Rights comprises ten amendments, each of which, presumably, is of substantial import. Yet, prior to the landmark 1965 contraceptive rights case, *Griswold v. Connecticut*, the Ninth Amendment had been cited in only a handful of Supreme Court opinions and had never—*Griswold* notwithstanding—been the basis of a Supreme Court decision.[2] Far from moribund, however, the Ninth Amendment is now more vital than ever.[3] As the guardian of fundamental rights unanticipated or underappreciated two centuries past, the Ninth Amendment transforms the Constitution from a static record of our forebears' political and moral understandings into a dynamic and evolving expression of our basic rights as women and men. In this book we argue that the freedom of sexual expression merits inclusion within the Ninth Amendment's framework of protected rights. Americans have a fundamental, "natural" right to make reproductive decisions, including the decision *not* to reproduce. They should be free to choose with whom they have sex, how they have sex, and under what circumstances they have sex. This freedom, we assert, is guaranteed by the Ninth Amendment of the Constitution.

This introductory chapter provides an overview of *Sexual Rights in America*. In it, we outline and highlight some of the main themes of the book. These themes include the historical foundations of our contention that sexual rights should be counted among the unenumerated rights protected by the Ninth Amendment, the inadequacy of protections based on ill-formulated notions of privacy, and the need to delimit sexual freedoms—just as all fundamental freedoms must be delimited—to ensure that one person's expression of his or her sexual rights does not encroach upon the fundamental rights of others.

We begin this chapter by recounting stories, rumors, and innuendo about the sex lives of the founding fathers. The fascinating and sometimes risqué personal histories of the men who shaped this country remind us that they were sexual beings, and not, as they often are characterized, a heavenly body of men void of the usual distractions of spirit and flesh. Although sex may not have been foremost in the minds of the constitutional delegates as they attempted to create a federal government, resolve the controversies surrounding states' rights, and navigate the aftermath of the Revolutionary War, it probably was never *that* far from their thoughts, if the historical accounts of their sexual escapades are any indication.

THE PHILANDERING FATHERS

It has become routine—and surprisingly banal—to uncover the sexual transgressions of twentieth-century American presidents, from John Fitzgerald Kennedy's numerous dalliances and Jimmy Carter's lusting in his heart, to the most recent and celebrated scandal, Bill Clinton's illicit affair with his intern, Monica Lewinsky. Although the phenomenal publicity surrounding our presidents' sexual misadventures is thoroughly modern, Bill Clinton was hardly the first great American to get caught with his pants down. The most prominent signer of the Declaration of Independence, John Hancock, maintained a mistress, as did many influential men of the day. The president of Harvard, Reverend Samuel Locke, was dismissed from office in 1773 after impregnating his housekeeper.[4] Thomas Jefferson and Benjamin Franklin both had children outside of marriage. And so on.

One of the most notorious incidents of sexual indiscretion involved Alexander Hamilton, an important figure in constitutional history. Hamilton was Secretary of the Treasury at the time, and a debonair—but very married—man of thirty. According to Hamilton's own account, during the summer of 1791, an attractive young lady presented herself at his home in Philadelphia. Mrs. Maria Reynolds, who claimed to be a member of a prominent New York family, related to Hamilton a sad tale of physical abuse and recent abandonment by her husband James.[5] Needing money to return to her family in New York, she asked Hamilton for a small loan. Hamilton was sympathetic and agreed to lend her the money. He promised he would deliver it to her that evening.

As it turned out, he delivered more than money. According to Hamilton, "some conversation ensued from which it was quickly apparent that other than pecuniary consolation would be acceptable."[6] The trap was set. Hamilton devoured the bait, repeatedly, over the course of the next several months, beginning a long-running sexual affair with Missus Reynolds. But then, in December of 1791, *Mister* Reynolds appeared, seeking restitution for Hamilton's "insult." In an earnest though semiliterate letter, Reynolds accused Hamilton of taking advantage of a "poor Broken harted woman. instead of being a Friend. you have acted the part of the most Cruelist man in existence. You have made a whole family miserable."[7]

Four days later, Hamilton received another letter from James Reynolds. The tone was similar to the first letter, but the intent was obviously different. Here's the punch line: "God knows I love the woman and wish every blessing may attend her. [But] I Don't think I can be Reconciled to live with her. when I know I hant her love . . . give me the Sum Of thousand dollars. . . . I will leve town . . . and leve her to Yourself."[8] Hamilton had been scammed!

Although one might expect Hamilton to put an end to the affair once the blackmail had commenced, in fact, he did quite the opposite. He thereafter *paid* for the privilege of the affair, in amounts ranging from $40 to $400, depending upon the negotiations between himself and Mr. Reynolds, who apparently did not "leve town."

Eventually, Hamilton found that he could no longer afford to support his own family *and* the Reynoldses, so he terminated the relationship. His problems, however, had just begun. As it turned out, soon thereafter Mr. Reynolds was arrested on an unrelated matter. Upon his arrest, Reynolds claimed to have evidence, including financial receipts, that proved Hamilton had defrauded the government.

Hamilton's political enemies were quick to exploit this "evidence," but congressional investigations ultimately concluded that the blackmail payments had nothing to do with governmental fraud. Even though Hamilton was officially exonerated of governmental improprieties, he still felt the need to publish a ninety-five-page confession of his affair. He was determined to wipe out any doubts about the reason for his payments to Mrs. Reynolds's husband. Hamilton concluded his confession with the hope that "bare perusal of the letters from Reynolds and his wife is sufficient to convince my greatest enemy that there is nothing worse in the affair than an irregular and indelicate amour."[9]

Hamilton's phraseology is instructive: his relationship with Mrs. Reynolds was "an irregular and indelicate amour." These words are hardly a remorseful admission of sexual impropriety. They suggest, instead, that he felt only that he had behaved somewhat indiscreetly. His motives and post-hoc rationalizations are telling indications of the contemporary sexual morality. Apparently, Hamilton believed that his *choice* to have an affair was a moral issue, in which the government had no standing. Although Hamilton's financial records were closely scrutinized, once the extramarital affair was corroborated, the matter was dropped. He was never prosecuted for fornication or soliciting prostitution, despite his admission of guilt.

Few men can lay claim to as varied and distinguished a litany of accomplishments as Benjamin Franklin. Franklin was a successful businessman; author of the revered *Poor Richard's Almanac*; a renowned scientist (he was a fellow of the Royal Society in London and developed a comprehensive theory of electricity); and an accomplished inventor (he is credited with inventing the lightning rod and the fireplace stove). According to David Hume, Franklin was the first great American man of letters. He was also America's first great statesman, serving as the American representative to both London and Paris, and the only person to sign all three essential founding documents: the Declaration of Independence (1776), the Treaty of Paris (1783), and the U.S. Constitution (1787).

Franklin's sexual exploits are no less impressive: he consorted with prostitutes and had affairs with unmarried women, fathered a child out of wedlock, and produced one of America's first pornographic works.

Franklin's first child, William, was born in either 1728 or 1729. Franklin was not married at the time, nor was he involved in a traditional romantic relationship. Rather, William was the product of Franklin's illicit affair with a prostitute. As A. Own Aldridge relates:

> Franklin, who had an illegitimate son from a prostitute, quietly accepted the situation and recognized the offspring, who eventually became the royal governor of New Jersey. The latter had an illegitimate

son of his own, whom Franklin in turn welcomed into the family; educated, and launched upon a respected career.[10]

An isolated indelicacy might be treated as an aberration. But there is ample evidence that Franklin was a strong proponent of sexual liberties, at least for himself. According to Aldridge, Franklin "thoroughly enjoyed wine, women, and song. . . . [Furthermore] Franklin's imagination . . . gave free rein to his sexual fantasies, and this can be documented."[11] Franklin himself worried that his frequent "Intrigues with low women" might have endangered his health.[12]

Franklin allegedly was the first American to own a copy of John Cleland's *Fanny Hill; or the Memoirs of a Woman of Pleasure* (a "lively piece of cheerful and literate hardcore pornography," according to English historian Lawrence Stone[13]). Moreover, he was widely known as the author of *Advice to a Young Man on the Choice of a Mistress*, which Aldridge called "the first indigenous work circulated as pornography."[14] (In this pamphlet, Franklin advised young men to consider the charms of older mistresses, because "they are more discreet in conducting an affair."[15] Perhaps Hamilton should have heeded this advice.)

Franklin's promiscuity was widely recognized, and possibly even exaggerated, particularly by his critics. In the *Memoirs of the Late Dr. Benjamin Franklin*, Andrew Allen and James Jones Wilmer claimed: "It is well known, he had mistresses plenty; and there are several living testimonies of his licentious amours."[16]

From Franklin's reputation we can infer that he was pure neither of thought nor of action. Franklin was an exceptional man, in both his public and his private lives. The critical question is whether the Constitution—and the Ninth Amendment in particular—was fashioned so as to protect the kinds of choices Franklin made, and the opinions he proffered. Given his prominence, it is hard to imagine the Constitution neglecting the rights of so great a man as Benjamin Franklin.

Thomas Jefferson presents another fascinating study in moral decision making. Perhaps the foremost libertarian of his day, Jefferson was also a full participant in the business of slavery. He inherited, purchased, and sold slaves. Furthermore, it appears that he was sexually involved with one of his slaves, a young lady named Sally Hemings. The available evidence suggests that Jefferson pursued an intimate long-term relationship with Hemings, and fathered six of her children.[17]

According to popular accounts, Jefferson's affair with Hemings blossomed in Paris, where Jefferson was serving as America's Minister to France.[18] Hemings had accompanied Jefferson's young daughter across the Atlantic at Jefferson's behest. At the time, Hemings was somewhere between fifteen and eighteen years of age, while Jefferson, a widower, was in his early to mid-forties.

A beautiful young lady of racially mixed parentage (her father and her maternal grandfather were white), Hemings must have made a striking impression in Europe. When it came time for Jefferson to return to America, Hemings wished to stay behind in Paris. Sally's son Madison later recalled:

> During that time my mother became Mr. Jefferson's concubine, and when he was called back home she was [pregnant] by him. He desired to bring my mother back to Virginia with him but she demurred. She was just beginning to understand the French language well, and in France she was free, while if she returned to Virginia she would be re-slaved. So she refused to return with him. To induce her to do so he promised her extraordinary privileges, and made a solemn pledge that her children should be freed at the age of twenty one years.[19]

Our objective in relating these examples of the founding fathers' sexual improprieties is not to condemn Hamilton, Franklin, or Jefferson, but to understand the choices they made and to shed some light on the variability of the moral climate of the times. The Hamilton-Reynolds affair illustrates that, in 1791, at least one prominent man exercised his right to regulate his own sexual behavior, in this case choosing an adulterous affair verging on prostitution. Although Hamilton was one of the principal architects of the Constitution, he was a vehement opponent of those who argued for appending a bill of rights to this document. A bill of rights was unnecessary, he believed, because the Constitution granted the federal government only limited powers. Did those powers include regulating the sexual behavior of consenting adults? It is hard to imagine a man who engaged in an "indelicate amour" believing that the federal (or state) government had the power to regulate citizens' private sexual decisions. Acting according to his own conscience in sexual matters appears to be a right that Hamilton himself chose to exercise.

Similarly, guided by *his* conscience, a forty-something Jefferson initiated a sexual relationship with his slave, a girl in her late teens. Though the circumstances were unique, the choice itself was not exceptional. Many American men chose to have sex with their slaves, often forcibly. They made such choices based upon their prerogatives as slave owners. This was a barbaric sexual choice to say the least, but it prevailed in the pre- and postrevolutionary periods for an obvious reason—the institution of slavery offered the potential of unlimited sexual access. Owners could demand whatever they wanted of slaves, including sex. Although retaliation in one form or another—refusing to work, family disruptions, or even violence—were distinct possibilities, the law was on the side of the slave owners—slavery and the sexual abuses it sanctioned were not crimes.[20]

Jefferson's affair with Hemings was not typical of master-slave relationships, of course. Not only was Hemings a free woman (in France, anyway); it appears that the attractions and affections were mutual.[21] Be that as it may, the facts remain. First, an innate power imbalance existed between the older Jefferson and the teenaged Hemings. Second, Hemings was a slave, and when she returned to America she once again became Jefferson's "property." And finally, by having sex with Hemings, Jefferson was guilty of fornication, at least in the Biblical sense. Nevertheless, Jefferson's moral conscience was able to reconcile these facts with his desires, and he maintained the relationship for many years.

Obviously, even in the late 1700s, there was considerable latitude for individual sexual decision making.[22] While Jefferson and slave owners throughout the southern states were exercising (or abusing) their prerogative to fornicate with their charges, Hamilton was exercising *his* right to engage in an adulterous affair, and Ben Franklin was busy musing on qualities of the ideal mistress. Apparently, the prerogative to make basic sexual and reproductive decisions was taken for granted, provided no laws were broken—and maybe even if they were. Many contemporaries condemned Hamilton as immoral, but few questioned his *right* to make his own decisions. (Samuel Adams was candid in his distaste for Hamilton, calling him a "proud-spirited, conceited, aspiring mortal . . . with as debauched morals as old Franklin.")[23]

James Madison, the principal architect of the Bill of Rights, escaped the public scrutiny experienced by Hamilton, Franklin, and Jefferson. His sexual morality was never an issue. Quite the opposite. The concern for

Madison was not wanton sexuality, but sexual infertility. The "father" of the Bill of Rights was a bachelor throughout the entire time he was fashioning the Constitution, thereby eschewing the prevailing ideal of "marriage and family." Eventually, at the age of forty-three, Madison married a twenty-six-year-old widow, Dolly. But the marriage was infertile. We can only speculate as to the cause, but at least three possibilities suggest themselves: the marriage was never consummated; the couple was sexually active, but James Madison was infertile (Dolly had a son from her previous marriage); or the couple practiced a rudimentary form of contraception, such as coitus interruptus.[24] Whatever the reason, Dolly and James Madison never conceived a child; thus the physical intimacy they shared had a different consequence, if not a different intent, than dictated by the "marriage and family" ideal.

The vigorous sexuality of founding fathers such as Hamilton, Jefferson, and Franklin is not reflected in the text of the Constitution, which omits any mention of sexual rights. This is not surprising. The Constitution did not have to spell out the right to have sex because, we believe, this right is transparent. All people have a fundamental, *natural* right to express themselves sexually.

The history of the Ninth Amendment (summarized in chapter 2) indicates that it was intended to safeguard from unwarranted governmental intrusion those basic rights of humanity that, according to John Adams, were "antecedent to all earthly government; rights that cannot be repealed or restrained by human laws; rights derived from the Great Legislator of the Universe."[25] The right to sexual expression and sexual self-determination, we maintain, is one such right. Sex is such an elementary and essential human activity that it ultimately would be ludicrous, as well as indiscreet, explicitly to proclaim private sexual rights in a public document like the Constitution. Instead, this essential right is simply "retained by the people."

SEXUAL RIGHTS

What, specifically, do we mean by "sexual rights," and why should they be protected by the Constitution? We begin by noting that Americans have a basic right to make reproductive decisions. The freedom to choose whether and when to have children, both within and without a marital relationship, is a basic human liberty, recognized throughout most of the world (tellingly, this is one of the freedoms wrested away from the citizenry in the authoritarian society described in Aldous Huxley's *Brave New World*).[26] Historically, reproduction has been central to familial prosperity, though it probably is less so today. Moreover, throughout the centuries, raising a family has been an important facet of the pursuit of happiness for many Americans.

Sexual reproduction is a primordial biological function and, as the foundation of evolution by natural selection, is responsible for the existence of intelligent minds capable of authoring the Constitution (or reading this book). Biologically speaking, the right to reproduce most assuredly ranks with the right to eat and sustain one's life as among the most fundamental. There is no evidence that the framers of the Constitution, or any other early Americans, favored relinquishing this right into the hands of government. Rather, as we discuss in chapter 4, the right to make reproductive decisions appears to be reserved by the people. This necessarily includes the right to have sex (which is essential for reproduction) as well as the right *not* to reproduce.

Having a child is an extraordinary responsibility. It requires substantial resources, perhaps the least of which are financial. Although money is certainly necessary for ensuring the welfare of children, the most significant expenditures are time, effort, and commitment. Children require a lifetime of devoted attention, without which they cannot thrive. Consequently, not everyone wants to have or raise a child. The responsibilities are daunting, and childbearing is not without physical and emotional risks. Some people choose not to have children for lifestyle or vocational reasons. Priests and nuns fall into this category, as do many gays and lesbians. These people are all exercising their right not to reproduce.

The decision not to reproduce is no less fundamental than the decision to reproduce or to engage in reproductive sexual activities. Without this symmetry, there is no choice. Decisions about whether and when to have children—and how many—are essential elements of the right to make reproductive choices. The right to make reproductive choices, of course, also includes the ability to make decisions of conscience with regard to contraception and abortion, thereby altering the odds of reproduction.

Choosing to delay reproduction is another form of sexual decision making, perhaps the most pervasive of all. The onset of sexual activity, at least in Western countries, usually precedes childbirth by several years. College students often wait longer before having a first child, and professional women sometimes wait twenty years (presuming initiation of sexual intercourse at eighteen and the birth of the first child at thirty-eight). Thus, in the United States alone, there are millions of women actively preventing conception without sacrificing their right eventually to reproduce.

We have argued elsewhere that long ago, deep in our evolutionary past, human sexuality bifurcated into pleasurable and reproductive functions.[27] Humans pursue myriad forms of sex, mainly to enjoy the attendant pleasures. Very little of this sexual activity is undertaken for the express purpose of procreation. Indeed, the possibility of conception often is viewed as a *risk* to be strenuously guarded against. The widespread use of contraceptives (e.g., condoms, birth control pills, etc.) testifies to the true intent of the greater part of contemporary sexual expression—namely, to enjoy the pleasures of the sexual experience without conceiving a child.

Contraception is not the only way to reduce the risk of pregnancy. Far more effective methods are available in the form of nonreproductive sexual activities. Oral and anal sex, for example, are inherently nonreproductive and often serve as substitutes for vaginal intercourse, particularly among teenagers. Similarly, vaginal intercourse without ejaculation (or ejaculation outside of the vagina) is meant to avoid conception, although it sometimes is spectacularly unsuccessful. Homosexual behavior (i.e., sex with a same-gendered partner) ultimately serves the same purpose, since there is *no* risk of pregnancy from these activities.

The Supreme Court has repeatedly acknowledged the centrality of reproduction in American life: "It is the right of the individual, married or single, to be free of unwarranted governmental intrusion into matters so fundamentally affecting a person as the decision whether to bear or beget a child."[28] One of the most important of these Supreme Court decisions, and certainly the most relevant to the present book, is the 1965 decision in *Griswold v. Connecticut*.[29] This case concerned the right of married couples to limit family size through contraception, which at the time was forbidden under Connecticut state law. The majority opinion by Justice William Douglas stressed the sanctity of the marital relationship and argued for the right of married couples to make private decisions about their reproductive futures. However, it is Justice Arthur Goldberg's concurring opinion that interests us most. In his written opinion, Justice Goldberg rescued the Ninth Amendment from nearly two centuries of obscurity and disuse, ultimately concluding that "the right to privacy in the marital relation is fundamental and basic—a personal right 'retained by the people' within the meaning of the Ninth Amendment."[30]

In marked contrast to the right to make reproductive decisions, there is no fundamental right to make elemental choices regarding one's *nonreproductive* sexual expression. Justice Byron White's majority opinion in *Bowers v. Hardwick* states unequivocally that the "proposition that any kind of private sexual conduct between consenting adults is constitutionally insulated from state proscription is unsupportable."[31] Chief Justice Warren Burger concurred, addressing the specifics of the *Bowers* case: "To hold that the act of homosexual sodomy is somehow protected as a fundamental right would be to cast aside millennia of moral teaching."[32]

The nonreproductive acts of oral sex (fellatio and cunnilingus) and anal intercourse enjoy considerable popularity in contemporary America.[33] Despite the ubiquity of these activities, they are illegal in many of the fifty states under extant "sodomy" laws (though the laws in question are seldom enforced). Utah's penal code, for example, states: "It is a misdemeanor called sodomy to engage in any sexual act involving the genitals of one person and the mouth or anus of another."[34] These laws, which derive from precedents in English common and church law,[35] attempt to force a reproductive sexual ideal on the American people, and especially to discourage homosexuality. Notably, several states specifically restrict the definition of sodomy to male-male or female-female sex (e.g., Tennessee: "It is a misdemeanor to engage in consensual sexual penetration with a person of the same gender").[36]

Because the government cannot legislate sexual orientation/preference, it has focused on behavior (hence: "don't ask/don't tell"). Nonreproductive acts such as oral sex and anal sex—especially anal sex—are targeted by sodomy laws despite the fact that both heterosexuals and homosexuals can engage in these acts. Although oral sex is now a ubiquitous feature of the American sexual landscape, there was a time when it was decidedly exceptional. Therefore, outlawing sodomy had the desired effect of criminalizing homosexual behavior and other nonnormative sexual activities without encroaching too severely on the sex lives of "proper" heterosexuals.

But the sexual landscape had changed by the 1980s, when the famous case of *Bowers v. Hardwick* was argued before the Supreme Court. Oral sex (with another man), the crime committed by Michael Hardwick under Georgia's arcane prohibition against sodomy, was no longer taboo. Likewise, anal sex had lost much of its stigma, becoming exotic rather than perverse. Yet, in his defense of Georgia's sodomy laws, Justice Byron White fell back upon historical precedence. As he factually noted: "Proscriptions against that conduct [sodomy] have ancient roots. . . . Sodomy was a criminal offense at common law and was forbidden by the laws of the original 13 States when they ratified the Bill of Rights."[37]

Nevertheless, the long judicial history and stubborn persistence of sodomy laws cannot be adduced to defend restricting sexual behavior to heterosexual intercourse. History was made to be rewritten based on lessons learned from the past. The founding of our great nation was a revisionist act *par excellence.* Quoting Madison:

> The glory of the people of America [is] that whilst they have paid a decent regard to the opinions of former times and other nations, they have not suffered a blind veneration for antiquity, for customs, or for names, to override the suggestions of their own good sense, the knowledge of their own situation, and the lessons of their own experience.[38]

Indeed, in 1967's *Loving v. Virginia,*[39] the Supreme Court struck down a law prohibiting interracial marriage *despite* the fact that the statute had "long historical roots."[40] Marriage is nowhere mentioned in the Bill of Rights and interracial marriage was illegal in most States in the nineteenth century, but the Court was no doubt correct in finding it to be an aspect of liberty protected against state interference by the substantive component of the Due Process Clause.[41] As the majority opinion in *Planned Parenthood of Southeastern Pennsylvania v. Casey* reaffirmed, "It is a promise of the Constitution that there is a realm of personal liberty which the government may not enter."[42]

There obviously are many longstanding religious and social prejudices condemning homosexual behavior—and interracial marriage, for that matter—that are best eliminated. Religious prejudice of any kind, including sexual prejudice in its various guises, has no place in our system of laws. Government cannot punish private behavior simply because it incurs religious hostility or contradicts the prevailing moral code. Madison recognized the threat that public morality or sentiment posed to the democratic principles enshrined in the Constitution: "I confess that I do conceive, that in a Government modified like this of the United States, the great danger lies . . . in the body of the people, operating by the majority against the minority."[43]

We believe it is time to take Madison's warning seriously and to address the sexual prejudices that pervade our legal and judicial systems. Despite the putative separation of church and state mandated in the First Amendment, the United States of America was founded as a Christian nation. Our legal biases reflect this heritage, particularly with regard to restrictions on sexual freedom. These restrictions include prohibitions on the types of sexual activities in which consenting adults may engage (sodomy laws); limitations on the content of sexually explicit materials available to the American populace ("pornography"), so as to discourage the supposedly heinous and unnatural practice of masturbation; and restrictions on the circumstances surrounding sexual expression, such as laws prohibiting the exchange of sex for money or other remuneration (prostitution) and public performances of a sexual nature (e.g., topless and nude dancing). Absent a compelling public interest in regulating these activities, the residuum is simply prejudice, borne of and sustained by our Christian moral heritage.

PROTECTING OUR SEXUAL RIGHTS

With no mention of sexual rights in the first eight amendments of the Bill of Rights, and an unwillingness to take the Ninth Amendment's unenumerated rights seriously,[44] commentators and litigants have been forced to look elsewhere for protection of sexual freedoms. What little constitutional standing sexual rights have attained arises mainly from the Supreme Court's construction of "privacy" as operationalized in *Griswold v. Connecticut*. As discussed above, the majority opinion in *Griswold* asserted the sanctity of the marital bedroom as the context for making "private" reproductive choices.[45] This "privacy" right underlies many subsequent sex-related Supreme Court decisions, ranging from abortion (*Roe v. Wade*),[46] in which privacy rights were upheld, to sodomy (*Bowers*),[47] in which they were denied.

In chapter 3 we address the critical question of whether the concept of privacy is relevant, or robust enough, to serve as an overarching, organizing principle for sexual rights—or conversely, for the legal regulation of human sexual behavior. As constructed from *Griswold*, privacy is textually nonexplicit and lacks a solid foundation in the Constitution.[48] Supreme Court justices have discovered privacy rights in the Fourth, Fifth, and Fourteenth Amendments, as well as in multiple "penumbras" arising from various provisions of the Constitution. Although Justice Goldberg resurrected the Ninth Amendment's "rights retained by the people" in *Griswold*,[49] the majority opinion largely ignored this amendment. Moreover, subsequent cases have not relied on the Ninth Amendment for constitutional support of privacy rights.

As a whole, Supreme Court sexual privacy cases suffer from conceptual incoherence. Privacy has been extended to women wishing to terminate pregnancies, but not to same-gendered lovers in their own homes. This inconsistency, we believe, is the result of a reproductive bias in the Court's construction of the concept of privacy—specifically, privacy appears only to protect reproductively-oriented sexual acts. The choice *not* to reproduce is but haphazardly protected by the privacy right, and the right to engage in inherently nonreproductive acts is not guaranteed at all.

Moreover, privacy is a stingy right. The concept of privacy delineated in *Griswold* was restricted to reproductive decisions made within a marital context. Although the privacy protections of *Griswold* were subsequently expanded to nonmarital relationships (in the 1972 *Eisenstadt v. Baird* decision),[50] the Court's reproductive focus has remained intact. As a consequence of this focus on reproduction, privacy protections have been limited to particular, mainly heterosexual, sex acts. For example, the Court's decision in *Bowers*—which as noted above involved consensual sex between two men—set a clear boundary on the protection of sexual practices, particularly those lacking reproductive potential. In short, the ill-defined notion of privacy developed in *Griswold* and subsequent cases is simply not broad enough to form a secure foundation for sexual rights. Indeed, the ubiquity of nonreproductive behaviors such as oral-genital sex and masturbation lends credence to the belief that many sex laws were made to be broken.

THE RIGHT TO SEXUAL EXPRESSION

The Court's reluctance to extend privacy protections to consensual sex between men (e.g., *Bowers*), or to nonreproductive sex more generally, highlights the critical weakness of this construct as a foundation for fundamental sexual rights. Sexual privacy has been oddly conceived as a right that couples in marital (or quasi-marital) relationships enjoy, premised on the sanctity of the family and the importance of procreation in sustaining the American way of life. But what if circumstances preclude a relationship? Should sexual rights be contingent upon having a sexual partner?

The obvious answer, we believe, is a resounding "no!" Sexual choices reflect *individual* rights, not rights that emerge only in relationships; these rights are not limited to dyads, whether heterosexual or homosexual, or to particular types of relationships (e.g., marriage). Privacy, as constructed by the Court in *Griswold* and subsequent cases, sidesteps sex in favor of relationships. By and large, it is the sanctity of the relationship that is protected within the privacy framework, not the individual's right freely to express his or her sexuality.[51] We believe that the Ninth Amendment offers a much more secure basis for individual sexual rights, one that respects the inherent human right to enjoy sex in its myriad forms and in various contexts.

A focus on individual sexual rights expands the discourse to encompass sexual activities outside the bounds of traditional relationships. Activities such as masturbation (the most frequent form of sexual behavior over the course of a male's lifetime), viewing pornography or erotic performances (either as an accompaniment to masturbation or as pure fantasy or entertainment), and having sex with a prostitute (a commercial substitute for a consensual sexual relationship) all fall into this category. In this book we examine two of these activities—masturbation within the context of telephone sex services ("dial-a-porn") and prostitution—as a means of explicating the potential role of the Ninth Amendment in protecting Americans' sexual freedoms.

Dial-a-porn, which includes both recorded telephone messages with explicit sexual content and "live" conversations with unseen telephone operators, serves one primary purpose. Like all pornography, dial-a-porn is meant to facilitate masturbation, primarily by men. Although dial-a-porn is already protected by the federal Right of Access—and therefore is permitted when not obscene—the simple fact remains: without masturbating customers, dial-a-porn would not exist. This is not to imply that, as speech, the basic "ideas" expressed by dial-a-porn (e.g., unbridled hedonism and the pursuit of sexual happiness) are not worth protecting. Quite the contrary: dial-a-porn and other forms of pornography serve to balance the many societal forces that pathologize sexuality.[52]

However, because dial-a-porn is primarily treated as a First Amendment issue, debates over this form of individual sexual expression seldom address the specific and very serious issue of undue infringement on sexual freedom, and by extension, the possibility of protecting fundamental sexual rights, such as the right to masturbate, through an appeal to the Ninth Amendment. In chapter 5 we bring masturbation out from the shadows and into the foreground through a consideration of the legal regulation of dial-a-porn and prohibitions on the sale of so-called "marital aids" (vibrators, dildos, and the like) in several states. Although masturbation itself is not criminalized in any state, the effect of restricting access to erotic materials—whether dial-a-porn, sex aids, or pornographic videos—is to discourage this non-procreative practice. Tellingly, Alabama defended its proscription on sexual aids by asserting that "the pursuit of orgasms by artificial means for their own sake is detrimental to the health and morality of the State."[53] Other states have justified similar laws by declaring that sexual aids are "obscene." Thus, the concept of obscenity figures prominently in the regulation of both sexual speech and sexual devices.

In chapter 5 we develop a behavioral analog to the obscenity/indecency distinction used to distinguish forms of expression deserving First Amendment protection from those that are denied constitutional standing. By analogy, "obscene" behaviors would be denied the protective shield of the Ninth Amendment in our framework. Masturbation, we conclude, may be indecent, but it is not obscene.

Masturbation represents the choice to self-stimulate and therefore is paradigmatic of the *individual* right to sexual expression. But sex, like many human activities, usually is more enjoyable with a partner. For various reasons, including convenience, the inability to attract a suitable partner, or a thirst for variety, some people choose to purchase sex to satisfy their sexual desires.[54]

Obviously, there are many implicit forms of sexual barter that escape the scrutiny of the law, such as the exchange of sex for jewelry, drugs, or a lifelong marital commitment. The law generally has little to say about such exchanges. But commercial sex, in which sex is traded at a set monetary price, is illegal throughout the United States, with the exception of a limited number of counties in Nevada. Why does the exchange of money make such a difference? As Polly Adler wryly observed in *A House Is Not a Home*, which chronicled her life as a whorehouse madam:

> The women who take husbands not out of love but out of greed, to get their bills paid, to get a fine house and clothes and jewels; the women who marry to get out of a tiresome job, or to get away from disagreeable relatives, or to avoid being called an old maid—these are whores in everything but name. The only difference between them and my girls is that my girls give a man his money's worth.[55]

The crucial question is whether Ninth Amendment sexual rights provide a basis for making an economic choice to exchange sex for financial considerations. Why should it be illegal to set an explicit price for sex, when the act of sexual intercourse is itself constitutionally protected?[56] In chapter 6 we argue that the Ninth Amendment's protection of sexual rights should preclude laws that criminalize an explicit financial relationship (e.g., $50 for oral sex) when implicit financial transactions (e.g., sex for free rent) are fully legal.

Prostitution and pornography exist because there is a market for these products and services. There will always be people who lack the social skills or personal characteristics necessary to create and sustain intimate relationships, or who prefer to engage in nonrelational sex. Are such people thereby precluded from exercising their nonreproductive sexual rights? Or, to put it another way, does the right to make sexual choices derive solely from the potential to reproduce? If we acknowledge that intimate relationships are not available to or necessarily desired by everyone, we must question the legitimacy of ultimately denying sexual access to a sizable portion of the population through unjustified legal restrictions on masturbation, pornography, and prostitution.

This line of reasoning raises the obvious question of limitations. When is sexual behavior *not* deserving of protection, constitutional or otherwise? It is often said that rights produce wrongs. Alarmists fear that any expansion of sexual rights could produce sexual mayhem, with exponential increases in incest, rape, sexual harassment, and so forth.

The task before us, then, is to develop a system that keeps the baby, while dumping the bath water.

This concern is not unique to sex. Capitalist economies, for example, are also prone to abuse. Fraud, counterfeiting, embezzlement, stock swindling, and so forth come with the territory. However, we do not manacle capitalism to avoid securities fraud; instead we create laws and establish procedures to define, detect, and discourage fraud and the like. The same logic, we argue, applies to sexual rights. Freedoms must be broadly maintained; laws must be enacted to distinguish unacceptable behaviors; and violations of the law must be duly punished.

The legal condemnation of prostitution rests on the "secondary effects" supposedly associated with commercial sex. Prostitution is accused of fostering crime and spreading sexually transmitted diseases. However, the evidence linking prostitution to these harms is inconclusive at best (see chapter 6). We believe that decriminalization coupled with regulation is a better strategy for reducing the putative downsides of prostitution. Similarly, there appears to be no overriding state interest in restricting adults' access to erotic or pornographic books, movies, videos, electronic media, or "sex toys," *provided* that appropriate steps are taken to ensure that minors do not have access to potentially harmful materials.

Nevertheless, there are areas in which substantial limitations and restrictions on sexual expression are clearly justified. In chapter 7 we examine the distasteful topic of child pornography as a means of illustrating the necessity of delimiting some sexual freedoms. *Consent* is the characteristic typically used to distinguish between legally protected and unprotected sexual rights, and it is particularly germane to child pornography. The concept of consent usually incorporates two requirements: first, the consenting party must act with volition, thereby making a willful choice; and second, he or she must have full knowledge and understanding of the nature and consequences of the act being consented to. The reason children cannot consent to sexual relations with adults is because, despite whatever desires they may or may not have, their cognitive and emotional immaturity precludes sufficient comprehension of the nature and consequences of sexual relations. For example, children cannot accurately assess the emotional sequelae, both short- and long-term, of engaging in sex with an adult, or participating in the production of pornographic materials. In short, they are not capable of providing consent because they cannot fully appreciate the consequences of their choices. Thus, as we elaborate in chapter 7, consent requirements act to place substantive limitations on the sexual freedoms protected by the Ninth Amendment.

SEXUAL RIGHTS IN AMERICA

Just as our genes interact with the social environment to shape our development as individuals, the Constitution (the genetic endowment of our great nation) interacts with its sociopolitical milieu to determine the eventual form of the laws and institutions under which we live. In the final chapter we expand this analogy further and examine how, in the more than two hundred years since the Constitution was ratified, our sexual rights could have diverged so far from the ideals of liberty and the pursuit of happiness encoded in the genetic blueprint of the Constitution and other foundational documents.

What changes are necessary to help the Constitution realize its full "genetic" potential, particularly with regard to better protecting our sexual rights? First, the courts must accord the Ninth Amendment the respect it deserves as an integral part of the Bill of Rights. The historical development of this amendment (reviewed in chapter 2) shows clearly the pivotal role it played in ensuring Constitutional ratification. The Ninth Amendment was not, as the courts have tended to regard it, a mere waste of parchment. It was meant to protect those basic rights, fundamental to liberty and the pursuit of happiness, that were not otherwise safeguarded by the Constitution. Thus, as a first step toward enhancing the status of sexual rights in America, the courts must give substance to the Ninth Amendment by recognizing the existence of unenumerated rights, sexual rights among them.

Of course, along with rights come responsibilities. The *right* to make choices about how we express ourselves sexually entails a *responsibility* to make intelligent, well-informed decisions. To ensure that Americans can effectively implement their sexual rights, we need societal changes that foster the development of a sexually literate population. By "sexual literacy" we mean the ability to understand the various implications of the many complicated sexual issues that arise when implementing fundamental sexual rights. Americans need to be able to make informed decisions and express coherent opinions on a range of sexuality-related topics, including such controversial issues as premarital sex, abortion, homosexuality, prostitution, pornography, and non-consensual sex. The goals of sexual literacy are twofold: to create a population capable of understanding and expressing their sexual rights and of respecting the sexual rights of others; and to arm the citizenry with the information they need to comprehend and actively participate in debates about the proper reach of sexual rights and the role of the government in safeguarding or regulating those rights.

Our hope is that *Sexual Rights in America* will encourage legal scholars and the judiciary to reevaluate the proper role of the Ninth Amendment in constitutional adjudication, especially in the adjudication of cases implicating sexual rights. We hope, in particular, to convince the reader that sexual rights should be counted among the unenumerated rights protected by the Ninth Amendment. Through advances on several fronts—changing how the judiciary views the Ninth Amendment, gaining recognition of the fundamental nature of sexual rights, and creating a politically aware, sexually literate populace—the Constitution's untapped potential for securing our sexual happiness might finally be realized.

2

History and Interpretation of the Ninth Amendment

ON JUNE 21, 1788, New Hampshire followed eight other former British colonies in ratifying the United States Constitution, making this remarkable document the law of the land. The months leading up to this day were filled with contentious debates over the appropriate exercise of federal powers in a diffuse republican government and the ability of the Constitution to safeguard the individual liberties the revolutionaries had fought so hard to win.

The primary source of this discord was the considered omission from the Constitution of a bill of rights to protect the liberties of the citizens and to reign in the powers of the federal government. This was the position adopted by Thomas Tredwell at the New York State ratifying convention:

> In this Constitution, sir, we have departed widely from the principles and political faith of '76, when the spirit of liberty ran high, and danger put a curb on ambition. Here we find no security for the rights of individuals, no security for the existence of our state government; here is no bill of rights, no proper restriction of power; our lives, our property, and our consciences are left wholly at the mercy of legislature, and the powers of judiciary may be extended to any degree short of almighty. Sir, in this Constitution we have not only neglected,—we have done worse,—we have openly violated our faith,—that is our public faith.[1]

Such concerns had gathered force in the wake of the Constitutional Convention, which had met in Philadelphia in the summer of 1787 to draft the Constitution but had adjourned without including a bill of rights in the six-page document or even giving serious consideration to the idea. James Wilson, a convention delegate from Pennsylvania, reported that "so little account was the idea [of a bill of rights] that it passed off in a short conversation, without introducing a formal debate or assuming the shape of a motion."[2]

Many notable Americans believed that a bill of rights was wholly unnecessary, superfluous at best and dangerous at worst. In a subsequent address to colleagues at the Pennsylvania ratifying convention on October 28, 1787, Wilson argued by example from the states that

> In a government possessed of enumerated powers, such a measure [adopting a bill of rights] would be not only unnecessary, but preposterous and dangerous. Whence comes this notion, that in the United States there is no security without a bill of rights? Have the citizens of South Carolina no security for their liberties? They have no bill of rights. Are the citizens on the eastern side of the Delaware less free, or less secured in their liberties, than those on the western side? The state of New Jersey has no bill of rights. The state of New York has no bill of rights. The states of Connecticut and Rhode Island have no bill of rights. I know not whether I have exactly enumerated the states who have not thought it necessary to add a bill of rights to their constitutions; but this enumeration, sir, will serve to show by experience, as well as principle, that, even in single governments, a bill of rights is not an essential or necessary measure.[3]

Of course, not everyone agreed with Wilson. For instance, Patrick Henry—who had refused to attend the Constitutional Convention, swearing that he "smelt a rat"—believed that it would take little effort to append a bill of rights to the Constitution, and thereby alleviate the fears, unfounded or not, of a large number of citizens. He stated his position as follows:

> A bill of rights may be summed up in a few words. What do they tell us? —That our rights are reserved. Why not say so? Is it because it will consume too much paper? . . . A bill of rights is a favorite thing with the Virginians and the people of other states likewise. It may be their prejudice, but the government ought to suit their geniuses; otherwise, its operation will be unhappy. . . . Unless the general government be restrained by a bill of rights, or some other restriction, [they may] go into your cellars and rooms, and search, ransack, and measure,

everything you eat, drink and wear. They ought to be restrained within proper bounds.[4]

But were such restraints necessary? Apparently most convention delegates thought not. They saw no need to impose explicit restrictions on the exercise of federal powers because the Constitution granted the government only very limited prerogatives. "Why declare that things shall not be done which there is no power to do?" asked Alexander Hamilton in *The Federalist* 84.[5] "Why, for instance, should it be said that the liberty of the press shall not be restrained, when no power is given by which restrictions may be imposed?" In short, the government had no power to intrude upon the rights of individuals unless expressly granted such powers in the Constitution, hence there was no need to safeguard against such encroachments.

Moreover, in several states, citizens' fundamental rights were already protected by their state constitutions. "The State Declarations of Rights are not repealed by [the U.S.] Constitution; and being in force are sufficient," insisted Roger Sherman of Connecticut.[6] A federal enumeration of such rights would be redundant, or worse, if the federal bill of rights in any way contradicted those of the states.

Further, singling out particular rights for protection within a federal bill of rights would by implication make insecure those that were not listed. The framers of the Constitution realized that any listing of protected rights would necessarily be incomplete, and they feared that the mere existence of such a list would imperil those rights inadvertently omitted. In the words, once again, of James Wilson:

> In all societies, there are many powers and rights which cannot be particularly enumerated. A bill of rights annexed to a constitution is an enumeration of powers reserved. If we attempt an enumeration, every thing that is not enumerated is presumed to be given. The consequence is, that an imperfect enumeration would throw all implied power into the scale of the government, and the rights of the people would be rendered incomplete.[7]

Although delegates to the Constitutional Convention could adduce several sound reasons to omit a bill of rights, this omission was to have severe repercussions as ratification proceeded, ultimately threatening the viability of the Constitution itself. For one thing, as noted by Wilson, many states did *not* have an extant bill of rights to guarantee their citizens' rights. And the quality of the states' declarations of rights, where they existed, was uneven. James Madison would later opine, "some states have no bills of rights, there are others provided with very defective ones, and there are others whose bills of rights are not only defective, but absolutely improper."[8]

The Constitution's lack of a bill of rights, "a favorite thing with the Virginians and the people of other states," provided the Anti-Federalists with a popular weapon in their attack on the integrity of the Constitution. In the ensuing debates, the Federalists' own arguments were turned against them. If the Federalists believed that a bill of rights was unnecessary, as they had professed at the Constitutional Convention and thereafter during the ratification process, then why, the Anti-Federalists asked, were certain protections (such as the right to a jury trial in criminal cases, bans on religious tests for political office seekers, etc.) incorporated into the text of the Constitution? If "any power not granted is retained," a favorite platitude of those who discouraged amending a bill of rights to the Constitution, then what of the constitutional stipulation that the writ of habeas corpus could be suspended under certain circumstances? Patrick Henry cannily deduced that "if it had not said so, they could suspend it in all cases whatsoever. It reverses the position of the friends of the Constitution, that every thing is retained which is not given up; for, instead of this everything is given up which is not expressly reserved."[9] The explicit protection of a limited number of rights was incongruent with the Federalists' warnings of the dangers of an incomplete enumeration of rights. Were all other freedoms placed in danger through omission?

The Anti-Federalists capitalized on this critical weakness of the Constitution, hoping to forestall ratification and possibly force a second constitutional convention. Indeed, by early 1789, no fewer than four states had joined in calling for a second convention. Others had ratified the Constitution, but with reservations. When Massachusetts became the fifth state to ratify, it recommended amending the Constitution to better secure the individual liberties of the people. Several other states followed Massachusetts's lead, with growing lists of amendments (many of which later found their way into the Bill of Rights).

JAMES MADISON'S BILL OF RIGHTS

The task of drafting a federal bill of rights eventually fell to James Madison, then serving as a representative from the state of Virginia. As a staunch Federalist, Madison did not much favor a bill of rights,[10] fearing that, by making selected rights explicit, any rights omitted from the enumeration would be insecure. As he stated in a letter to Thomas Jefferson in November 1788, he was not "anxious to supply it even by subsequent amendments."[11] (Jefferson's pragmatic reply: "Half a loaf is better than no bread. If we can not secure all our rights, let us secure what we can."[12]) Nevertheless, Madison recognized the imminent danger to the ratification process posed by the absence of a bill of rights. He therefore came to support (at least publicly) adding a bill of rights to the Constitution. A bill of rights would "give satisfaction to the doubting part of our fellow citizens"[13] and would quiet the fears of those crucial states where ratification had been in doubt.[14]

On June 8, 1789, Madison delivered a politically astute and historically momentous speech before the House of Representatives, in which he elucidated his reasons for supporting a bill of rights and outlined several potential amendments to the Constitution:

> I will state my reasons why I think it proper to propose amendments, and state the amendments themselves, so far as I think they ought to be proposed. . . . It cannot be a secret to the gentlemen in this House, that, notwithstanding the ratification of this system of Government [i.e., the Constitution] by eleven of the thirteen United States, in some cases unanimously, in others by large majorities; yet still there is a great number of our constituents who are dissatisfied with it; among whom are many respectable for their talents and patriotism, and respectable for the jealousy they have for their liberty, which though mistaken in its object, is laudable in its motive. There is a great body of the people falling under this description, who at present feel much inclined to join their support to the cause of Federalism, if they were satisfied on this one point. We ought not to disregard their inclination, but, on principles of amity and moderation, conform to their wishes, and expressly declare the great rights of mankind secured under this constitution.[15]

Before listing his proposals to protect specific rights, Madison gave voice to a more general sentiment, expressing the prevailing belief that governments exist to serve the governed, and not, as we so often observe today, the other way around:

> The amendments which have occurred to me, proper to be recommended by Congress to the State Legislatures, are these:
>
> First. That there be prefixed to the constitution a declaration, that all power is originally vested in, and consequently derived from, the people.
>
> That Government is instituted and ought to be exercised for the benefit of the people; which consists in the employment of life and liberty, with the right of acquiring and using property, and generally of pursuing and obtaining happiness and safety.[16]

Here Madison is simply summarizing the prevailing philosophical position of the day, which held that governments are instituted by agreements ("social compacts") among freely acting individuals and that the role of government is to protect the rights and interests of the people. (This conception of government is further explored later in this chapter.)

After elaborating his proposals for amendments safeguarding the freedoms of religion, speech, assembly, and so forth, Madison came to his final point, which served as the precursor to the Ninth and Tenth Amendments:

> The exceptions here or elsewhere in the Constitution, made in favor of particular rights, shall not be so construed as to diminish the just importance of other rights retained by the people, or as to enlarge the powers delegated by the Constitution; but either as actual limitations of such powers, or as inserted merely for greater caution.[17]

This proposal was meant to address explicitly the concerns of the Anti-Federalists that "everything is given up which is not expressly reserved." As Madison explained:

> It has been objected also against a bill of rights, that, by enumerating particular exceptions to the grant of power, it would disparage those rights which were not placed in that enumeration; and it might follow by implication, that those rights which were not singled out, were intended to be assigned into the hands of government, and were

consequently insecure. This is one of the most plausible arguments I have ever heard against admission of a bill of rights into this system; but, I conceive, that it may be guarded against. I have attempted it, as gentlemen may see by turning to the last clause of the fourth resolution.[18]

The clause to which Madison referred his brethren was, of course, destined to become the Ninth Amendment. Madison's solution to the problem of a finite bill of rights was to introduce an additional class of rights that, though not expressly enumerated in the Bill of Rights, were nonetheless protected against governmental interference.

Congress, which had much more pressing issues to address, adopted Madison's proposed amendments with little debate and only minor modifications. In final form, the Ninth and Tenth Amendments read, respectively: "The enumeration in the Constitution, of certain rights, shall not be construed to deny or disparage others retained by the people" and "The powers not delegated to the U.S. government, nor prohibited by it to the states, are reserved to the states respectively, or to the people." The amended Constitution was submitted to the states on September 25, 1789, and ratified by the requisite number by December 15, 1791.[19]

RIGHTS AND POWERS:
THE NINTH AND TENTH AMENDMENTS

Several commentators have dismissed the Ninth Amendment as redundant in light of the Tenth.[20] In this interpretation, rights are "retained by the people" only insofar as the federal government is denied the power to act against them. Even Madison, in his preliminary thinking on the relationship between rights and powers, seems to have viewed them as complementary, two sides of the same coin. In a letter to his fellow Virginian, George Washington, he explained:

> If a line can be drawn between the powers granted and the rights retained, it would seem to be the same thing, whether the latter be secured by declaring that they shall not be abridged, or that the former shall not be extended. If no such line can be drawn, a declaration in either form would amount to nothing.[21]

But the final draft of the Bill of Rights belies this notion of strict complementarity by embracing *both* the Ninth and the Tenth Amendments. As Knowlton Kelsey observed in his 1936 *Indiana Law Journal* article, "The Ninth Amendment of the Federal Constitution":

> When the two provisions are laid beside each other, it becomes evident that there was some distinction in the minds of the framers of those amendments between *declarations of right* and *limitations on* or *prohibitions of power*. If no distinction had been in mind, the Ninth Amendment would have been unnecessary. The Tenth Amendment, reserving powers to states and people, would have been enough.[22]

Rights and powers are fundamentally distinct though necessarily interrelated concepts. The concept of "power" refers to the permission, ceded by the people to the government, to act on their behalf. To protect its citizens, each state has a general police power with which to regulate and guarantee the health, safety, and general welfare of its residents. Although the federal government has no police power per se, it makes use of several of its powers to regulate many aspects of daily life. The federal power to impose taxes is one obvious example. The government was given the power of taxation—meaning that it has the permission, and hence the ability to act upon, a system for taxing businesses, individuals, and so forth—because it ultimately serves the people. The same is true for the power of regulating commerce. However, the Tenth Amendment makes it clear that the people (or the states, acting as the people's agent) still retain the "permission," hence control, over all powers not explicitly granted to the federal government by the U.S. Constitution.

Rights are undoubtedly related to the exercise of power, since rights often are implemented through actions (e.g., making a speech) that are not constrained by governmental power. However:

> The idea that constitutional rights are simply what is left over after the people have delegated powers to the government flies in the face of the [Ninth and Tenth] amendments themselves. For example, it is impossible to find a right to "a speedy and public trial by an impartial jury," a right against double jeopardy or self-incrimination, or a right to be free from "unreasonable searches and seizures" by closely examining the limits of the enumerated powers of the national government.[23]

According to Randy Barnett, one of America's preeminent Ninth Amendment scholars, constitutional rights do more than simply delineate the boundaries of federal powers—they also place limitations on the means by which the government can pursue legitimate ends.[24] Thus, rights can limit the exercise of powers explicitly granted the government by the Constitution, potentially placing constitutionally protected rights in conflict with constitutionally granted powers. Importantly, when such conflicts arise, "rights can cut across or 'trump' powers,"[25] regardless of whether those rights are explicitly listed in the first eight amendments or implicit in the Ninth. The Ninth Amendment therefore adds potency to the protection of individual liberties over and beyond that implied by the Tenth Amendment's reservation of unenumerated powers.

In short, the first eight amendments preserve explicit rights, whereas the Ninth Amendment protects the unenumerated ones. The Tenth Amendment completes this logic by insisting that undelegated *powers* are retained by the people (or the states in service of guarding the people's liberties). In combination, the Ninth and Tenth amendments make it clear that the unenumerated rights and the undelegated powers reside with the people, not with the federal government.

THE MEANING OF THE NINTH AMENDMENT

But what did the framers *mean* by the rather vague proposition that "the enumeration in the Constitution, of certain rights, shall not be construed to deny or disparage others retained by the people"? Some commentators have attempted to strip the Ninth Amendment of any substance by interpreting it as a simple statement of the obvious fact that there might, indeed, be rights other than those listed in the preceding eight amendments of the Bill of Rights. Kelsey has suggested, rhetorically, that perhaps the Ninth Amendment was meant only as a cast-off phrase, much like the "other articles too numerous to mention" disclaimer on a bill of sale, the sole purpose of which is to protect the seller on the off chance that he or she forgot to specify something in the contract.[26] On this reading the Constitution does not *deny* the possible existence of unenumerated rights, but neither does it recognize the substantive implications of the existence of such rights, nor offer any constitutional guarantees against their infringement.[27]

This interpretation of the Ninth Amendment as functionally impotent or merely tautological has been vigorously rejected time and again.[28] The greatest and most obvious weakness of this view is that it ignores and negates the prevailing constitutional interpretive process, first laid out by Chief Justice John Marshall in 1803 in the landmark case *Marbury v. Madison*. In *Marbury*, Chief Justice Marshall declared: "It cannot be presumed that any clause in the Constitution is intended to be without effect. . . . If any other construction would render the clause inoperative, that is an additional reason for rejecting such other construction, and for adhering to their obvious meaning."[29]

This analysis is especially apropos for the Ninth Amendment in particular. Most assuredly, Madison and colleagues meant to convey something more than simply that there were rights other than those listed in the first eight amendments. We can assume that "The utterers of this language were not talking just to hear their heads rattle."[30] As Justice Arthur Goldberg stated in his concurring opinion in *Griswold v. Connecticut*: "In interpreting the Constitution, 'real effect should be given to all the words it uses' [quoting *Myers v. United States*]. . . . Since 1791 [the Ninth Amendment] has been a basic part of the Constitution which we are sworn to uphold."[31]

Granting "real effect" to the language of the Ninth Amendment requires respecting the substantive meaning of those words. Kelsey offers:

> Surely [the Ninth Amendment] is more than a mere negative on implied grants of power that might otherwise be asserted because of the express enumeration of rights in respect of matters where no power was granted. It must be more than a mere net to catch fish in supposedly fishless water. It is certainly more than a mere emphasis on the doctrine of delegated and enumerated powers. It must be a positive declaration of existing, though unnamed rights, which may be vindicated under the authority of the amendment whenever and if ever any governmental authority shall aspire to ungranted power in contravention of "unenumerated rights."[32]

Kelsey therefore concluded that we must "assume that in the minds of the framers of [the Ninth] amendment, other rights than those 'enumerated' did, and supposedly do now, exist."[33] Nearly fifty years later, Charles Black stated the case more forcefully:

[The] preponderance of reason leaves us with the conclusion, about as well-supported as any we can reach in law, that the Ninth Amendment declares as a matter of law—of constitutional law, overriding other law—that some other rights are "retained by the people," and that these shall be treated as *on an equal footing* with rights enumerated.[34]

Granting that unenumerated rights exist and are retained by the people, the critical question becomes: can these rights be identified in a principled, judicially enforceable manner? One notable critic of expansive interpretations of the Ninth Amendment, Judge Robert Bork, addressed this issue during his 1987 Supreme Court confirmation hearings. In Judge Bork's opinion, the Ninth Amendment is too ambiguous to support any definitive conclusions regarding the nature of unenumerated rights. It is, in essence, "an amendment that says 'Congress shall make no' and then there is an inkblot, and you can't read the rest of it, and that is the only copy you have."[35] Without knowing what is under the inkblot, judicial enforcement of unenumerated rights is impossible, and the amendment is rendered meaningless. Judge Bork's cautious approach to judicial review is commendable, but the Ninth Amendment is not nearly so opaque as he implies. The historical record makes clear that this amendment was intended to protect those *natural* rights not otherwise mentioned in the Constitution. The Ninth Amendment is not an inkblot. The words are legible, though their meaning requires careful elucidation.

Raoul Berger is another staunch critic of recent (post-*Griswold*) efforts to resuscitate the Ninth Amendment. Berger's analysis in his article, "The Ninth Amendment," focuses on the pairing of the Ninth and Tenth Amendments in Madison's original formulation (quoted above), in which Madison disavows any intention "to enlarge the powers delegated by the Constitution."[36] In Berger's view, judicial enforcement of unenumerated rights violates this proviso and therefore constitutes an usurpation of powers expressly disallowed the government by the Ninth and Tenth Amendments:

Madison's disclaimer of intention "to enlarge the powers delegated by the Constitution" by non-enumeration of "other rights" and his emphasis on enumeration as "actual limitations" on such powers bars a construction which would endow the federal government with the very powers that were denied to it.[37]

The phrase at the center of Berger's analysis ("The exceptions here . . . shall not be so construed . . . as to enlarge the powers delegated by the Constitution") reflects the concern, cited earlier, that the mere presence of a Bill of Rights might be misconstrued as implying the existence of federal powers not explicitly granted within the Constitution ("Why declare that things shall not be done which there is no power to do?"). There is no reason to believe, as Berger apparently does, that by this phrase Madison meant to abnegate any possibility of judicial protection for the liberties encompassed by the Ninth Amendment.[38]

Berger also is critical of Justice Goldberg's *Griswold* opinion, which, he feels, "leaps too lightly from the 'existence of rights' retained by the people to a federal power to *protect* them."[39] Berger is unwilling to grant the government this power not only because he believes that doing so would be in direct violation of Madison's injunction against "enlarg[ing] the powers delegated by the Constitution," but also because of a curious interpretation of Madison's address before Congress, in which Madison stated that the purpose of the Ninth Amendment was to quell any and all fears "that those rights which were not singled out [for enumeration] were intended to be assigned into the hands of the General Government, and were consequently insecure."[40] The obvious reading of this statement suggests that the omission of any particular right from the Bill of Rights did not imply a grant of power to infringe upon the legitimate exercise of that right. Quite the contrary: even unenumerated rights were secure against such infringement, lest they be "disparaged."

Rejecting the obvious, Berger interprets "assigned into the hands of the General Government" to mean "'assigned' to the federal government, *for enforcement or otherwise.*"[41] We find this a peculiar reading of Madison's stated concern that such rights might "consequently [be] insecure." Could Madison have intended that government should be barred from *protecting* unenumerated rights? We find this doubtful. Instead, we agree with Simeon McIntosh: "It is Berger and not Justice Goldberg who is missing the point. For the power to protect (enforce) must indeed follow from the presumption that a right exists."[42]

NATURAL RIGHTS PHILOSOPHY

Importantly, the Ninth Amendment was not meant to create new rights. It does not, in the words of Justice Goldberg, "[constitute] an independent source of rights protected from infringement by either the States or the Federal Government. Rather, the Ninth Amendment shows a belief of the Constitution's authors that fundamental rights exist that are not expressly enumerated in the first eight amendments and an intent that the list of rights included there need not be deemed exhaustive."[43]

The purpose of the Ninth Amendment was to protect existing rights, which according to the amendment were "retained by the people." These included the *natural rights* of mankind: those privileges that exist at birth and therefore persist independent of any government or other social arrangement.[44] Man's natural rights include elusive and ineffable concepts like "freedom," "justice," and the Declaration of Independence's "life, liberty, and the pursuit of happiness." The source of these rights is not the government, or the Constitution. They arise, instead, from nature herself: people "have rights antecedent to all earthly government; rights that cannot be repealed or restrained by human laws; rights derived from the Great Legislator of the Universe."[45]

Governments are not the source of natural rights, but are instead vehicles for protecting these rights, both enumerated and unenumerated. As Bennett Patterson argues in his seminal monograph, *The Forgotten Ninth Amendment*: "The broad and historic concept of human rights and human liberty establishes such unenumerated rights as preconstitutional rights, and such rights were not abridged by the Constitution of the United States, or any State constitution, or any power, Government or person whomever."[46] Here Patterson restates the prevailing eighteenth-century concept of rights as innate and inviolate. In 1766, John Dickinson, a Pennsylvania legislator and future governor of Pennsylvania, declared: "[natural rights] are created in us by the decrees of Providence, which establishes the laws of our nature. They are born with us; exist with us; and cannot be taken away from us by any human power without taking our lives."[47] This conclusion is echoed in the Ninth Amendment, which ensures that those natural rights granted us "by the decrees of Providence" cannot be abridged merely because they were not enumerated in the first eight amendments.

∎

The concept of natural rights was articulated in the works of seventeenth- and eighteenth-century social philosophers such as William Blackstone, Edmund Burke, Edward Coke, and John Locke. Locke deserves extra emphasis because his writings were highly influential during the colonial and revolutionary epochs. Locke's influence is clearly evident in Thomas Jefferson's Declaration of Independence, which justified the colonies' rebellious actions as necessary to preserve the people's "inalienable rights." Like all well-read men of the time, Jefferson was intimately familiar with Locke, but he denied the accusations of contemporaries who branded him an intellectual plagiarist: "Richard H. Lee charged [the Declaration] as copied from Locke's treatise on Government. . . . I know only that I turned to neither book nor pamphlet while writing it."[48] Instead, according to Carl Becker, author of the classic treatise, *The Declaration of Independence: A Study in the History of Political Ideas*, the philosophy expounded in this famous document's preamble "was intended to be an expression of the American mind."[49] That this collective mind had drunk deep and long at the wellspring of seventeenth- and eighteenth-century philosophical thought is indubitable. Indeed, Becker has suggested that by the onset of the Revolution, "most Americans had absorbed Locke's works as a kind of political gospel."[50]

Lockean theory was the product of social and political forces very different from those that prevailed in colonial and postrevolutionary America. As a longstanding monarchy, Britain had spent hundreds of years putting the privileges of kings and queens above the rights and responsibilities of the common man. In medieval England, it was generally accepted that monarchs should be free to make laws, reorganize governments, and reward and punish completely at their own discretion. Their ultimate authority was not to be questioned by their subjects, who were required to submit to royal edicts, just or otherwise. Royals, it was held, ruled by divine right and divine counsel, not by the consent of the governed: "kings derive not their authority from the people but from God. . . . To Him only are they accountable."[51]

God's allegiances underwent a fundamental shift with the adoption of Magna Carta in 1215, and later, the Glorious Revolution of 1688. Although kings and queens continued to implement the goals and expectations of God, it was grudgingly acknowledged that common folk also possessed rights emanating from a much higher authority than their hereditary rulers. These "natural rights," which arose from the natural state of man as fashioned by their Creator, transcended royal desires and edicts. Burke's writings emphasize this point: "The rights of men—that is to say the natural rights of mankind are indeed sacred things; and if any public measure is proved mischievously to affect them, the objection ought to be fatal to that measure."[52] In the natural rights context, monarchs assume a different role. Their purpose is to create laws (and governments) to safeguard these rights and facilitate civil harmony. Though the process may be different from a democracy, the ultimate objectives are the same: to protect rights and keep the peace.

Natural rights philosophy formed the cornerstone of Locke's views on the relationship between government and the governed. In his *First Treatise of Government* he challenged the ultimate authority of kings and emphasized the need to resist arbitrary monarchs. In his *Second Treatise*, he again emphasized the importance of resistance and revolt, as well as the value of a limited constitutional government and the importance of preserving the right to life, liberty, and property.

At the heart of Locke's *Second Treatise* is the premise that people form a "social compact" whereby they assent to government as a means of assuring mutual respect and protection of their natural rights. As a result of the compact, some individual rights are necessarily relinquished or curtailed for the collective good. However, when people band together to form societies, they never cede to government absolute or arbitrary power because doing so would negate their natural rights, which ultimately are inviolable. The noted constitutional scholar Leonard Levy provides the following eloquent summary:

> The social compact theory hypothesized a prepolitical state of nature in which people were governed only by the laws of nature, free of human restraints. From the premise that man was born free, the deduction followed that he came into the world with God-given or natural rights. Born without the restraint of human laws, he had a right to possess liberty and to work for his own property. Born naked and stationless, he had a right to equality. Born with certain instincts and needs, he had a right to satisfy them—a right to the pursuit of happiness.[53]

Thus, although governments are formed to secure the collective weal, people still retain natural rights to liberty, property, happiness, and so forth, as well as the right to alter the frame of the government when it no longer serves their needs.[54] Jefferson's Declaration of Independence stated the Lockean case as follows:

> We hold these truths to be self-evident. That all men are created equal, that they are endowed by their creator with certain inalienable rights; that among these are life, liberty, and the pursuit of happiness; that to secure these rights governments are instituted among men, deriving their just powers from the consent of the governed; that whenever any form of government becomes destructive of these ends, it is the right of the people to alter or to abolish it, and to institute new government, laying its foundation on such principles and organizing its powers in such form, as to them shall seem most likely to effect their safety and happiness.[55]

Although the American conception of rights was originally derived from ideas espoused by Locke and other natural rights philosophers, they were adapted to the unique American experience. By 1787, America had dispensed with its king. It also had resisted the imposition of a state religion, and indeed had exercised great care to craft a government that encouraged a separation of church and state. As a nascent state with vast, untapped resources, America was closer than the motherland to the original state of nature in which social compacts initially were formed. The broad expanse of the American continent, extending well beyond the boundaries of the original thirteen colonies, was a primitive, uncharted wilderness with seemingly endless possibilities for settlement, economic growth, and unencumbered self-determination.[56] Likewise, America was navigating uncharted waters in the political realm, creating a nation in which all men were equal and imbued "with certain inalienable rights." These "inalienable rights" were the natural rights of man, and the Constitution was the modern embodiment of the social contract. The Bill of Rights, which is the positive affirmation of these rights, consists of eight amendments with explicit guarantees; the Tenth Amendment, which reserves undelegated powers to the people and the states; and the all-important Ninth Amendment, which secures those natural rights left unprotected by the remainder of the Constitution.

AN INCOMPLETE ENUMERATION

Locke did not provide an exhaustive list of natural rights, nor does he give explicit criteria for distinguishing natural rights from other types of rights. Locke generally was vague—and sometimes contradictory—regarding the nature and origin of natural rights. But, whatever these rights are and wherever they come from, Locke was adamant in his insistence that there *are* rights that neither kings nor governments can deny or ignore. If they do, the people can, and should, resist.

Locke should be excused for failing to advance a comprehensive listing of natural rights. Perhaps he realized, as the framers of the Constitution undoubtedly did, that the natural rights of mankind are *inherently* unenumerable. As Barnett states:

> Rights are unenumerable because rights define a private domain within which persons have a right to do as they wish, provided their conduct does not encroach upon the rightful domains of others. As long as their actions remain with this rightful domain, other persons—including the government—should not interfere. Because people have a right to do whatever they please within the boundaries defined by natural rights, this means that the rights retained by the people *are limited only by their imagination* and could never be completely specified or enumerated.[57]

Indeed, the unfeasibility of providing an exhaustive enumeration of rights is the *raison d'être* of the Ninth Amendment. Madison recognized that it was not only unwise, but patently impossible, to attempt an exhaustive enumeration of the great rights of mankind. Clearly, if there were only a finite number of such rights, then the Bill of Rights would have been expanded to encompass them all, rendering the Ninth Amendment moot. The Ninth Amendment is an explicit acknowledgment of the infinitude of potential rights and the impossibility of a complete accounting thereof.

As our understanding of human nature continues to grow, so does our understanding of natural rights. Advances in such areas as human biology, psychology, sociology, genetics, and so forth have changed how we view ourselves and our place in the world. We have no reason to believe that we can accurately predict the social, scientific, or technological future. Consequently, we cannot accurately predict the human rights that will be recognized in response to scientific and technological advancements.

Nor can we predict the future evolution of our moral understanding:

> We believe that the Ninth Amendment was intended to protect the un-enumerated rights, not only as they have now appeared, but also as such rights may appear as history and the future shall unfold. As the human race becomes more evolved, and as respect for the dignity of human life increases; as we become more intelligent and spiritual human beings, then we shall learn more of the fundamental truths about human nature.[58]

The abolition of slavery, which persisted for a significant and shameful portion of our national history, and the long-overdue enfranchisement of women provide concrete examples of how our evolving moral understanding led to monumental social and legal changes in the status of African Americans and women, respectively. Although the Ninth Amendment was not the basis for the expansion of African Americans' and women's rights, the rights guaranteed by the Thirteenth and Nineteenth Amendments are entirely consistent with the spirit of the Ninth Amendment's unenumerated natural rights.

In short, the category of unenumerated rights necessarily remains open-ended. This open-endedness is essential to protect our rights in unanticipated contingencies. But does this indeterminacy foreclose the possibility of identifying unenumerated Ninth Amendment rights? Certainly, it makes it a daunting task:

> Madison's contention that the "natural rights [are] retained by the people" is consistent with the theory that natural rights find their source in the immutable, inalienable rights of mankind, possessed apart from and transcendent to government. It is the transcendent authority of these rights that makes them important to confront; it is their gossamer nature that makes them virtually impossible to discern by neutral principles.[59]

Edmund Randolph, then governor of Virginia, raised this same objection to the proposed Ninth Amendment. As Madison recounted in a letter to Washington, Randolph was concerned "that there was no criterion by which it could be determined whether any particular right was retained or not."[60]

Nevertheless, as Black asserts: "we have for a very long time been protecting unnamed rights."[61] The right to privacy articulated in *Griswold* is perhaps the most famous example—a right founded, in part, by an appeal to the Ninth Amendment. Another example is the freedom of association, which is derived from the First Amendment.

Various methods can be used to identify fundamental or natural rights, including the application of rationality,[62] similarity to existing constitutional rights and consistency with the overall constitutional scheme,[63] appeals to the theory of justice underlying the Constitution,[64] and elaboration of current understandings of the fundamental nature of humankind.[65] The quest to enumerate the unenumerated may be arduous, but, "with the carefulness that is a condition of the law's rationality, we may be able to discern and validate 'other rights retained by the people' as latent in, and therefore susceptible of being drawn from the noblest of the concepts to which our nation is committed."[66] We return to this difficult topic in chapter 4, where we construct a Ninth Amendment foundation for sexual rights in America.

APPLICATION OF THE NINTH AMENDMENT TO THE STATES

The Supreme Court decided early on, in *Barron v. The Mayor and City Council of Baltimore* (1833), that the Bill of Rights applied *only* to the federal government and not to the states. Had Congress intended otherwise, it "would have declared this purpose in plain and intelligible language."[67]

But, with regard to the Ninth Amendment specifically, is this what Madison and colleagues intended, or were Ninth Amendment protections meant to extend to the states as well? Russell Caplan, Calvin Massey, and Bennett Patterson[68] argue that the framers meant the Ninth Amendment to apply to the states as much as, if not more than, to the federal government. Patterson in particular offered a litany of reasons for believing that the Ninth Amendment "was not intended solely as a restrictive inhibition against the National Government, but as a great declaration of the liberty of mankind."[69] Among these, perhaps the most persuasive is his appeal to the amendment's underlying logic: "We either believe in inherent rights, or we do not believe in them; if we believe in such inherent rights, then such rights must be protected against the unwarranted power of either the National or State Governments, otherwise they fail and cannot be classified as inherent rights at all."[70] Norman Redlich disagrees with Patterson's analysis, citing historical evidence that elsewhere in Madison's proposals for the Constitution, when he meant to restrict the powers of the states, he was quite explicit in doing so.[71]

Whatever the original intent, vis-à-vis applicability to the states, of the Ninth Amendment (and the Bill of Rights more generally), the situation was radically altered with the adoption, in the years from 1865 to 1870, of the Thirteenth, Fourteenth, and Fifteenth Amendments. These "reconstruction amendments" were intended to prevent state discrimination against individuals, most notably newly freed slaves. Importantly, the Fourteenth Amendment includes a due process clause (virtually identical to that of the Fifth Amendment) stipulating that no person be deprived of life, liberty, or property without due process of law. This crucial clause has served as a conduit for application of the Bill of Rights to the states.

Although the Court could have decided that, by means of its due process clause, the Fourteenth Amendment simply extended the Bill of Rights to include protection against state interference (certainly a clean and easy way to restrict state action against individual liberty), this approach did not find favor. Instead, the Court has taken a "fundamental rights" approach in which "liberty" has been taken as the standard by which rights are judged: "The Fourteenth Amendment protects against state violation those liberties 'so rooted in the traditions and conscience of our people as to be ranked as fundamental.'"[72]

In practice, nearly all of the constitutional guarantees contained in the first eight amendments of the Bill of Rights have been found to be fundamental aspects of liberty and therefore applicable to the states.[73] The wording and intent of the Ninth Amendment suggests that the first eight amendments do not exhaust the fundamental liberties of the American people. Therefore, these unenumerated liberties, too, should be protected by the due process clause of the Fourteenth Amendment. This was the position adopted by Justice Goldberg in *Griswold*:

> While the Ninth Amendment—and indeed the entire Bill of Rights—
> originally concerned restrictions upon *federal* power, the subsequently
> enacted Fourteenth Amendment prohibits the States as well from

abridging fundamental personal liberties. And the Ninth Amendment, in indicating that not all such liberties are specifically mentioned in the first eight amendments, is surely relevant in showing the existence of other fundamental personal rights, now protected from state, as well as federal, infringement. In sum, the Ninth Amendment simply lends strong support to the view that the "liberty" protected by the Fifth and Fourteenth Amendments from infringement by the Federal Government or the States is not restricted to rights specifically mentioned in the first eight amendments.[74]

Applying the Ninth Amendment to the states, via the Fourteenth, is simply to require of the states due process with respect to Ninth Amendment rights.[75] "If the rights encompassed by the ninth amendment are the natural rights of man, analogous to speech and religion, surely they must be ranked as 'fundamental.' . . . Therefore, it is almost axiomatic that if an unenumerated right is good against the federal government by virtue of the ninth amendment, it is good against the state governments by virtue of the fourteenth amendment."[76]

THE NINTH AMENDMENT AND THE COURT

The Ninth Amendment is intentionally vague, which was simultaneously its strength as an instrument to facilitate ratification of the Constitution, and its bane as a protector of fundamental rights. The difficulty, as noted above, is that the amendment provides no guidance on how to distinguish an unenumerated right that is worthy of constitutional protection from pretenders to this status. Consequently, the Supreme Court has adopted a conservative solution to identifying fundamental rights, essentially eschewing the Ninth Amendment and only rarely enlarging the scope of constitutional protections. Supreme Court references to the Ninth Amendment are rare, appearing principally *in dicta*, or as part of the opinions of individual justices. Among the few noteworthy cases in which the Ninth Amendment was cited are *Griswold v. Connecticut* and *Roe v. Wade*, both of which were in reference to privacy and, significantly, to human sexual behavior (see chapter 3).

In fundamental rights jurisprudence, the role of the judiciary is to determine, guided by the Constitution, the boundary between the set of rights "implicit in the concept of ordered liberty"[77] and those rights that could be sacrificed without undue harm to liberty and justice. The Supreme Court has generally construed the universe of fundamental rights very narrowly, starting with the first eight amendments of the Bill of Rights and expanding slowly, one at a time, as new rights are recognized as meriting constitutional protections (the right to privacy being a paradigmatic example). Rather than acting from a "presumption of liberty," in which persons are free to act without fear of government interference provided they do not violate the rights of others, the Court has instead favored a "presumption of constitutionality,"[78] whereby new laws are upheld provided that they do not violate a fundamental right, such as those enumerated in the first eight amendments, and provided that they are rationally related to a legitimate end.[79]

As a consequence of this "presumption of constitutionality," the Supreme Court has recognized very few "rights retained by the people" beyond those explicitly enumerated in the Bill of Rights. Apparently, the Court has found it too daunting, and too overwhelming, to make constitutional decisions in accordance with the broad dictates of the Ninth Amendment. Even in the exceptional cases, such as *Griswold*, caution has reigned. Note Justice John Marshall Harlan's concurrence in *Griswold*, which called for adherence to "judicial self-restraint . . . [to keep] judges from roaming at large in the constitutional field."[80] The substance of Justice Harlan's warning, while commendable in theory, has in practice been taken too far. Not only have judges inclined toward restraint, they have generally pretended that the Ninth Amendment does not exist or have distorted its meaning, thereby rendering it impotent. We suggest that it now is time to hold the Supreme Court accountable to the words and spirit of the Ninth Amendment to the Constitution.

Articles Three and Six of the Constitution provide the framework for and describe the responsibilities of the judicial branch of the government. For example, Article Six states: "This Constitution . . . shall be the supreme law of the land, and judges in every state shall be bound thereby." Notice that no exception was made for any article or amendment of the Constitution. Thus, the failure of judges to adhere to a specific part of the Constitution, such as the Ninth Amendment, is a direct violation of the Constitution, in letter and in spirit.

Similarly, Article Three, Section Two states that "The Judicial power shall extend to all cases, in law and equity, arising under the Constitution." This does not mean "part of" the Constitution, or "most of" the

Constitution. No qualifier was stated nor intended. Supreme Court justices, who are granted the power to interpret the Constitution and to make decisions about the constitutionality of laws, must base their findings on the whole of the Constitution, and cannot exclude those parts they find inconvenient or bothersome. By ignoring the Ninth Amendment, the Court has effectively denied Americans their inalienable but unenumerated rights.

As a result, Anti-Federalist fears about the Constitution—whereby the government would take everything not explicitly retained by the people—have to some extent been realized, at least where the Ninth Amendment is concerned. The failure to spell out unenumerated rights (which would be paradoxical, to say the least) or to establish criteria for identifying such rights has allowed the judiciary to withhold "rights retained by the people." Perhaps justifiably, judges are concerned that if they behaved otherwise, they might be accused of abusing their power of judicial review. Moreover, they worry that under a contrary system, people might fill the courts with unreasonable claims for alleged "rights." These fears, though understandable, have allowed the government to abuse its power, invading individual freedoms and withholding protection of liberties, by ignoring the explicit intent of the Ninth Amendment.

3

The Poverty of Privacy

THE SEARCH FOR enumerated sexual rights within the text of the U.S. Constitution is futile. Sexual rights are nowhere to be found in this venerable document. Nevertheless, certain sexual rights, such as the right to utilize contraceptives and the right to an abortion, have gained a footing within the Constitution under the general rubric of the "right to privacy."

What is the basis for this vague "right to privacy?" There is, in fact, no explicit privacy guarantee written into the Constitution or the Bill of Rights. Instead, this right arose as a "penumbra" (emanation) of various other constitutionally guaranteed rights, such as the right of association and protections against unreasonable search and seizure. The Court later placed the privacy right within the "liberty" of the Fourteenth Amendment's due process clause, but the boundaries of this right are no less muddled for this putative clarification.

Privacy seems like a right we *should* have, especially as a demarcation between "the people" and their government. Privacy provides a bulwark against perpetual intrusion. It also seems reasonable to consider the absence of a clear-cut privacy reference in the Constitution an unfortunate oversight.

Sex and privacy make natural bedfellows. Sex, after all, is a private behavior; indeed, public sexual performances are uniformly criminalized. As such, constitutionally guaranteed privacy has formed the basis for several high-profile sexual rights cases, such as *Griswold v. Connecticut* (concerning a married couple's right to use contraceptives), *Roe v. Wade* (a woman's right to an abortion), and *Bowers v. Hardwick* (the right to engage in sodomy).[1] Thus, if sexual rights are to be expanded, one could certainly argue that it would be much more frugal, and keeping with precedence, to widen the privacy umbrella to encompass a greater diversity of sexual rights, instead of advancing, as we do herein, the somewhat radical proposition that sexual rights are—or should be—rooted in the Ninth Amendment.

However, as we argue below, the concept of privacy as articulated in *Griswold* and subsequent cases is vague and contradictory, thereby making the corresponding rights insecure, as demonstrated by the Court's refusal in *Bowers* to recognize a right to engage in consensual homosexual activity. Moreover, by treating contraception, abortion, and sodomy as privacy issues, the Court has sidestepped the fundamental question of sexual rights per se. While this problem could be rectified if the Court were to treat these cases as instances of natural, sexual rights elemental to the "liberty" of the due process clause, the Court has shown great reluctance to adopt this approach. We believe that this reluctance may be reasonably overcome by considering these cases under the Ninth Amendment. Reliance on the Ninth Amendment, rather than the vague notion of privacy proffered by the Court, adds the constitutional protection needed to ensure our sexual rights in all their breadth, and does so in a most parsimonious manner.

GRISWOLD V. CONNECTICUT

For the first half of the twentieth century, it was a crime in the State of Connecticut to use contraceptives. Connecticut General Statute 53-32 stated that "Any person who uses any drug, medicinal article or instrument for the purpose of preventing conception shall be fined not less than fifty dollars or imprisoned not less than sixty days nor more than one year or be both fined and imprisoned." The State of Connecticut believed that contraceptives facilitated fornication and adultery, and, moreover, considered contraception to be "immoral in itself."[2] Thus, under the presumption that they were preserving marriages and the moral fiber of the community, Connecticut outlawed the use of contraceptives. To further discourage immorality (and, we cynically note, to prevent citizens from making informed reproductive decisions), the state also prohibited health care professionals from dispensing contraceptive advice.

It was within this context that, in 1961, the Executive Director of Planned Parenthood in New Haven, Mr. Griswold, and a respected Yale Medical School professor, Dr. Buxton, were arrested and subsequently convicted for providing married couples with medical advice on how to prevent conception. Griswold and Buxton appealed their convictions twice to higher courts in Connecticut (the Circuit Court and the Supreme Court of Errors). Both times their convictions were upheld. Finally, in 1965, the U.S. Supreme Court agreed to consider the case. *Griswold et al. v. Connecticut*[3] was argued on March 29–30, 1965. The Supreme Court made its final decision on June 7, 1965.

Griswold ultimately was framed as a question of privacy. It was not a matter of whether couples (or persons) have a fundamental right to make decisions about reproductive or sexual behavior. Instead, *Griswold* addressed the question of whether there is a domain of privacy wherein married couples can make decisions about their sexual behavior without government intrusion. *Griswold*, in essence, attempted to create a guarantee of privacy that applied specifically to married couples and protected their "private" decisions.

Although privacy is not explicitly guaranteed in the Constitution, in *Griswold* the Supreme Court concluded that such a right exists. Writing for the majority, Supreme Court Justice William Douglas argued that the rights enumerated in the Bill of Rights have "penumbras." Penumbras, according to Justice Douglas, were additional rights which "emanated" from the central rights specified in the Constitution. For example, the "freedom of association" has been protected as a First Amendment right, even though it is not explicitly mentioned in the First Amendment. The same is true for the right to educate a child in a school of the parent's choice. Justice Douglas emphasized that though many such concepts are not actually included in the wording of the First Amendment, they are necessary for making the express guarantees of the First Amendment fully meaningful.

Taking this logic a step further, Justice Douglas argued that there are, in fact, *several* amendments to the Constitution which have penumbras creating "zones of privacy." For example, the First Amendment's freedom of association guarantee protects the right of individuals to participate privately in organizations such as the ACLU, the NRA, or the Communist Party. The Third Amendment also protects privacy by prohibiting the quartering of soldiers "in any house" without the owner's consent. The Fourth Amendment affirms the "right of the people to be secure in their persons, houses, papers, and effects, against unreasonable searches and seizures," again suggesting a "zone of privacy." So does the Fifth Amendment, which prohibits self-incrimination, thereby limiting governmental intrusion into the lives of the citizenry. Finally, Justice Douglas concluded that the right to privacy was implied in the Ninth Amendment's rights "retained by the people."

According to Justice Douglas, history also supported his contentions regarding privacy. Citing a previous Supreme Court case, *Boyd v. United States*,[4] Justice Douglas documented that the Fourth and Fifth Amendments were explicitly described as protecting "the sanctity of a man's home and the privacies of his life."[5]

Convinced that he had established a firm Constitutional basis for a "zone of privacy," Justice Douglas then turned his attention to the defendants Griswold and Buxton. Both men were highly esteemed individuals whose only "crime" was providing contraceptive advice to married couples. The question for Justice Douglas was whether their fine should be upheld, or whether they had a constitutional right to provide contraceptive information, with a corresponding right for married couples to hear this information and use it accordingly.

It is important to note that the defendants were *not* themselves making private decisions. They were offering a service to the public by helping couples make decisions about their sexual behavior and the reproductive consequences thereof. Although the Court allowed standing to Griswold and Buxton to assert the rights of the couple they counseled, this sleight of hand diverts attention from the defendants to the recipients of their information. Privacy per se is irrelevant to Griswold and Buxton—*confidentiality* is another matter. Doctors, lawyers, psychologists, and other professionals have privileged (confidential) relationships with their clients that allow for the discussion of private matters. Thus, the issue before the Supreme Court was, or should have been, whether these gentleman had a constitutional right to counsel couples on their reproductive options; this seems like a freedom of speech question. Instead, the Court focused on the marital relationship, which had nothing whatsoever to do with the defendants, Griswold and Buxton. The Court's decision in this case postulated a "zone of privacy" in which married couples could think, discuss, and make private choices about reproduction. However, it did *not* create or secure a particular sexual right to make informed reproductive decisions, except insofar as this right was protected within the zone of privacy.

Justice Douglas concluded that *Griswold* concerned a relationship—specifically, marriage—falling within a constitutionally guaranteed zone of privacy. Furthermore, he proclaimed that the Connecticut law forbidding the use of contraceptives had a "maximum destructive impact upon that relationship." Continuing, he asked, "Would we allow the police to search the sacred precincts of marital bedrooms for telltale signs of the use of contraceptives? The very idea is repulsive to the notions of privacy surrounding the marriage relationship."[6]

Persuaded by these arguments, the Supreme Court voted to reverse the convictions of Griswold and Buxton. Justice Douglas concluded his opinion with the following statement, which is among the first constitutionally relevant statements designed to give married couples rights related to their sexual behavior, if only tangentially:

> We deal with a right to privacy older than the Bill of Rights—older than our political parties, older than our school system. Marriage is a coming together for better or for worse, hopefully enduring, and intimate to the degree of being sacred. It is an association that promotes a way of life, not causes; a harmony in living, not political faiths; a bilateral loyalty, not commercial or social projects. Yet it is an association for as noble a purpose as any involved in our prior decisions.[7]

Although six other justices agreed with the result in *Griswold*, Justices Hugo Black and Potter Stewart dissented strongly. Their arguments would later play an important role in other major decisions about sexuality, such as abortion (*Roe v. Wade*) and homosexual behavior (*Bowers v. Hardwick*). Justice Stewart opened his dissent by noting that

> Since 1879 Connecticut has had on its books a law which forbids the use of contraceptives by anyone. I think this is an uncommonly silly law. . . . But we are not asked in this case to say whether we think this law is unwise, or even asinine. We are asked to hold that it violates the United States Constitution. And that I can not do.[8]

Moreover, Justice Stewart was not persuaded by the "penumbra" justification for privacy rights proffered by Justice Douglas. Justice Stewart complained that he could "find no such general right of privacy in the Bill of Rights, in any other part of the Constitution, or in any case ever before decided by this Court" and concluded, therefore, that no such right exists.[9] Apparently, he found implausible the notion that new rights might emanate from explicit constitutional guarantees. Clearly, Justice Stewart's opinion contradicts the spirit, if not the word, of the

Ninth Amendment, which permits the expansion of constitutionally protected rights.

Justice Stewart's dissent notwithstanding, the right to privacy gained a leg (albeit a feeble one) to stand on, thanks to the majority decision in *Griswold*. Shortly thereafter, privacy took on new meaning in the now famous abortion debates of *Roe v. Wade*, which resulted in the nullification of another state law with relevance to sexuality, reproduction, and the sanctity of the body.

ROE V. WADE

In August 1969, a twenty-one-year-old carnival worker, nicknamed Pixie, was allegedly gang-raped by three men and a woman near Augusta, Georgia. Three weeks later, Pixie (whose real name was Norma McCorvey) discovered she was pregnant. Norma went back to her home state of Texas hoping to get an abortion.[10]

Abortion was illegal in Texas, except to save the life of the mother. McCorvey discovered that "no legitimate doctor in Texas would touch me. . . . I found a doctor who offered to abort me for $500. Only he didn't have a license, and I was scared to turn my body over to him. So there I was—pregnant, unmarried, unemployed, alone and stuck."[11]

McCorvey kept her pregnancy, had her child, and gave her up for adoption. Shortly thereafter, she met two recent University of Texas law school graduates, Sarah Weddington and Linda Coffee. Together these three women (with McCorvey taking the fictional name of "Jane Roe") decided to challenge the constitutionality of the Texas abortion law. Their goal was to establish a woman's constitutional right to control her body, by appealing to the "right to privacy" from *Griswold*.

Curiously, nearly twenty years after *Roe v. Wade*, McCorvey admitted that, though she was poor and single, she was never raped. She invented the gang rape because she thought it might help her get an abortion in Texas. "I said it because I was desperate and wanted an abortion very, very bad and thought that would help the situation. It didn't."[12]

It is significant that McCorvey was poor, for the poor bore the greatest burden of the Texas abortion law. At the time, abortion was legal in several states, including New York. Thus, Texas women with sufficient assets could, if they desired, obtain legal abortions from licensed gynecologists in New York City. Poor Texas women, however, could afford neither the travel nor the medical intervention itself, leaving them with two options: unwanted children or risky "back alley" abortions. They could also try to self-abort, which was *not* a crime in Texas. It was only a crime for a physician to perform an abortion. For all the obvious reasons, few women chose to self-abort.

The Texas law did not intentionally discriminate against poor women. Rather, the purpose of the Texas abortion law was to protect the "rights" of the fetus or embryo, on the premise that life begins at the point of conception and therefore proto-humans at all stages of development share with already born persons a fundamental right to life.

Henry Wade, district attorney of the criminal division for Dallas County, defended the Texas law before the Supreme Court. But Wade met a harsh critic in Justice Stewart, who took immediate exception to the law, noting that Texas does not punish a woman who self-aborts. Surely, if the state were protecting fetal life, it would not matter who performed the abortion.

Justice Stewart's concern was consistent with Weddington's argument that the Texas law ultimately constrained doctors from considering the effects of pregnancy on a woman's health, and thereby protected the fetus to the potential detriment of the mother. Weddington was particularly aware of these concerns because she, like many other women in the late 1960s, had crossed the border into Mexico to obtain an abortion from a licensed doctor.[13]

In her argument, Weddington primarily emphasized the issue of a woman's right to exercise control over her life and her body. As noted, there was a fundamental incongruity in Texas state law: Texan women could legally perform abortions on themselves, but they could not enlist the assistance of Texan doctors. Thus, the ultimate question in *Roe* was whether women had a right to make reproductive decisions (including abortion) and, if so, whether doctors had a right to perform medically sound procedures to implement those decisions. This highlights an important facet of abortion "rights": if they are to be meaningful, such "rights" must reside in both sides of the doctor-patient relationship. That is, not only must women have the right to abort, doctors must have the right to perform abortion procedures. In Texas, the right to abort was technically not in question, but the right to seek a safe abortion was.

As millions of "pro-choice" women and men have done since, Weddington argued that the issue was not whether abortion was right or wrong, but whether abortion decisions belonged in the personal or the public sphere:

> We are not here to advocate abortion. . . . We do not ask this Court to rule that abortion is good, or desirable in any particular situation. We are here to advocate that the decision as to whether or not a particular woman will continue to carry or will terminate a pregnancy is a decision that should be made by that individual; that, in fact, she has a constitutional right to make that decision for herself; and that the State has shown no interest in interfering with that decision.[14]

The Supreme Court agreed that Texas's interests were insufficient to justify its near total ban on abortions and so ruled in favor of "Jane Roe." The majority opinion concluded that the "right to privacy" was "broad enough to encompass a woman's decision whether or not to terminate her pregnancy." Consequent to *Roe*, states could no longer make abortions categorically illegal during the first two trimesters of pregnancy, and even in the third trimester abortions were required to be permitted where necessary to preserve the life or health of the mother.[15]

Although *Roe* broadened the concept of the right to privacy, which now encompassed abortion, the Supreme Court reversed this expansive trend in *Bowers v. Hardwick,* in which the Court concluded that privacy need not extend to homosexual relationships. The majority opinion in this case was written by Justice Byron White, who, along with Justice William Rehnquist, had authored a dissenting opinion in *Roe.*

BOWERS V. HARDWICK

Michael Hardwick was arrested for drinking in public. He was supposed to go to court, and he should have gone to court, but he didn't. An arrest warrant was issued, and a police officer went to his house to serve it. When the officer knocked on the door, Hardwick's roommate answered. The roommate told the police officer that he didn't think Hardwick was at home, but if the officer wanted to check the bedroom to make sure, he could. When the officer opened the bedroom door, he discovered Hardwick having sex with another man. Hardwick was then arrested under the Georgia statute for sodomy (which usually refers to anal intercourse, but sometimes also refers to oral-genital sex).

Shortly thereafter, the district attorney dropped the sodomy charges. It was not the kind of criminal case he wanted to pursue. However, the indignity of being arrested was sufficient to motivate Hardwick to contact the American Civil Liberties Union to challenge the constitutionality of Georgia's sodomy law. Although a federal court initially dismissed the case, the Eleventh Circuit Court of Appeals reversed the arrest, concluding that the right to privacy protects all individuals from punishment for their "consensual sexual behavior." This ruling was immediately appealed by Georgia's Attorney General, Michael Bowers.

Bowers v. Hardwick[16] was argued before the Supreme Court on March 31, 1986, and was decided three months later. Writing for the majority, Justice White made very clear that he had no sympathy for homosexuals. He viewed *Bowers* as questioning whether the federal Constitution gave homosexuals a fundamental right to engage in sodomy. White was adamant that the Supreme Court was not going to announce such a right: "This we are unwilling to do."[17] Although he acknowledged that the privacy rights established in *Griswold* and *Roe* were in keeping with the "liberty" of the due process clause of the Fourteenth Amendment, in his opinion those rights were irrelevant to *Bowers*, as the Georgia statute entailed no great loss in liberty. Justice White did not feel that justice was sacrificed by making sodomy illegal for homosexuals, and he did not believe that tolerance for homosexual sodomy was "deeply rooted in this Nation's history and tradition."[18] Indeed, he noted that there have always been laws against homosexuality and sodomy and argued that there was no reason to reverse this historical trend.

In the end, only one vote separated the majority from the minority in the Supreme Court's five-to-four decision to uphold Georgia's anti-sodomy statute. It easily could have gone the other way, however. When the Supreme Court first voted on this case in conference, it was five to four to *overturn* the ban on sodomy. Four justices were prepared to overturn the Georgia law as infringing the right to privacy, with Justice Lewis Powell ready to follow suit on grounds that the law ran afoul of the Eighth Amendment's prohibition of cruel and unusual punishment (violations of the sodomy law were punishable by up to twenty years in prison!). However, the following day, Chief Justice Warren Burger sent Justice Powell a three-page letter pleading with him to change his vote. In this letter, which Justice Powell described as mostly nonsense, Burger argued that revoking the Georgia law would create a slippery slope ("are we to excuse every Jack the Ripper?" asked Chief Justice Burger[19]) and concluded that there was no reason for indulging Hardwick's desire for "sexual gratification." Such nonsense notwithstanding, this letter persuaded Justice Powell to change his vote on the day the final tally was taken.[20]

Justice Powell was ambivalent about the social ramifications of homosexual behavior. On the one hand, he worried about the implications of homosexuality for the continuation of the species:

> In view of my age, general background and convictions as to what is best for society . . . I think a good deal can be said for the validity of statutes that criminalize sodomy. If it becomes wide-spread, civilization itself will be severely weakened as the perpetuation of the human race depends on normal sexual relations just as is true in the animal world.[21]

The silliness of this argument is transparent. Homosexual activities represent only a small fraction of human sexual behavior and certainly do not preclude heterosexual reproduction. Same-sex sexual behavior is evident in all historical epochs, and in many mammalian species, and in no instance is there any suggestion that such behavior interferes with the ability of the species to perpetuate itself. Yet, Justice Powell also recognized the futility of criminalizing sodomy:

> If I were in the state legislature I would vote to decriminalize sodomy. It is widely practiced in some places (e.g., San Francisco), and is a criminal statute that almost never is enforced. Moreover, police have more important responsibilities than snooping around trying to catch people in the act of sodomy.[22]

Thus, Justice Powell was deeply conflicted over *Bowers*. This, perhaps, explains why he voted against Georgia's law in conference but, after a bit of coaxing by Chief Justice Burger, eventually voted to uphold the law. Amazingly, he was not yet done flip-flopping. In another reversal, he later conceded that he had made a mistake and should have voted that the Georgia law was unconstitutional, as he had originally intended.[23] This would have tipped the balance of justice in favor of Hardwick, and nullified Georgia's antisodomy law.

Although Justice White, writing for the Court, focused on the particular sex acts at issue (anal and oral sex) and framed the debate in moralistic terms, Justice Harry Blackmun insisted in his dissenting opinion that *Bowers* was *not* about "a fundamental right to engage in sodomy" but instead about "the right to be let alone."[24] Justice Blackmun refuted Justice White's appeal to history as a marker of the constitutionality of the Georgia law. Quoting former Chief Justice Oliver Wendell Holmes, Blackmun stressed that it is foolish to keep a law simply because it "persists from blind imitation of the past."

Justice Blackmun was also very concerned with the Supreme Court's "obsessive focus on homosexual activity," pointing out that the Georgia law itself makes no mention of the sex of the participants. In fact, it states only that a "person commits the offense of sodomy when he performs or submits to any sexual act involving the sex organs of one person and the mouth or anus of another."[25] Obviously, this could as easily apply to heterosexual as to homosexual couples, making sexual orientation irrelevant as a matter of law. As such, Justice Blackmun concluded that Hardwick's claim of "unconstitutional intrusion into his privacy and his right of intimate association" was unrelated to his sexual orientation.

Even more forcefully, Justice Blackmun used his written dissent to craft constitutional language that would give broad-based support to sexual rights under the banner of the right to privacy. Because this language is extraordinarily significant in the way it argues for sexual rights, it is quoted here in its entirety:

> Only the most willful blindness could obscure the fact that sexual intimacy is "a sensitive, key relationship of human existence, central to family life, community welfare, and the development of human personality" [quoting *Paris Adult Theatre I v. Slaton*[26]]. The fact that individuals define themselves in a significant way through their intimate sexual relationships with others suggests, in a Nation as diverse as ours, that there may be many "right" ways of conducting those relationships, and that much of the richness of a relationship will come from the freedom an individual has to choose the form and nature of these intensely personal bonds. . . . The Court claims that its decision today merely refuses to recognize a fundamental right to engage in homosexual sodomy; what the Court really has refused to recognize is the fundamental interest all

individuals have in controlling the nature of their intimate associations with others.[27]

Finally, putting it in a basic rights perspective, Justice Blackmun concluded:

> It is precisely because the issue raised by this case touches the heart of
> what makes individuals what they are that we should be especially
> sensitive to the rights of those whose choices upset the majority.[28]

Rarely do sexual rights, broadly characterized, receive such highly
placed champions or such heartfelt eloquence, especially from someone
with no obvious personal interest in the outcome of the debate. Although we are in complete agreement with the sentiment and logic of
Justice Blackmun's interpretation, we would make one adjustment. We
would give him another weapon with which to overcome the "great resistance" of the majority in *Bowers* to "expand the substantive reach" of
fundamental rights.[29] That weapon is the Ninth Amendment.[30]

THE POVERTY OF PRIVACY

In this chapter, we have reviewed three momentous Supreme Court
decisions and found three quixotic interpretations of privacy. In *Griswold v. Connecticut*, two defendants, one of them a doctor, were convicted of dispensing information as part of a public service. The conviction was overturned because it was held that married couples—not
Griswold or Buxton—have a "zone of privacy" in which to make decisions about contraception. Contraceptives thereby became legal in Connecticut through an appeal to privacy. Had this case been brought to
overturn the conviction of a married couple charged under Connecticut's law forbidding the use of contraceptives, then the Supreme
Court's ruling would have been entirely sensible and appropriate. Although we applaud the Court for protecting the rights of couples to
make their own reproductive and contraceptive decisions, the relevance of privacy to the charges against Griswold and Buxton remains
unclear.

The next case, *Roe v. Wade*, concerned a woman, Jane Roe, who had
the right to an abortion (a self-conducted abortion, that is), but lived in

a state (Texas) that forbade doctors from performing the procedure. The Court found the Texas law prohibiting doctors from performing abortions unconstitutional because it impeded women's exercise of their privacy-derived right to have a doctor assist with the abortion.

Finally, in *Bowers v. Hardwick*, the Court upheld a law that clearly permits intrusion into the private sex lives of Georgia citizens. Although this law has no particular relevance to sexual orientation per se, since both heterosexuals and homosexuals can engage in sodomy, the Court based its decision on its personal distaste for homosexuality and the belief that restricting homosexual behavior entails no great loss of liberty. Homosexuals, it appears, do not have the cherished right to privacy, making this right stingy, rather than pithy, particularly as it relates to sexual decision making.

Thus, in these cases we find that protecting a person's (or couple's) right to privacy requires doctors who are able to dispense information on contraceptives (*Griswold*) and perform abortions (*Roe*)—activities that seem somewhat tangential to the sexual decision making that lies at the heart of the privacy debate. Yet strangely, the right to privacy does *not* protect someone from being prosecuted for engaging in *private*, consensual sexual behaviors that others might find distasteful or unconventional (*Bowers*).

Part of this conundrum is undoubtedly related to the judicial history of privacy as a legal concept. Although we have discussed privacy as it relates to sexual freedoms, the typical context in which the Supreme Court addresses privacy concerns is outside the sexual realm. The concept of privacy has been applied to debates about investigative powers of legislatures (e.g., requiring doctors to identify patients who receive hazardous but legal drugs, such as opiates[31]); newspapers' rights to report factually true but professionally damaging information about individuals[32]; the right to block receipt of offensive mail[33]; and so on.

The Court is perhaps on the most familiar ground when it invokes "privacy" as part of the Fourth Amendment's restriction on governmental searches and seizures (i.e., "The right of the people to be secure in their persons, houses, papers, and effects against unreasonable searches and seizures, shall not be violated"). Privacy rights in this context flow from a supreme regard in American jurisprudence for the sanctity of the home. Indeed, the Fourth Amendment was designed to preclude "writs of assistance," which were used by British officers to enter private property and search for contraband.

When the Court invokes privacy rights under the aegis of the Fourth Amendment, it usually is in good stead. There was considerable precedence for this amendment in our English law heritage, such as the Magna Carta (i.e., "No freeman man shall be taken . . . except by lawful judgement of his peers"), the 1604 *Semayne* case ("the house of everyone is to him his castle and fortress"), and the writings of William Blackstone, who in 1767 concluded that a person's house deserved deference that the state could not violate without justification.[34]

Given the relevance of the Fourth Amendment to privacy doctrine, it seems natural that the Court in *Griswold* would look to the amendment's privacy guarantees as a means to bolster marital rights. Not only did Justice Douglas mention the Fourth Amendment conspicuously among his penumbras, but Justice Arthur Goldberg in his concurrence also pointed out the relevance of the Fourth Amendment to marital privacy:

> Certainly the safeguarding of the home does not follow merely from the sanctity of property rights. The home derives its pre-eminence as the seat of family life. And the integrity of that life is something so fundamental that it has been found to draw to its protection the principles of more than one explicitly granted Constitutional right. . . . Of this whole "private realm of family life" it is difficult to imagine what is more private or more intimate than a husband and wife's marital relations.[35]

Nonetheless, as we have seen from *Griswold* and its progeny, the extension of the Fourth Amendment specifically, and constitutional guarantees more generally, to sexual rights has bred disorder.

The difficulty of applying conventional privacy doctrine to the arena of sexual freedoms is further illustrated by 1969's *Stanley v. Georgia*.[36] In this case the authorities searched the home of a Georgia man and, while looking for evidence of his alleged bookmaking activities, came across several 8-millimeter films. A cursory review of the films found them to be obscene and the man was charged under Georgia's law with "knowingly hav[ing] possession of . . . obscene matter." The principle issue in *Stanley* was whether private possession of obscene material was criminal. The Court conceded that states may have an interest in regulating possession of obscenity but maintained that this interest was trumped by the right of individuals, in the privacy of their homes, to read and watch obscene matter as they please (with the exception of child pornography). Nevertheless, producing or distributing obscene materials remained illegal.

Comparing *Stanley* to *Bowers*, one might think that if the regulation of obscenity may not reach into the privacy of one's home, then Hardwick's private life would similarly be beyond the pale of governmental intrusion. However, as Michael Hardwick sadly discovered, this was not the case.

The Supreme Court's confusion over sexual rights began years before the privacy cases discussed here. The Court had, in fact, established in the 1942 case *Skinner v. Oklahoma*[37] that reproduction is a constitutionally protected fundamental right. But the Court secured this right in a rather awkward way, by relying solely on the equal protection clause of the Fourteenth Amendment, which declares: "No state shall . . . deny to any person within its jurisdiction the equal protection of the laws." The law in question permitted sterilization of repeat offenders who committed crimes of "moral turpitude." Thus, it concerned a fundamental right (reproduction), which the Court pointed out is "one of the basic civil rights of man. Marriage and procreation are fundamental to the very existence and survival of the race."[38] As such, the law was strictly scrutinized. In adjudicating this case, the Court found that Oklahoma's law disproportionately affected "blue-collar" (as opposed to "white-collar") criminals and therefore concluded that Oklahoma's uneven approach to sterilization violated the "equal protection of the laws" afforded by the Fourteenth Amendment.

Only fifteen years prior to *Skinner*, in *Buck v. Bell*[39] the Court had upheld a law, over both equal protection and due process claims, that allowed involuntary sterilization of institutionalized, "mentally defective" persons. The plaintiff in *Buck* was described as "a feeble minded white woman . . . the daughter of a feeble minded mother . . . and the mother of an illegitimate feeble minded child."[40] Chief Justice Holmes, in one of his less shining moments, justified the law by remarking: "It is better for all the world, if instead of waiting to execute degenerate offspring for crime, or to let them starve for their imbecility, society can prevent those who are manifestly unfit from continuing their kind. . . . Three generations of imbeciles are enough."[41] Compared with *Buck*, *Skinner* was a notable (if awkward) step forward for fundamental sexual rights. It was notable because, for the first time, the Court affirmed a basic right to reproduce, but it was awkward in basing this right on the Fourteenth Amendment's equal protection clause (not the most relevant source of fundamental reproductive rights).

The more general right to privacy poses a similar difficulty: what is the constitutional basis for this right? In *Griswold*, Justice Douglas professed to find support for this right throughout the text of the Constitution: "This notion of privacy . . . emanates from the totality of the constitutional scheme under which we live."[42] As noted above, Justice Stewart disagreed, stating in his dissent that he could "find no such general right of privacy in the Bill of Rights, [or] in any other part of the Constitution."[43] Later, in *Roe v. Wade*, Justice Stewart would discover the missing right to privacy within the "liberty" interest protected against state action by the Fourteenth Amendment. In his concurrence, Justice Stewart asserted that *Griswold* "can be rationally understood only as a holding that the Connecticut statute substantively invaded the 'liberty' that is protected by the Due Process Clause of the Fourteenth Amendment."[44] Since *Roe*, the Court has generally adhered to this view.

This position leaves the Court open to accusations that it has simply injected its own values into the Constitution. Set adrift from more settled privacy doctrine, with only the "liberty" of due process to guide them, judges have been charged with moral philosophizing. This accusation seems particularly apropos for Justice Douglas's construction of privacy in *Griswold*. Opposition to the majority decision, such as Justice Black's dissenting opinion, noted that there are no explicit constitutional provisions supporting a right to privacy:

> The Court talks about a constitutional "right of privacy" as though there is some constitutional provision or provisions forbidding any law ever to be passed which might abridge the "privacy" of individuals. But there is not. There are, of course, guarantees in certain specific constitutional provisions which are designed in part to protect privacy at certain times and places with respect to certain activities. . . . I get nowhere in this case by talk about a constitutional "right of privacy" as an emanation from one or more constitutional provisions. I like my privacy as well as the next one, but I am nevertheless compelled to admit the government has a right to invade it unless prohibited by some specific constitutional provision.[45]

Justice Douglas denied the implication that, in its majority opinion, the Court had "invented" a right to privacy. As he explained, "We deal with a right of privacy older than the Bill of Rights—older than our political parties, older than our school system."[46] Thus, privacy is—to borrow Bennett Patterson's phrase—a "pre-constitutional right" that antedates and transcends the specific provisions of the U.S. Constitution,[47] or any constitution, for that matter. Indeed, Patterson, like Knowlton Kelsey[48] before him, considered privacy to be a fundamental, natural right of mankind, eligible for *Ninth Amendment* protections:

> Our thesis is that human rights which are not enumerated in the Constitution will be revealed and become apparent in the future, and it is within the spirit of the Constitution, and the letter of the Ninth Amendment, that these rights should be recognized and protected. . . . The right to privacy may be such a right. If there is such a right, it is difficult to classify it under any right that is enumerated in the Constitution. This is a right that is of comparatively recent recognition. Some courts call it a fundamental right. While the courts seem to feel that it should exist, there is a great timidity and lack of forthrightness in the protection of this right, because its existence is not to be found in the written and enumerated law.[49]

If privacy is a fundamental "pre-constitutional" liberty, as proposed by Patterson, then Justice Douglas is absolved: a right to privacy didn't need to be invented, it already existed in the implicit guarantees of the Ninth Amendment. This was Justice Goldberg's argument in *Griswold*. His concurring opinion, he explained, was meant to "emphasize the relevance of [the Ninth] Amendment to the Court's holding,"[50] which listed this amendment among the penumbras supportive of the posited right to privacy. After briefly reviewing the historical development of the Ninth Amendment, Justice Goldberg returned to the case at hand:

> To hold that a right so basic and fundamental and so deep-rooted in our society as the right to privacy in marriage may be infringed because that right is not guaranteed in so many words by the first eight amendments to the Constitution is to ignore the Ninth Amendment and give it no effect whatsoever.[51]

Marital privacy is a fundamental Ninth Amendment right, he argued, and therefore susceptible to the due process guarantees of the Fourteenth Amendment, as applied against the state of Connecticut. He concluded:

> In sum, I believe that the right of privacy in the marital relation is fundamental and basic—a personal right "retained by the people" within the meaning of the Ninth Amendment. Connecticut cannot constitutionally abridge this fundamental right, which is protected by the Fourteenth Amendment from infringement by the States. I agree with the Court that the petitioners' convictions must therefore be reversed.[52]

Justice Goldberg's astute analysis of the history of the Ninth Amendment and its applicability to the *Griswold* case "catapulted the Ninth into sudden respectability."[53] However, it is important to emphasize that this *concurring* opinion supported only a vague notion of privacy, limited to married couples, that permitted them to make reproductive decisions without interference by the state. It did not proclaim a general right to sexual choice, within marriage or without. According to Justice Goldberg: "The Court's holding today . . . in no way interferes with a State's proper regulation of sexual promiscuity or adultery."[54]

Contraceptive rights were finally extended to unmarried couples in 1972's *Eisenstadt v. Baird*.[55] At issue was a Massachusetts law forbidding anyone other than a registered physician or pharmacist from dispensing contraceptive devices or information. When, in the course of a Boston University lecture, William Baird (who was neither a physician nor a pharmacist) provided a female student with contraceptive foam, he was charged under this statute and brought to trial. He was initially convicted both for exhibiting contraceptives and for giving the young woman the foam. The Massachusetts Supreme Judicial Court set aside the first conviction as a violation of Baird's First Amendment rights, but, by a four-to-three vote, upheld the conviction for dispensing contraceptive foam. In November 1971, the debate over the constitutionality of the second conviction reached the U.S. Supreme Court. The Court, relying on *Griswold*, held that Baird's conviction should be set aside. The Massachusetts statute, "viewed as a prohibition on contraception, per se, violates the rights of single persons under the Equal Protection Clause of the Fourteenth Amendment."[56] Marital status was immaterial, the Court ruled, with regard to the protections afforded reproductive decisions by *Griswold*:

> It is true that in *Griswold* the right of privacy in question inhered in the marital relationship. . . . [But] if the right of privacy means anything, it is the right of the individual, married or single, to be free from unwarranted governmental intrusion into matters so fundamentally affecting a person as the decision whether to bear or beget a child.[57]

Despite this promising trend toward greater recognition of the fundamental nature of *individual* sexual rights, the Court's privacy decisions retained elements of a reproductive bias, as illustrated by its stance on homosexual sodomy. Just months before the *Bowers* decision denying homosexual couples the right to engage in consensual oral or anal sex, the Oklahoma Court of Criminal Appeals set aside a criminal conviction for *heterosexual* sodomy, ruling in *Post v. Oklahoma* that "the right to privacy, as formulated by the Supreme Court, includes the right to select consensual adult sex partners."[58] Presumably, the Oklahoma court was aware that the issue of homosexual sodomy would soon be decided by the Supreme Court. Consequently, the appeals court took pains to limit its holding, explicitly disavowing the obvious implications of its findings for consensual sex between same-sex partners. In combination, *Post* and *Bowers* suggest that whether or not a particular sex act is considered "private" depends on the sexes of the persons involved.

PRIVACY VERSUS THE NINTH AMENDMENT

For sexual freedom to be truly meaningful it must extend not only to those reproductive acts encouraged by the dominant morality, but also to those nonreproductive expressions of sexual intimacy upon which society sometimes frowns. At present, our (somewhat limited) sexual freedoms are protected against state action by the "right to privacy" and the "liberty" guarantees of the Fourteenth Amendment's due process clause. Conceivably, the privacy doctrine could be expanded to secure our sexual rights in all their breadth. But, as our review of the development of privacy doctrine demonstrates, the right to privacy provides a weak and unstable basis for sexual rights in general. This weak foundation no doubt contributed significantly to Richard Posner's contention that "there is no more troubled field of law today than the regulation of sexual behavior."[59] Posner notes that where sex is concerned, courts "have little idea of what they are doing," "conventional legal reasoning carries them nowhere," and "common sense [is] an unreliable guide" because of the emotional and taboo nature of sex.[60]

Calvin Massey expresses a similar opinion, offering the Ninth Amendment as a possible solution to the privacy morass: "Current constitutional privacy jurisprudence is unnecessarily muddled. Rather than grounding privacy rights squarely amid the unenumerated natural rights secured by the ninth amendment, it uses as its constitutional anchor the Due Process Clauses of the fifth and fourteenth amendments."[61] We agree with both Posner and Massey but believe that sexual rights *themselves* should be grounded directly in the bedrock of the Ninth Amendment.

The problem with sexual privacy rights as constructed by the Supreme Court is that "the term 'privacy' is a misnomer for what is really being protected"—namely, sexual intimacy.[62] What is needed is a clean break from privacy jurisprudence coupled with a recognition of the fundamental right to engage in consensual acts of sexual intimacy, whether reproductive or nonreproductive, heterosexual or homosexual, married or unmarried. The concept of privacy, as developed by the Court, is much too ill-defined to serve as an effective basis for protecting our sexual rights. The natural home for such rights, as for all fundamental rights not explicitly enumerated in the Constitution, is the Ninth Amendment.

As we explain in the next chapter, the Ninth Amendment provides a solid foundation on which to secure our rights to make intimate sexual choices, reproductive or not, within marriage or without, and regardless of sexual orientation, preference, or happenstance. Firmly securing these rights by direct appeal to the unenumerated rights of the Ninth Amendment is more natural, parsimonious, and transparent than making procreation rights a spin-off of the equal protection guarantees of the Fourteenth Amendment, as the Court did in *Skinner*, or the various penumbras construed as protecting privacy, as in *Griswold*. The "basic civil right" to reproduce, or not—which most certainly existed long before it was affirmed in *Skinner*—seems an obvious candidate for Ninth Amendment protections. Likewise, the freedom of intimate expression—whatever form this expression assumes—seems to us a natural right, given by nature and inviolate by human government.

The Constitution grants the federal government no power to regulate sex, the most intimate of human activities. Yet, the right to make reproductive and nonreproductive choices, *and to act upon these choices*, is not explicitly guaranteed either. From our vantage point, the right to sexual expression is obviously and unquestionably retained by the people, and therefore is constitutionally protected—not indirectly by the equal protection clause, nor at bottom by the "liberty" of the due process clause, but originally and fundamentally, by the Ninth Amendment. What could be more basic, more natural, than the right to choose how, when, and with whom we have sex?

4

A Solid Foundation for Sexual Rights

SEVERAL YEARS PRIOR to its ruling in *Griswold v. Connecticut*,[1] which upheld the right of married couples to use contraceptives in the privacy of the marital relationship, the Supreme Court had dismissed a similar appeal challenging the constitutionality of Connecticut's contraceptives statute. Here are the pertinent facts in *Poe v. Ullman*: After suffering through three consecutive pregnancies, each of which resulted in the birth (and death soon thereafter) of a child with a congenital abnormality, Mr. and Mrs. Poe sought the advice of an eminent gynecologist, Dr. Buxton (the same Dr. Buxton who was later to figure prominently in *Griswold*), regarding applicable methods of contraception. In their complaint, the Poes asserted that they were unable to obtain the requested information because "its delivery and use may or will be claimed . . . to constitute offenses against Connecticut law."[2] However, because neither the Poes nor Dr. Buxton had yet been charged with a crime under this law—and possibly because the statute had been around for eighty years with only one reported prosecution—the Court felt that it could not rule on its constitutionality.

Believing that "the appellants have presented a very pressing claim for Constitutional protection," Justice John Marshall Harlan dissented. His dissent foreshadowed the central argument in *Griswold*: "it is difficult," he wrote, "to imagine what is more private and intimate than a husband and wife's marital relations."[3] Although one might question the relevance of marital status to the degree of privacy or intimacy involved in sexual relations, the more intriguing question is why, in this case and its successors (e.g., *Griswold*), the Court chose to focus on privacy, leaving the relations themselves largely unexamined.[4] By "relations," of course, we infer that Justice Harlan meant sex.

"Privacy" refers to the privilege of being able to act unobserved by others, or to the personal nature of the act itself. In its decision that married couples have a right to privacy in their reproductive choices (in *Griswold*) and that this right also extends to unmarried couples (in *Eisenstadt v. Baird*) the Court was saying, literally, that couples could make reproductive decisions without undue scrutiny by the government. By protecting their right to privacy in making contraceptive decisions, the Court intended that these couples should, in fact, be protected in their *use* of contraceptives. In effect, the Court was protecting *sexual conduct* (the act) through *privacy* (the context surrounding the act, or the nature thereof).

Rather than protecting the private circumstances or context in which sexual conduct occurs, it would be much more parsimonious, direct, and *honest* for the Court to have declared that particular sexual acts (e.g., contraceptive use) are themselves protected. As we hope to establish in this book, this protection should extend to all the choices individuals make with regard to how they express their sexuality. Some couples express their sexual unity by electing to conceive children, others by practicing contraception during heterosexual intercourse, and still others by engaging in nonreproductive sexual acts, including oral and anal sex, mutual masturbation, erotic massage, deep kissing, sadomasochistic role play, and so on, ad infinitum. These behaviors should be protected out of a basic regard for personal autonomy, and not simply because they are "private" or "intimate." Many times, sexual relations are not especially intimate (e.g., commercial sex encounters). At other times, whatever intimacy exists is completely self-directed (e.g., solo masturbation). Does the lack of intimacy make this conduct any less worthy of constitutional protection? The answer clearly is "no," other than to enforce a vision of moral conduct that, by way of our Christian heritage, discourages nonintimate—and especially, nonreproductive—sexuality in its many forms.

Although the state may legislate for the health, safety, and general welfare of its constituency, it does not have unfettered authority to promote its particular view of proper moral conduct, particularly where a fundamental right is concerned. Chief Justice Earl Warren's dissenting opinion in *Jacobellis v. Ohio* broadly summed up the issue:

> In this and other cases in this area of the law [i.e., privacy rights], which are coming to us in ever-increasing numbers, we are faced with the resolution of rights basic both to individuals and to society as a whole. Specifically, we are called upon to reconcile the right of the

Nation and of the States to maintain a decent society and, on the other hand, the right of individuals to express themselves freely in accordance with the guarantees of the First and Fourteenth Amendments.[5]

The Court's analysis in *Eisenstadt v. Baird* (discussed in the previous chapter) illustrates Chief Justice Warren's point. The most interesting aspect of *Eisenstadt*, for our purposes, is not the Court's finding upholding the right of single people to obtain contraceptive devices (with which we wholeheartedly agree), but the Court's interpretation of the legislative *intent* behind the Massachusetts contraception law. The statute in question, which was subsequently amended to incorporate the *Griswold* exclusion for married couples, originally was included in a legislative act dealing with "Crimes against chastity, morality, decency, and good order," and was cast in strictly moralistic terms. The original stated purpose of the law was "to protect purity, to preserve chastity, to encourage continence and self restraint, to defend the sanctity of the home, and thus to engender in the State and nation a virile and virtuous race of men and women,"[6] or, more succinctly, to protect morals by "regulating the *private* sexual lives of single persons."[7] The Supreme Court found this rationale specious, citing the "dubious relation" of the contraceptive law to the stated goal of preventing fornication. Among other things, the Court wondered why, if Massachusetts truly sought to prevent extramarital sex, the penalty structure of its laws afforded only a ninety-day jail sentence to those who violated its direct prohibition on fornication while meting out a five-year prison sentence to persons convicted of illegally distributing contraceptive devices.[8]

The Court also considered the lower court's finding in this case:

> To say that contraceptives are immoral as such, and are to be forbidden to unmarried persons who will nevertheless persist in having intercourse, means that such persons must risk for themselves an unwanted pregnancy, for the child illegitimacy, and for society, a possible obligation of support. Such a view of morality is not only the very mirror image of sensible legislation; we consider that it conflicts with fundamental human rights. In the absence of demonstrated harm, we hold it is beyond the competency of the state.[9]

Ultimately, the Court concluded that it need not "decide that important [moral] question in this case because, whatever the rights of the individual to access to contraceptives may be, the rights must be the same for the unmarried and the married alike."[10] Obviously, we concur with the Court regarding the equal accessibility of condoms to married and single persons,[11] but we agree as well with the lower court's suggestion that Massachusetts's contraceptive law "conflicts with fundamental human rights." These fundamental sexual rights, we assert, are tantamount to the natural rights of humankind, and therefore are embedded within the unenumerated rights of the Ninth Amendment.

The right to sexual autonomy, we believe, should also extend to the choice to engage in sex with a person of one's own gender. In a 1996 case, *Romer v. Evans*,[12] the Court invalidated on equal protection grounds a Colorado amendment that foreclosed to homosexual persons legal protection against discrimination (e.g., in employment or housing), concluding: "If the constitutional conception of 'equal protection of the laws' means anything, it must at the very least mean that a bare ... desire to harm a politically unpopular group cannot constitute a *legitimate* governmental interest."[13] Denying gay men and women their right to sexual expression for reasons of animus is unlawful, and denying them sexual rights for reasons of morality (generally a mask for animus) is no more sensible than the denial of rights to unmarried persons overturned in *Eisenstadt*. If same-gender sexual conduct is offensive to some (as was the conduct of unmarried persons in *Eisenstadt*), so be it. These are not people who are broadcasting their conduct into the homes and lives of others. This is not "a 'live' performance of a man and woman locked in a sexual embrace at high noon in Times Square" (*Paris Adult Theater v. Slaton*[14]). These are people engaging in private, protected sexual relations. Equal protection of the laws requires that gay men and lesbians enjoy the same opportunities as heterosexuals to enrich their lives with intimate sexual encounters.

Just as the Court in *Moore v. East Cleveland*[15] struck down a state ordinance that defined "family" too narrowly, freedom of sexual expression is unduly limited if it does not extend to minority sexual choices, such as a preference for same-gender partners. Significantly, the plurality opinion in *Moore* conceded the relevance of the *Griswold* line of cases to its decision and, quoting Louis Pollak,[16] avowed: "In due course we will see *Griswold* as a reaffirmation of the Court's continuing obligation to test the justifications offered by the state for state-imposed constraints which significantly hamper those modes of individual fulfillment which are at the heart of a free society."[17] As the *Moore* plurality anticipated, it is the right of the *individual* to sexual self-expression, regardless of sexual orientation, that warrants constitutional protection. This right is fundamental to our happiness as individuals and, as we establish below, is precisely the sort of preeminent right James Madison meant the Ninth Amendment to safeguard.

THE PURSUIT OF HAPPINESS

The pursuit of happiness is central to the American way of life. It is one of the basic entitlements upon which our country was founded and is among the most cherished freedoms that we, as Americans, enjoy. Although we (arguably) may take credit for advancing the pursuit of happiness farther than any other nation in recorded history, we were not the first to propose happiness as an organizing principle of government. Happiness has a long history.

The concept of "happiness" was a cornerstone of eighteenth-century philosophical thought, finding voice in the works of John Locke, Francis Hutchinson, and Jean-Jacques Burlamaqui, among others. Colonial America famously expressed its high regard for happiness in Thomas Jefferson's Declaration of Independence, which asserts that "all men are created equal [and] are endowed by their creator with certain inalienable rights, [among them] life, liberty, and the pursuit of happiness."[18] Constitutional Convention delegate James Wilson echoed Jefferson; "The happiness of society is the first law of every government," wrote Wilson in 1774.[19]

"Happiness" encompasses a diverse constellation of concepts, from the satisfaction of material needs for food and shelter to the more ethereal satisfactions of the mind and of the flesh. In his influential *Second Treatise of Government*, Locke equated "happiness" with sensible pleasure and graded it from "the utmost pleasure we are capable of" to "so much ease from all pain, and so much present pleasure, as without which anyone can not be content."[20] For Locke, "the pursuit of happiness" was the ultimate determiner of people's actions. Actions were undertaken, or not, as they tended to increase or decrease a person's overall happiness.

As Lockean thought dominated the political discourse in postrevolutionary America,[21] it is not surprising that "happiness" language should appear in the state constitutions of the newly independent nation. Consider, for example, this excerpt from the New Hampshire Constitution of 1783:

[Part 1, Article I]: All men are born equally free and independent; therefore all government of right originates from the people, is founded in consent, and instituted for the general good.

II. All men have certain natural, essential and inherent rights; among which are—the enjoying and defending life and liberty—acquiring, possessing and protecting property—and in a word, of seeking and obtaining happiness.[22]

These same themes were later reflected in the resolutions passed by the states' constitutional conventions. For instance, on July 26, 1788, the New York state constitutional convention resolved

That all Power is originally vested in and consequently derived from the People, and that Government is instituted by them for their common Interest Protection and Security. That the enjoyment of Life, Liberty and the pursuit of Happiness are essential rights which every Government ought to respect and preserve. That the Powers of Government may be reassumed by the People, whensoever it shall become necessary to their Happiness.[23]

The concept of *happiness*, and the inherent right thereto, is repeated throughout the foundational documents.[24] For example, when Virginia ratified the Constitution in 1788, it did so with the suggestion that a declaration or bill of rights be added asserting the "essential and inalienable rights of the people," among them "the enjoyment of life and liberty, [the] means of acquiring, possessing and protecting property, and pursuing and obtaining happiness and safety."[25] Moreover, Madison's original proposal for a federal bill of rights included a prefatory statement proclaiming that governments are formed to secure their citizens "in the enjoyment of life and liberty . . . and generally of pursuing and obtaining happiness."[26] However, these general principles were omitted from the final version of the Bill of Rights adopted by the House, and are nowhere to be found in the Constitution. "Conceivably," Leonard Levy suggests, "the [Congressional] committee that eliminated Madison's prefatory principles believed them to be implicit in its streamlined version of what became the Ninth Amendment."[27] Edward

Corwin makes a similar point: happiness and the other general rights emphasized in Madison's proposed preface "insofar as they are rights, and insofar as they contain elements not embraced within the enumerated rights, may be protected by the Ninth Amendment."[28] If so, this historically neglected amendment becomes the reservoir for the myriad rights required to ensure all Americans the opportunity to seek their individual happiness.

In equating pleasure with happiness, Locke followed the lead of the Greek philosopher Epicurus (342–270 B.C.E.), who taught that pleasure is the supreme good and the attainment thereof is the ultimate goal of life.[29] According to Epicurus, people should (and naturally do) seek out pleasurable experiences and avoid painful ones. English philosophers such as Jeremy Bentham (1748–1832) and John Stuart Mill (1806–1873) expanded upon and codified this Epicurean notion in the now famous *Greatest Happiness Principle*:

> Utility, or the Greatest Happiness Principle, holds that actions are right in proportion as they tend to promote happiness, wrong as they tend to produce the reverse of happiness. By happiness is intended pleasure, and the absence of pain; by unhappiness, pain, and the privation of pleasure.[30]

Notice how the Greatest Happiness Principle equates happiness with pleasure. That which brings pleasure is good. Consensual sex that creates mutual pleasure clearly falls into this category.

Indeed, pleasure is one of the two main functions of sex, along with reproduction. As we discuss in our book, *With Pleasure: Thoughts on the Nature of Human Sexuality*, although the *ultimate* function of sex is the reproduction of the species (or more accurately, the perpetuation of the individual's genes[31]), the *proximal* function is to provide pleasure to the sexual participants.[32] Sexual pleasure is an evolved motivational system that was "designed" to ensure that our evolutionary ancestors reproduced. Pleasure provided the benefit needed to offset the sizable costs associated with sexual intercourse, such as time and energy expenditures, vulnerability to attack, the dangers of sexually transmitted diseases, pregnancy and childbirth, and so on. Natural selection therefore favored those who experienced greater pleasure in sex because they tended to invest more of their energies in the pursuit of sex and thus begat more offspring, many of whom inherited copies of the enhanced pleasure-seeking genes. In this way, the desire for sexual pleasure spread throughout the human race.

In the many millions of years since this exquisite and flexible sexual system first evolved, humans have co-opted it to serve various purposes other than reproduction. Although the pursuit of pleasure is undoubtedly the most prevalent rationale for engaging in sex, it is by no means the only function, or meaning, of sex. Sex is an integral component of interpersonal relationships, serving as an expression of love, commitment, and intimacy. Some people use sex to relieve stress or to reduce interpersonal tensions. Others use it to make money, and a few use it in very unhealthful ways. Very seldom, however, is sex used for its "intended" purpose, procreation: "while procreation is indisputably the ultimate function of sex, this reproductive aspect alone cannot account for the variety of meanings and practices encompassed by human sexuality."[33]

To promote the happiness of its citizens, a government has a duty to respect their pleasures—sexual and otherwise—or at the very least, not to interfere unduly with the pursuit thereof. Sexual freedom, we maintain, is crucial to the happiness of society. As the instrument meant to safeguard our liberties and to facilitate the individual pursuit of happiness, the Constitution is the natural place to seek a foundation for sexual freedoms.

Importantly, the framers' concept of happiness did not neglect the corporeal dimensions of happiness. Justice Louis Brandeis offered the following interpretation of the framers' intent:

> The makers of our Constitution undertook to secure conditions favorable to the pursuit of happiness. They recognized the significance of man's spiritual nature, of his feelings, and of his intellect. They knew that only a part of the pain, pleasure and satisfactions of life are to be found in material things. They sought to protect Americans in their beliefs, their thoughts, their emotions and their sensations.[34]

Madison himself held the preservation of intensely personal acts in highest regard—not simply the communication of ideas, but also the discharge of human "passions."[35] He considered the free exercise of the passions irreproachable so long as it "leaves to everyone the like advantage."[36] Moreover, assuming the passions are a matter of human conscience, which Madison labeled "the most sacred of all property,"[37] then the preservation of the passions takes its place at the top of Madison's hierarchy of values.

SEX AS A NATURAL RIGHT

The Constitution of the newly formed nation, particularly the Bill of Rights, is the concrete embodiment of the revolutionaries' vision of an America in which men (and women) could pursue their individual ideals of happiness, unfettered by unnecessary governmental intrusions. Roger Sherman's working draft of the Bill of Rights expressed this vision in the language of natural rights and social contract theory: "The people have certain natural rights which are retained by them when they enter into Society. Such are the rights of Conscience in matters of religion; of acquiring property and pursuing happiness and Safety."[38] Some of these rights are protected by the first eight constitutional amendments; the others are secured by the Ninth. Thus, "the Ninth Amendment is the repository of natural rights, including the right to pursue happiness."[39]

But is there a natural right to pursue *sexual* happiness? Obviously, we believe there is. Knowlton Kelsey, who years before us tried to impose a sense of order on the tangle of Ninth Amendment rights, identified the following classes of natural rights:

1) such rights as appertain originally and essentially to man, such as are inherent in his nature, and which he enjoys as a man, independent of any particular act on his side;
2) those which grow out of the nature of man and depend upon personality as distinguished from those created by law;
3) those rights which are innate, and which come from the very laws of nature, such as life, liberty, pursuit of happiness, and self-preservation.[40]

By any of Kelsey's criteria, sexual expression would appear to be a natural right. Sex is an innate biological capacity that derives "from the very laws of nature" and is essential to our happiness. The desire to express ourselves sexually is inherent in our nature and would exist with or without the social contract that forms the philosophical underpinning of our nation. Sex predates modern human society by millennia upon millennia. It is eminently natural—the birds do it, the bees do it, and every mammalian species does it as well.

One might argue that the only truly natural function of sex is procreation, and therefore only heterosexual intercourse properly should be considered a natural right. This is silliness, plain and simple. Although the sexual pleasure mechanism evolved to motivate people to reproduce, the desire for sexual pleasure can be satisfied in a variety of nonreproductive ways, from masturbation to anal intercourse.[41] If these activities were "unnatural," or a threat to the species' survival, they would have been eliminated through the process of natural selection many thousands of years ago. Since these behaviors have persisted, and are observed in many other primate species, they undoubtedly are "natural."

But did the framers recognize a natural right to sexual expression? We begin the discussion with the obvious: heterosexual intercourse. The significance of heterosexual intercourse for procreation was of course appreciated in eighteenth-century America. Procreative sexuality was encouraged by the church ("be fruitful and multiply"), with obvious economic advantage accruing to a vastly underpopulated America.[42] In the two hundred years since, the Court has vigorously resisted attempts to encroach upon the "sacred" realm of marital relations. There can be little serious doubt, therefore, that procreative sexuality would have been classed a "natural right" by anyone who gave the matter careful thought.

But even if heterosexual intercourse was recognized as a natural right, it is largely inconceivable that homosexual sodomy would have been categorized likewise. The long history of sodomy prohibitions in America (and earlier, in England) testifies to the general abhorrence to the populace of these "unnatural acts." Significantly, the laws of many states define sodomy as "the abominable and detestable crime against nature."[43] We conclude that it is unlikely that the architects of the Constitution would have acknowledged a natural right to engage in sodomy. But is this dispositive of the issue? We think not. "The natural rights of Americans should not be static and fixed as of the date of the adoption of the Constitution and the Bill of Rights," wrote Bennett

Patterson in 1955. "To interpret the Ninth Amendment in this manner would take it out of its clearly intended meaning."[44] As society evolves, so too does its understanding of humankind's essential nature and the corresponding rights required to ensure that this nature is not trampled underfoot. There is ample evidence, both historical and by analogy to our primate relatives, that nonprocreative sexuality is not antithetical to essential human nature.[45] The time seems ripe to cease ignoring this evidence and to admit nonprocreative sexuality, sodomy included, as a natural right of humankind.

This natural right to sexual expression in all its myriad forms was not ceded upon our entry into society, except insofar as needed to protect the rights of our fellow citizens. Private, consensual sexual expression is at best a victimless crime, infringing on the rights of no one. Calvin Massey eloquently summarizes this argument:

> The right to engage freely in private, consensual sex is a paradigmatic natural right. Can it be seriously contended that the social compact *creates* the right to have sexual relations? What private right, to which the state is the successor, could be asserted to circumscribe private, consensual sexual behavior? Whatever arguments may be made concerning the efficacy of natural rights theory, sex is one right which is undeniably, and powerfully, natural.[46]

In short, sexual rights were not sacrificed when we entered into the social compact. Rather, they were, and remain, "retained by the people."

Obviously, not everyone will agree with us. The Supreme Court, in particular, has refused to recognize a fundamental (or natural) right to participate in homosexual activities. In a series of cases the Court has acknowledged that childbearing, child-rearing, and marital relations deserve constitutional protection as fundamental rights (see chapter 3) but has denied the "right of homosexuals to engage in acts of sodomy."[47] Notwithstanding its decision in *Eisenstadt*, the Court seemingly has been reluctant to countenance nonmarital sexuality.

The Court's insistent focus on marital relations reflects the centrality of marriage as a social institution, not only in America, but in cultures worldwide. But marriage is not a "natural" state; it is a quasi-religious pact in which consenting persons agree to "forsake all others and keep only unto" each other, as well as a "contract made in due form of law, by which a free man and a free woman reciprocally engage to live with each other during their joint lives." Although many animal species mate for life (gibbons being the closest to humans in evolutionary terms), matrimony is a distinctly human invention, and one that translates poorly into "mating for life," as indicated by the high divorce rates in the United States and elsewhere.

In nature, sex sometimes occurs within the context of a devoted relationship, sometimes not. Often it is restricted to a male-female pair; sometimes it occurs in other dyadic combinations, and occasionally it extends to groups of three or more.[48] The right to sexual expression is an *individual*, natural right that does not depend on marriage or any other legal or social arrangement for legitimacy. As the Court duly noted in *Eisenstadt*: "The marital couple is not an independent entity with a mind and heart of its own, but an association of two individuals each with a separate intellectual and emotional makeup."[49] This is equally true for unmarried couples, threesomes, and so forth.

In summary, the individual freedom to chose how, when, and with whom we express our sexuality is a natural right that is critical to our happiness and fulfillment as human beings. Sexual rights do not derive from the social compact or from the sociolegal institution of marriage. They are, as Alexander Hamilton wrote of natural rights more generally, "written as with a sunbeam, in the whole volume of human nature . . . and can never be erased or obscured by mortal power."[50] As such, sexual rights clearly merit Ninth Amendment protection.

THE UNENUMERATED RIGHT TO SEX

Although we have emphasized sexual expression's claim to natural rights status, the concept of natural rights is not the only framework in which unenumerated rights can be articulated. Charles Black, for example, suggests that we "take the Ninth Amendment as a command to use any rational methods available to the art of law"[51] to identify these rights. In particular,

we may be able to discern and validate 'other rights retained by the people' as latent in, and therefore susceptible of being drawn from, the noblest of the concepts to which our nation is committed. The two best sources for such concepts are the Declaration of Independence and the Preamble to the Constitution.[52]

We already have noted the centrality of the concept of "happiness"—evident in numerous foundational documents (including the Declaration of Independence)—in shaping the Constitution and American society. The freedom to express oneself sexually, we maintain, is critical to happiness, which as we noted above has often been equated with, or held to include, the sensible pleasures. Similarly, it would be difficult to realize the Preamble's vision of promoting "the general welfare" of the country absent a constitutional right to sexual relations. The survival of the species and the integrity of intimate relationships are obviously dependent upon the emotional and reproductive consequences of our sexual behavior. Again drawing from the Constitution's Preamble, it seems reasonable to conclude that securing "the blessings of liberty to ourselves and our posterity" incorporates the sexual choices we make in the context of our most cherished interpersonal relationships. On this basis, we conclude that sexual rights lay strong claim to Ninth Amendment protection as "unenumerated rights" under Black's strategy for locating such rights among the "the noblest of the concepts to which our nation is committed."

Norman Redlich suggests a similar strategy, focused on the underlying themes expressed in the Constitution itself:

> Our Constitution provides the basic text for the delineation of rights retained by the people with respect to which the state and federal governments have been denied the power to act. Accordingly, the Ninth and Tenth Amendments should be used to define rights adjacent to, or analogous to, the patterns of rights in the Constitution.[53]

What pattern, if any, is discernible among the rights enumerated in the Constitution? First and foremost is the right to personal autonomy or "liberty," which figures prominently in the First Amendment (freedom of religious choice, freedom of speech, freedom of assembly) and the due process guarantees of the Fifth and Fourteenth Amendments. The right to make choices for oneself and to act upon those choices absent demonstrable harm to others (or, possibly, to one's own person) certainly ranks among the most basic human rights. The posited right to choose when and under what circumstances to participate in sexual conduct is entirely consistent with personal autonomy. Sex is inherently personal, engaging the whole of our beings: mind, body, and soul. The Court time and again has rejected legislation that invades the private sanctum of the bedroom, most famously in *Griswold v. Connecticut* and *Eisenstadt v. Baird* (but notably not in *Bowers v. Hardwick*). Interference with private, consensual sexual conduct is a clear violation of the principle of autonomy and the "right to be let alone."[54]

Both Black's suggestion that we look to the most noble principles to which our nation is committed and Redlich's method of inferring unenumerated rights from the explicit guarantees of the Constitution resemble in substantial application to the issue of sexual rights Barnett's proposal that we view the Ninth Amendment as "establishing a general constitutional presumption in favor of individual liberty."[55] Liberty, as noted above, is one of the cherished ideals upon which this nation was founded, as well as one of the preeminent themes of the Constitution as a whole.

Barnett's presumptive approach assumes that "individuals are constitutionally privileged to engage in rightful behavior—acts that are within their sphere of moral jurisdiction—and such behavior is presumptively immune from government interference."[56] The role of the judiciary is then to assess the validity of claims to the rightfulness of behaviors in the face of opposing governmental claims to regulate said behaviors in the interest of the state. Recognition of a particular right as deserving of Ninth Amendment protection would confer upon that right the same status enjoyed by the enumerated rights of the Constitution. Like enumerated rights, unenumerated rights would be amenable to judicial scrutiny and possible restriction, but the government would be required to demonstrate a compelling state interest to justify any abridgment. Thus, Ninth Amendment rights would be granted a "presumption of liberty" that would place the burden of justification on the government rather than accede a "presumption of constitutionality" to governmental regulation. "We must choose," Barnett concludes, "between two fundamentally different constructions of the Constitution, each resting on a different presumption. We either accept the presumption that in pursuing happiness persons may do whatever is not justly prohibited or we are left with a presumption that the government may do whatever is not expressly prohibited. The presence of the Ninth Amendment strongly supports the first of these two presumptions."[57]

Having reviewed several relevant perspectives, we now turn to sketching a possible framework for sexual rights in America. We hope by this point to have convinced the reader that sexual rights are worthy of Ninth Amendment protection, either as prototypical natural rights or as unenumerated rights more generally. In either instance, a "presumption of liberty" would be established that would guide adjudication in any case implicating sexual liberties. As such, *all* consensual sexual behaviors, of whatever form, would deserve the equal protection of the law. If government were to disparage any consensual sexual behavior, it would need to demonstrate "an exceedingly persuasive justification" motivated by an actual state purpose, and not merely a post hoc rationalization. This same standard currently is used to judge gender-based classification schemes, which, like restrictions on sexual conduct, often are accused of relying on outdated stereotypical notions.[58]

To justify infringing upon a sexual right, the government would be compelled to demonstrate the existence of harms associated with the sexual conduct in question. That the behavior might be distasteful to the majority of Americans, or violate traditional moral proscriptions, would not be sufficient justification for abridging a constitutionally protected sexual right, nor would a claim that regulation rationally serves a legitimate state interest.[59] In Redlich's words:

> We are concerned here with areas where there would normally be a presumption of constitutionality and a willingness to uphold the statute if it appears reasonably related to a valid legislative end. When the individual asserts rights recognized under the Ninth and Tenth Amendments, however, the Court should sound a different note: These are rights which a free society reserves to the people. You many not "deny or disparage" them by a mere showing of reasonableness.[60]

In subsequent chapters of this book we review particular aspects of governmental interest in regulating sexual conduct and conclude that insufficient justification exists to proscribe private sexual activities between consenting adults. Consequently, were sexual expression granted a "presumption of liberty" based on its standing as a Ninth Amendment right, then, as more and more sexuality-related statutes were challenged in court, the lack of persuasive state interests in regulating sexual conduct would gradually lead to an expansion of sexual freedoms.

PROTECTION FROM HARM

When Madison conceived the Ninth and Tenth Amendments, he meant to address the appropriate extent of individual freedom in our society and the government's power to restrict such freedoms. The boundary between the two, as Madison most certainly recognized, was harm to others. When individual liberty unduly infringes on the rights of others, the government may intervene in service of the public welfare. This is the basis of Lockean natural rights theory, with parties to the "social contract" relinquishing power to the common collective only insofar as is necessary to prevent each from violating the others' rights. In Locke's own words, governmental power, "in the utmost bounds of it, is limited to the public good of society. It is a power that hath no other end but preservation, and therefore can never have a right to destroy, enslave, or designedly to impoverish the subjects."[61]

In short, the proper role of the Lockean government is to protect individuals from harm, to preserve the public good, and not to otherwise interfere in the private lives of its citizens, lest individual rights be insecure. The Bill of Rights, and the Ninth and Tenth Amendments in particular, embodies this Lockean ideal by limiting the power of the government to act against the citizenry. To safeguard our sexual rights, "the courts should keep in mind the Lockean principle which the Ninth Amendment was intended to effectuate: the state can only exercise coercive powers which its constituent members could legitimately exercise in self-defense."[62] Because the Lockean state derives its power from its constituents, with rights ceded to the government only as necessary to protect the liberty of all, the government may only regulate individual freedoms to the extent that they intrude upon the rights of others. The critical question is whether and in what way sexual conduct might harm or otherwise encroach upon the rights of other citizens.

Restrictions on sexual conduct sometimes are justified on the basis of the harmful ancillary effects associated with said conduct. The validity of claims that a particular sexual activity is associated with harmful secondary effects, and the extent of the alleged harms, must be assessed on a case-by-case basis. For example, the ostensible rationale for prohibiting prostitution is to limit the spread of sexually transmitted diseases and to reduce criminal activities that are believed to accompany the sale of sex for cash. In chapter 6 we evaluate the secondary harms putatively associated with prostitution and conclude that the available evidence is insufficient to support a complete prohibition of this commercial sex activity.

The second main class of potential harms is broadly defined as injury to the public morality, or as expressed in *Jacobellis*, "the right of the Nation and the States to maintain a decent society."[63] But the prejudicial imposition of one moral/religious framework over another cannot be adduced in support of ostensibly secular legislation. In his dissent in *Bowers*, Justice Harry Blackmun rejected Georgia's assertion that "traditional Judeo-Christian values" justified the state's prohibition of sodomy:

> That certain, but by no means all, religious groups condemn the behavior at issue gives the State no license to impose their judgements on the entire citizenry. The legitimacy of secular legislation depends instead on whether the State can advance some justification for its law beyond conformity to religious doctrine. . . . A State can no more punish private behavior because of religious intolerance than it can punish such behavior because of racial animus.[64]

Justice Blackmun also rejected the notion that legitimating the private sexual behavior of homosexual individuals might create a slippery slope leading to the complete disintegration of public morality. Quoting H.L.A. Hart's article, "Immorality and Treason,"[65] Justice Blackmun concluded,

> Reasonable people may differ about whether particular sexual acts are moral or immoral, but "we have ample evidence for believing that people will not abandon morality, will not think any better of murder, cruelty, and dishonesty, merely because some private sexual practice which they abominate is not punished by the law."[66]

A "moral majority" cannot impose its vision of correct moral conduct upon the nation as a whole without encroaching upon the legitimate rights of others. The ever-prescient Madison foresaw the threat posed to individual freedom by the collective will of the majority. In a letter to Jefferson, Madison expressed this concern:

> Wherever the real power in a Government lies, there is the danger of oppression. In our Governments the real power lies in the majority of the Community, and the invasion of private rights is chiefly to be apprehended, not from acts of Government contrary to the sense of its constituents, but from acts in which the Government is the mere instrument of the major number of the Constituents.[67]

The Bill of Rights was intended as a remedy to this potential threat to individual liberty. The several amendments explicitly protect certain rights from infringement by the government acting as the agent of the majority, while the Ninth Amendment protects the unenumerated rights of individuals. In their book, *On Reading the Constitution*, Laurence Tribe and Michael Dorf reached a similar conclusion:

> If we are to take seriously the Ninth Amendment's requirement that "[t]he enumeration in the Constitution, of certain rights, shall not be construed to deny or disparage others retained by the people," at a minimum we must consider the possibility that rights which are consistent with the enumerated rights—as a right to choose unconventional sexual behavior is, and as a "right" to theft surely is not—may be required by the Constitution.[68]

The significance of this quote lies not only in the prospect that sexual rights might find a constitutional basis in the Ninth Amendment (a sentiment with which we wholeheartedly agree), but in Tribe and Dorf's particular suggestion that the Ninth might guarantee the right to choose "unconventional" sexual behavior. "Unconventional" implies the threat of prejudice and the potential need for shelter from the tyranny of the majority.

One function of the Bill of Rights is to protect unconventional behaviors and unconventional choices. Adhering to the tenets of the Kabbalah, for example, represents an unconventional religious choice in our predominantly Christian nation, but followers of this mystical Jewish tradition need not fear governmental interference in their religious practice, thanks to the First Amendment. This amendment ensures all Americans the freedom to choose their own religions.

Likewise, the Ninth Amendment secures our freedom to choose unconventional forms of sexual expression. Although religion governs our spiritual satisfactions, the choices we make for love, sexual attraction, and sexual pleasure have profound influences on the personal and experiential realms of happiness, and on how we define ourselves as human beings (e.g., gay, straight, or in-between). When the government prohibits Americans from making choices about how and with whom they express their sexuality, it institutionalizes a practice no less injurious than denying religious choices.

In contrast to dubious ancillary harms and supposed injuries to the dominant morality are the very real (and sometimes severe) physical, psychological, and emotional damages inflicted upon nonconsensual participants in sexual conduct. Because we address the topic of consent in chapter 5, here we present only a brief synopsis of the key issues. Nonconsensual sex can assume any of a number of forms, from the paradigmatic example of rape, to being the involuntary witness to an exhibitionistic display. The traumatic effects of rape and other forms of sexual assault are well documented and need no further elaboration.[69] Sexual abuse is all the more horrific when the victim is a child or adolescent.[70] Sexual harassment, though less drastic than sexual assault, often leaves its mark, sometimes in profound and disturbing ways. Likewise, although exhibitionists are sometimes dismissed as harmless "dirty old men," witnessing an act of exhibitionism (whether someone exposing him- or herself or a public sexual act) can be an unsettling experience. For these reasons, nonconsensual and abusive sexual conduct is rightly prohibited.

But do *consensual* sexual acts, *conducted* in private, invade the rights of others, and thereby create tangible harm? We assert that they do not. Private sexual acts of personal determination, same-gender sex included, do not tangibly invade the rights of others. Consequently, they need not be countered by a legitimate use of self-defense, and their exercise does not require the government to mobilize on the people's behalf. Rather, in the name of personal dignity and individual liberty, the government is directed *not* to intervene. This conclusion is consistent with Madison's intent that the Bill of Rights should "limit and qualify the powers of Government, by excepting out of the grant of power those cases in which the Government ought not to act, or to act only in a particular mode."[71] According to Massey, "By its terms the [ninth] amendment is the final counterweight, to be used against governmental intrusion upon the people when all else fails."[72]

In our framework for protecting sexual rights, sexual expression would be legitimate provided it is done in private and no harm to others ensues, exactly as the Ninth Amendment intended. This would exclude all manner of nonconsensual sexual activity, including rape, adult-child sex, bestiality, and so forth, from the domain of constitutionally protected sex. Public displays of sex also would be left unprotected. In contrast, homosexual sex and acts of heterosexual sodomy, if private behaviors between consenting adults, would be unimpeachable.

LESSONS FROM FIRST AMENDMENT LAW

In this chapter we have proposed a foundation for Ninth Amendment adjudication based on protecting private sexual acts that effect no material harm on the public welfare. But is a legal analysis based on the character of the act (public versus private) and the harm effected on others truly practicable? If First Amendment jurisprudence is any indication, it certainly is. In defamation cases, for example, different rules of law apply to public versus private figures. To apply the correct rule of law, judges must be able to distinguish the one from the other. To guide them in this endeavor, the Supreme Court has provided that public figures come in several forms, including government officials, those with "notorious" achievements, and those who have vigorously and successfully sought out public attention. Some are regarded as public figures in limited contexts; others achieve public status more broadly. "In some instances an individual may achieve such pervasive fame or notoriety that he becomes a public figure for all purposes and in all contexts. More commonly, an individual voluntarily injects himself or is drawn into a particular public controversy and thereby becomes a public figure for a limited range of issues."[73]

For public figures to recover for defamation, they must prove that the defendant acted with "actual malice."[74] By contrast, in defamation suits brought by private figures, a negligence standard is permissible (*Gertz v. Robert Welch, Inc.*[75]). Moreover, where a private individual brings suit on a matter of private concern (as opposed to one of public interest), unique rules apply that are even more protective of individual rights (*Dun and Bradstreet, Inc. v. Greenmoss Builders*[76]).

The heightened protection available for private figures reflects in large part the fact that they have not "voluntarily exposed themselves" to injury. As a general matter, the Court has been reluctant to find that someone has "inject[ed] himself . . . into a public controversy." The *Gertz* case illustrates this point. Elmer Gertz, who had represented in a civil suit the family of a boy who had been shot by a policeman, was subsequently accused in a magazine article of instigating a communist "frame-up" of the officer. Despite the obvious public controversy surrounding this case, Gertz was deemed by the Court to be a private figure, even though he was a well-known local attorney who had "long been active in community and professional affairs," had published several books and articles, and had previously served on housing committees appointed by the mayor of Chicago.[77]

In upholding the rights of private persons (in *Gertz* and *Dun*), the Court was guided by the sentiments of Justice Potter Stewart in a prior defamation case. "The protection of private personality," Justice Stewart opined, concurring in *Rosenblatt v. Baer*, "like the protection of life itself, is left primarily to the individual States under the Ninth and Tenth Amendments. But this does not mean that the right is entitled to any less recognition by this Court as a basic of our constitutional system."[78]

The law of defamation clearly illustrates that judges are both willing and able to make distinctions between issues of private determination and those of public controversy. Moreover, in both *Gertz* and *Dun*, the Court was quite protective of personal rights (even in the face of competing freedom of the press concerns). Significantly, the Court acknowledged the overarching role of the Ninth Amendment in the protection of personal autonomy in both these cases.

It remains for us to demonstrate that, where personal expression is concerned, judges are capable of deciding where private rights must cede to social harm. Again, First Amendment adjudication suggests that judges are more than able to fix the line where personal expression must yield to public injury. Although First Amendment protections are extensive, words that are likely to incite to violence the person to whom they are addressed (e.g., "fighting words") are constitutionally proscribable.[79] Words that merely offend, however, are not. As Justice Harlan famously declared: "One man's vulgarity is another's lyric."[80] In *Ohralik v. Ohio State Bar Association* the Court remarked that there are numerous examples of

Communications that are regulated without offending the First Amendment, such as the exchange of information about securities, corporate proxy statements, the exchange of price and production information among competitors, and employers' threats of retaliation for the labor activities of employees. Each of these examples illustrates that the State does not lose its power to regulate commercial activity *deemed harmful to the public* whenever speech is a component of that activity.[81]

The line separating obscenity from constitutionally protected speech is determined by reference to whether the work, taken as a whole, harms people by appealing to unhealthy sexual desires.[82] Whether or not we approve of this definition or the tack courts have taken with regard to specific obscenity determinations is immaterial. The important point is that judges do not shy away from the task of distinguishing the obscene from the nonobscene, a task described by Justice Stewart as "trying to define what may be indefinable"[83] ("but I know [obscenity] when I see it," he added).

JUDICIAL REVIEW

The main difficulty with applying the Ninth Amendment in juridical practice is "that rights not enumerated are not enumerated," as Charles Black wryly observed.[84] A few brave judges have approached the Ninth Amendment with some interest, but without rules of interpretation to guide them, most have gone back. The Court understandably has been hesitant to give substance to the Ninth Amendment's unenumerated rights for fear of interjecting its own values in constitutional doctrine, thereby usurping the proper role of the legislature. Justice Byron White, writing for the majority in *Bowers v. Hardwick*, noted: "The Court is most vulnerable and comes nearest to illegitimacy when it deals with judge-made constitutional law having little or no cognizable roots in the language or design of the Constitution."[85]

Judge Learned Hand (perhaps the most revered judge *never* to serve on the Supreme Court) captured the Court's discomfort with an overactive judiciary in the following quip: "For myself it would be most irksome to be ruled by a bevy of Platonic guardians, even if I knew how to choose them, which I assuredly do not." While we, no less than Judge Hand, are cautious of "Platonic guardians," it seems evident that the best antidote to a domineering judiciary is to prescribe definable, workable limits to legal doctrines, something we have formulated as regards to the Ninth Amendment. Although constitutional interpretation is a difficult job, *someone* has to do it. From our perspective, who better than an informed judiciary? The legislature by and large serves the whim and will of the majority. Consequently, legislation can (and does) intrude upon individual rights, notably the rights of minorities, the very rights Madison was at pains to protect. Judges are generally appointed for life and therefore are insulated from the social and political pressures of the majority. By design, they are the most objective interpreters of the Constitution we as a nation have available to us.

Nevertheless, the judiciary generally has been reluctant to give substance to the Ninth Amendment, instead treating it as an obscurative and uninterpretable "ink blot."[86] However, other constitutional provisions that seem just as murky as the Ninth Amendment have not engendered similar resistance. The due process clauses of the Fifth and Fourteenth Amendments, for example, essentially state that no person shall be deprived of "life, liberty or property, without due process of law," but provide no further guidance. Even so, "the cases are legion in which those Clauses have been interpreted to have substantive content, subsuming rights that to a great extent are immune from federal or state regulation or proscription."[87] As such, the Court has been accused of using a "we'll protect it because it seems important" standard to decide which liberty interests shall be deemed fundamental.[88] Even the "specific" provisos of the Constitution, such as the Fourth Amendment's prohibition against unreasonable searches and seizures, are open to a wide latitude of interpretation. Indeed, as Justice Harlan stated, concurring in *Griswold v. Connecticut,* "'Specific' provisions of the Constitution, no less than [ambiguous provisions such as] 'due process,' lend themselves as readily to 'personal' interpretations by judges whose constitutional outlook is simply to keep the Constitution in supposed 'tune with the times.'"[89]

The main difference between the Ninth Amendment and the others is that, of all the amendments, only the Ninth has no underlying theme through which to funnel relevant legal discourse.[90] Even the due process clause has been granted fixed (though uncertain) limits. In response to the open-ended nature of due process, judges have tried to restrict themselves to the dictates of history and tradition in interpreting it. In particular, "The Due Process Clause protects against state infringement those liberties 'so rooted in the traditions and conscience of our people as to be ranked as fundamental.'"[91]

Unfortunately, history and tradition are poor defenders of sexual rights; American heritage is riddled with instances of prejudice finding form in laws injurious to minority rights, sexual rights prominent among them. Given the Court's reliance on due process during the last several decades of sexual rights jurisprudence, it is understandable that any expansion of sexual rights thought imminent in *Griswold* and *Roe* (see chapter 3) has since been stalemated. Because, as a nation, we traditionally have condemned sex outside the confines of marriage and procreation, we have reached an impasse where sexual rights are concerned. The Supreme Court in *Bowers* essentially drew a line in the sand, saying "we will go this far, but no further" (with homosexual individuals left stranded on the far side of the line).

The Ninth Amendment provides an alternative to due process adjudication of sexual rights. Ninth Amendment adjudication would not be so dissimilar, nor necessarily less principled than its due process counterpart, yet it would be exceedingly more relevant. As with substantive due process, Ninth Amendment adjudication of sexual issues would be informed by an appreciation of natural, fundamental rights. But instead of being confounded by our history of discrimination or getting bogged down in conventional privacy doctrine, Ninth Amendment jurisprudence would go to the heart of the matter and would base sexual rights on the firm foundation of the amendment's original intent: to safeguard the fundamental liberties of the people.

Judges generally are not shy when it comes to assessing challenges to constitutional provisions *other* than the Ninth Amendment. As judges are required to uphold the Constitution, we would ask that they acknowledge their Ninth Amendment responsibilities. John Hart Ely asserts, rather pessimistically, that "if a principled approach to judicial enforcement of the Constitution's open-ended provisions cannot be developed, one that is not hopelessly inconsistent with our nation's commitment to representative democracy, responsible commentators must consider seriously the possibility that courts simply should stay away from them."[92] We believe that the framework we have proposed for adjudicating sexual rights and for placing practicable limits on those rights adequately addresses Ely's concerns. The next several chapters describe how we would apply this framework to specific realms of sexual conduct. The reader can judge for her- or himself whether we have succeeded in putting Ely's fears to rest.

5

What Can We Learn from Dial-a-Porn?

MASTURBATION IS A TOPIC most people are reticent to discuss. As Dan Conner, a character on the hit 1980s television show *Roseanne*, explained to his son D. J.: "Everybody does it but *nobody* talks about it." Nevertheless, upwards of 90 percent of men admit having masturbated at some point in their lives, with a mean frequency of between four and nine times a month.[1] This makes masturbation one of the most common and most frequent sexual behaviors among men, if not *the* most common and frequent. Fewer women report having masturbated (60 percent or more), and those that do, do so less frequently (approximately two to four times each month, on average) than men.[2]

Masturbation has been observed in virtually all primate species.[3] Ethologists and psychologists believe that masturbation is a necessary step toward healthy sexual development, both physiologically and psychologically.[4] Masturbation is an incipient form of sexual exploration among both human and nonhuman primates, often occurring within the first year of life, or even earlier. It is a behavior that is neither learned nor easily suppressed, suggesting that it is a natural and inherent form of primate sexual behavior.[5]

Masturbation is the means by which we and other primates learn about sexual arousal and orgasm, and, at least for humans, it helps to establish our psychological associations to sexual stimuli and sexual activities, including feelings of ecstasy, contentedness, guilt, and shame. Masturbation serves many important functions beyond the obvious generation of pleasure. It teaches us about our bodies and how we react to specific sexual stimuli, it helps to relieve tension, it provides a sexual outlet when willing sexual partners are unavailable, it is an expression of self-love (*not* self-abuse!), and so forth. Therefore, it is not surprising that many men and women masturbate throughout their lifetimes, regardless of whether or not they are engaged in an active sexual relationship with another person.

In short, masturbation is an integral, enduring, and important component of the sex lives of many Americans, young and old.[6] Yet, there is no mention of masturbation in the U.S. Constitution, nor in any other constitution of which we are aware. There are at least two plausible explanations for this "oversight." Perhaps masturbation is such a ubiquitous human behavior that it qualifies as an obvious and inherent human right, rather like the right to eat or sleep. Or maybe masturbation is such a reprehensible and nearly always clandestine behavior that it warrants neither protection nor encouragement.

As the reader has no doubt anticipated, we believe that masturbation is a fundamental natural right and an obvious candidate for Ninth Amendment protection as a right "retained by the people." Although there are undoubtedly other social scientists and legal scholars who agree with us, to our knowledge no one has previously argued that a right to masturbate follows from the Ninth Amendment. (On the other hand, to our knowledge there are no laws that *directly* infringe on the right to masturbate.)

The American populace has been masturbating for centuries without an explicit constitutional right entitling them to do so. Why, one might ask, do we need to argue for such a right now? Our position is simple. We believe that much of the dialogue about "free speech" rights as it relates to pornography and obscenity is a discussion (albeit a convoluted one) about the right to masturbate while viewing or hearing pornographic "speech." Masturbation, ultimately, is the silent partner in the debates about the First Amendment as it applies to adult pornography.[7]

Nowhere is this more evident than in the furor over dial-a-porn, a form of telephone pornography that includes both prerecorded X-rated messages and "live" conversations with a paid telephone sex operator. Certainly, if we limited ourselves to the legal rhetoric, we would conclude that the primary concern was whether the American populace has the right to *hear* X-rated dialogue over the phone and whether that dialogue has "value." Although these issues certainly are important, they ignore the *purpose* of dial-a-porn. Customers do not call phone sex lines to gain political insight or to enhance their knowledge of world affairs; they do so to obtain sexual stimulation while masturbating.

Consider the following prerecorded message:

I'm just sitting here, playing with my pussy.
It's getting REAL wet.
Oooh, I want your BIG cock right NOW!

What, we ask, is the purpose of such wordplay? In short: money and orgasm. Dial-a-porn is a multinational, multi-billion-dollar industry that
creates a product intended solely to enhance masturbation—primarily
male masturbation. As opposed to Internet products, which often are
more complex and sophisticated (involving video, audio, photographs,
and animation), dial-a-porn is an inexpensive populist product, available to anyone with a telephone. In the typical prerecorded dial-a-porn
service, callers pay several dollars to listen to a three-minute message
featuring a sultry and sexy female (or male) voice aurally simulating
one or more sexual acts, with the focus on the listener's sexual satisfaction. Or, for those with a bit more money, the caller can speak "one-on-
one" with a live model who will tailor the content of the phone call to
the listener's individual sexual fantasies.

Judging by the preponderance of advertisements that fill the back
pages of men's magazines such as *Penthouse, Hustler,* and *High Society,*
and the phone sex ads that proliferate on late-night television, the target audience is primarily male. However, contrary to popular imagery,
the audience for dial-a-porn is not solely teenage boys and partnerless
men. A man might "dial-a-porn" when his primary sexual partner is not
interested in sex or is away on business, out of boredom or a desire for
sexual variety, or through a selfish desire to avoid reciprocal pleasuring
of his partner. Sometimes masturbation is less of a choice than one
might think: having a regular sexual partner does not necessarily imply
consistently available sex (as the joke goes, "just ask a married guy").
Finally, regardless of one's sexual opportunities, there will be times
when masturbation is the *preferred* sexual outlet. It can be quick, it can
refresh an old memory, it can be done without troubling anyone else,
and it is the epitome of safe sex.

Undeniably, there exists a powerful impetus toward sexual self-
satisfaction. This is evident not only in the success of the dial-a-porn
industry, but in the proliferation of sexually explicit sites on the World
Wide Web, many of which offer the visual equivalent of dial-a-porn:
"live" video interactions with sexually desirable men and women. Because access to "phone sex" resembles access to sex on the Internet,
the following exegesis of dial-a-porn may also serve as a model for

contemporary and future discussions of Internet pornography regulation.

THE FAIRNESS DOCTRINE

Before we consider the legal wrangling over dial-a-porn, it will be instructive to review and distinguish the related area of public broadcasting (i.e., television and radio), where government regulation of communications media first commenced in earnest. Legal regulation of the communications industry centers on the concepts of indecency and obscenity and the Right of Access to communications media. According to the prevailing definition of "obscenity," established in *Miller v. California*,[8] a work is obscene if: (1) the "average" person applying "contemporary community standards" would find that the work, taken as a whole, appeals to prurient interest; (2) the work depicts or describes, in a patently offensive way, sexual conduct specifically defined by the applicable state law; and (3) the work, taken as a whole, lacks serious literary, artistic, political or scientific value.[9] Books, films, videos, television and radio broadcasts, paintings, and so forth that are judged to be obscene are denied constitutional protection. Indecent materials, in contrast, are generally protected. (However, as we will see, "indecency" never has been clearly defined.)

The Right of Access refers to the right of individuals to express themselves over the public airwaves, and the right of others to "access" this expression. Unlike orators at a public park, however, speakers on TV and radio are a select and limited group. Whereas William F. Buckley and Howard Stern can jabber away ad nauseam, most of us have a very hard time accessing the radio and television airwaves. How, then, can a Right of Access be asserted with regard to public broadcasting in the face of practical restrictions on *who* can talk?

The answer involves application of the Fairness Doctrine, which is intended to protect listeners and viewers. The underlying logic is simple: Although broadcasters (who have enormous sway over public opinion) are few, listeners are many. Therefore, this doctrine regulates the former to protect the latter. The doctrine requires that broadcasters allow individuals air time to reply to personal attacks or political editorials[10] and allows regulation of the context in which indecent speech is aired in order to shelter younger listeners and persons who might be offended by such material.[11] This doctrine is "fair" to the extent that it allows the rights of the many to outbalance the privileges of the few.

The Fairness Doctrine developed out of the Federal Communications Commission's (FCC) recognition of two problems with the Right of Access vis-à-vis public broadcasts. First, it was readily apparent that only a small number of individuals (or entities) possess the resources required to procure a broadcast license. Thus, access to broadcast media is limited, and control is circumscribed. Second, because the number of broadcast frequencies is finite, broadcast monopolies are a tangible risk. This risk, if realized, would place further restrictions on who would be able to talk, and ultimately on what points of view would be heard. These problems are of course less pressing today, with the advent of cable and satellite television, the proliferation of FM radio, the introduction of satellite radio, and so forth, but they remain relevant nonetheless.

The downside to fairness is increased governmental intrusion. Does the government have a right to control the electronic media in general, and broadcasters in particular, especially where *their* First Amendment rights are concerned? This issue came to the forefront in *Red Lion Broadcasting Co. v. Federal Communications Commission*. The petitioner, Red Lion Broadcasting Company, operated a radio station under FCC license that broadcast a much-too-spirited debate between the Reverend Billy James Hargis and author Fred J. Cook. Cook, who felt he had been personally attacked by Hargis without being given an opportunity to respond in full, requested free airtime to reply. The station refused, believing that the First Amendment granted them the right to choose who could use their frequency and when. But the FCC sided with Cook and ordered the station to air his rebuttal. The station refused again, asserting their First Amendment rights; the case then went all the way to the Supreme Court. The Court rejected Red Lion's argument, noting that "Where there are substantially more individuals who want to broadcast than there are frequencies to allocate, it is idle to posit an unbridgeable First Amendment right to broadcast, comparable to the right of every individual to speak, write or publish."[12] Furthermore, "It is the right of the public to receive suitable access to social, political, aesthetic, moral and other ideas and experiences which is crucial here. That right may not constitutionally be abridged either by Congress or by the [FCC]."[13] Thus, the Court upheld the FCC's contention that broadcasters could be regulated in order to protect the rights of listeners.

SEVEN DIRTY WORDS

Along similar lines, the FCC has concluded that it must protect listeners from indecent speech, and especially from the seven dirty words: "shit, piss, fuck, cunt, cocksucker, motherfucker and tits." Those words were part of a monologue, broadcast on the radio, by the irreverent comedian George Carlin. With tongue planted firmly in cheek, Carlin said there were seven words that you can't say on the public airwaves, and then proceeded to say the seven aforementioned words, repeatedly.[14] A complaint was registered by a man who heard the Carlin monologue on his car radio while taking an early afternoon drive with his son. Here, in part, is what he heard:

> I was thinking one night about the words you couldn't say on the public airwaves, the ones you definitely wouldn't say, ever. . . . The original seven words were: shit, piss, fuck, cunt, cocksucker, motherfucker, and tits. Those are the ones that will curve your spine, grow hair on your hands and maybe, even bring us, God help us, peace without honor. . . . The big one, the word fuck, that's the one that hangs them up the most. 'Cause in a lot of cases that's the very act that hangs them up the most. So, it's natural that the word would have the same effect. It's a great word, fuck. Nice word, easy word, cute word, kind of. Easy word to say. One syllable, short u. Fuck. . . . It's an interesting word too, 'cause it's got a double kind of a life—personality—dual, you know, whatever the right phrase is. It leads a double life, the word fuck. First of all, it means, sometimes, most of the time, fuck. What does it mean? It means to make love. Right? We're going to make love, yeh, we're going to fuck. . . . And it also means the beginning of life, it's the act that begins life, so there's the word hanging around with words like love, and life, and yet on the other hand, it's also a word that we really use to hurt each other with, man. It's a heavy. It's one that you have toward the end of the argument. Right? You finally can't make out. Oh, fuck you man. I said, fuck you. Stupid fuck. Fuck you and everybody that looks like you!

When the FCC heard the monologue, it issued a declaratory order against Pacifica, the company that held the broadcast license for the station that aired the comedy routine. The order warned that if subsequent complaints were received about the Carlin monologue, the FCC could impose one of several sanctions. Among other options, the FCC was empowered by a congressional statute to issue a cease and desist order, impose a fine, or revoke the station's license. Pacifica took issue with the FCC's declaratory order and filed suit.

The case reached the Supreme Court in 1987. In *FCC v. Pacifica Foundation*,[15] the Court considered three main constitutional issues: (1) whether the FCC's order constituted impermissible censorship; (2) whether the FCC can prohibit "indecent" as opposed to obscene speech; and (3) whether the order infringed upon the broadcasters' First Amendment rights. They concluded the following. First, although the FCC cannot engage in *prior* censorship (i.e., setting preemptive rules about suitable broadcasts), it can review and impose sanctions on completed broadcasts in fulfilling its regulatory duties. Moreover, the FCC could prohibit both obscene and indecent speech, where indecent speech was defined as "nonconformance with accepted standards of morality." Finally, the Court concluded that broadcasters were entitled only to "the most limited" free speech protections. The Court held that broadcasts could be extensively regulated because this form of speech is "a uniquely pervasive presence in the lives of all Americans" and "is uniquely accessible to children, even those too young to read."[16]

With regard to the Carlin monologue specifically, the Court upheld the FCC's right to impose sanctions on Pacifica. In his plurality opinion, Justice John Paul Stevens offered the following, somewhat loose, analogy to principles of nuisance law: "We simply hold that when the Commission finds that a pig has entered the parlor [instead of the barnyard], the exercise of [the FCC's] regulatory power does not depend on proof that the pig is obscene."[17]

In a rather deft maneuver, the Court provided the FCC with the right to combat indecency without giving it a workable definition of "indecency." In a national broadcast, for example, what moral standards are to be used in the determination of indecency? Those of West Hollywood, California, or those that prevail in Montgomery, Alabama? The FCC's declaratory order against Pacifica tried to add some substance to this rather nebulous concept, defining indecency as "intimately connected with the exposure to children of language that describes in terms patently offensive as measured by contemporary community standards for the broadcast medium, sexual or excretory activities and organs at times of the day when there is a reasonable risk that children will be in the audience."[18] Nevertheless, this definition, which obviously was lifted and condensed from the Court's character-ization of obscene speech in *Miller*, defies detailed analysis and orderly enforcement.

Several justices disagreed with the result in *Pacifica*. In his dissent-ing opinion, Justice William Brennan, joined by Chief Justice John Mar-shall, continued Justice Stevens's barnyard metaphor, suggesting that the majority had "burn[ed] the house to roast the pig." Justice Brennan argued that when someone turns on the radio, that person has *chosen* to participate, as a listener, in a public discourse. Further, he did not be-lieve it was the government's business to decide what was appropriate for children. Rather, that role falls to parents. Justice Brennan noted that, "as surprising as it may be to individual members of the Court, some parents may actually find Mr. Carlin's unabashed attitude towards the seven dirty words healthy, and deem it desirable to expose their chil-dren to the manner in which Mr. Carlin defuses the taboo surrounding the words."[19] Justice Brennan also felt that the government was over-stepping its bounds by denying *adults* the right to listen to speech sim-ply because that speech was considered indecent for children, even though it was not obscene.[20]

In a separate dissenting opinion, Justice Potter Stewart (joined by Justices Brennan, Marshall, and Byron White) found the very concept of "indecent speech" to be problematic. He contended that Congress, in empowering the FCC to regulate the airwaves, had intended to limit the meaning of indecent to "obscene." Justice Stewart noted that, in inter-preting a closely related Congressional statute that prohibits the send-ing of "obscene, lewd, lascivious, indecent, filthy or vile" mail,[21] the Court had construed "indecent" to mean "obscene." He saw no reason for a different interpretation in the *Pacifica* case. Therefore, in his opin-ion, the FCC lacked authority to regulate Carlin's admittedly nonob-scene monologue.

DIAL-A-PORN AND THE FCC

The FCC also has regulatory jurisdiction over the telephone industry. However, the constitutional concerns surrounding potentially offensive telephonic communications are much weaker than for broadcast media. Dial-a-porn is not nearly as "pervasive" as broadcast material, nor is it as "accessible to children." It does not catch people unaware when they pick up their phone, as might happen when someone inadvertently tunes in an offensive radio or television broadcast.[22] But the same rules apply. Dial-a-porn, like material broadcast over the public airwaves (including Carlin's amusingly offensive monologue), is constitutionally protected speech, provided that it is not judged to be obscene according to the *Miller* guidelines. The American populace has a First Amendment right to listen to such speech, no matter how indecent it might be. In order for the government to defend content-based regulation or censorship of protected speech, it must offer a *very* compelling justification. Furthermore, it must implement any restrictions it places on such speech in the *least restrictive* way available.

The FCC's "compelling interest" for regulating dial-a-porn is to protect children from the perceived harms of exposure to indecent speech.[23] Consequently, it has exercised its regulatory powers to restrict minors' access to dial-a-porn, justifying its actions by citing "the concern of parents and congressmen that teenagers and pre-teenagers may have access to offensive recordings."[24] This position, in and of itself, is certainly reasonable, given that the purpose of dial-a-porn is not to air opinions per se, but to facilitate masturbation. Parents *should* have the right to prohibit access to dial-a-porn in their homes. The real issue for debate, however, is *how* best to regulate access, thereby permitting the "speech" and the subsequent "conduct" (adult masturbation) in the least restrictive manner.

Even though across-the-board termination hardly seems the "least restrictive" means of regulating dial-a-porn, many who oppose dial-a-porn want to be rid of this "scourge" completely and finally. With this goal in mind, some pursue legal action and push for greater and greater restrictions, with the hope that the combination of exorbitant legal fees and burdensome restrictions will ultimately put dial-a-porn out of business. This strategy can be remarkably effective, as the Second Circuit recognized in *Carlin Communications* (discussed below), remarking that "the inconvenience associated with [instituting an effective system of age verification] might . . . conceivably place [dial-a-porn's] financial viability in jeopardy."[25] The same strategy often is used, successfully, against producers and distributors of X-rated videos.

Others have taken a more direct tack by appealing directly to the FCC. This was the approach adopted by Peter F. Cohalan, the County Executive for Suffolk County, who in 1982 joined with Thomas J. Bliley, a Republican Congressman from Virginia, in an attempt to persuade the

FCC to terminate *High Society* magazine's dial-a-porn service through administrative action.[26] Bliley and Cohalan argued that the New York Telephone Company was in violation of the Communications Act of 1934 by tacitly permitting *High Society* to transmit obscene communications. But the FCC cannot easily compel dial-a-porn providers to cease operating legal, money-making ventures. Thus, Cohalan and Bliley's effort failed when the FCC declined to force *High Society* to discontinue its dial-a-porn service.

At about the same time, forty-six congressmen signed a letter addressed to the FCC chairman urging him to stop the growth of the dial-a-porn industry.[27] Under growing pressure from many quadrants, in September 1983 the FCC issued a Notice of Inquiry seeking public opinion regarding the possible prosecution of telephone companies under Section 223 of the Communications Act (the statute that regulates obscene and harassing telephone calls). But the FCC was upstaged just two months later when Congress amended Section 223 to address dial-a-porn. As amended, Section 223 states that it is a crime for anyone to knowingly "[make] (directly or by recording device) any obscene or indecent communication for commercial purposes to any person under eighteen years of age or to any other person without that person's consent, regardless of whether the maker of such communication placed the call." Congress also included a "parachute clause" within this section. No doubt compelled by the requirement of utilizing the least restrictive means of denying adult access to protected speech, Section 223 provides the following loophole: "It is a defense to a prosecution under this subsection that the defendant restricted access to the prohibited communication to persons under 18 years of age or older in accordance with procedures which the [FCC] shall prescribe by regulation."

The promised regulations were issued by the FCC in June of the following year. According to the regulations, dial-a-porn providers could protect themselves against conviction under the Section 223 provisions dealing with access by minors if they operated their service only between the hours of 9:00 P.M. and 8:00 A.M., or if they required adult customers to pay by credit card. However, these seemingly minor requirements were judged to be overly restrictive by the Second Circuit Court of Appeals in *Carlin Communications, Inc. v. FCC*.[28] The Court of Appeals declared that the FCC regulations were poorly drawn. On the one hand, they too greatly abridged freedom of speech by denying access to adults during certain hours. On the other, they inadequately protected children, who could access the services with relative ease during their hours of operation. In response, the FCC modified its procedures once again, in October 1985. At that point, for a credible defense, dial-a-porn providers had only to require customers to use a credit card for payment or to use a previously authorized identification code to gain access to the dial-a-porn service.

PORNOGRAPHY, MASTURBATION, AND VIBRATORS

According to FCC regulations, then, dial-a-porn services can operate without additional governmental interference provided they take appropriate steps to ensure that underage persons cannot access their services. Section 223 respects dial-a-porn operators' right to provide indecent content to customers over the telephone, and the First Amendment protects those customers' right to hear such material. But is their right to *masturbate* while listening to dial-a-porn sufficiently protected?

Although the freedom to masturbate in the privacy of one's own home *might* be granted constitutional protection based on the right to privacy established in *Griswold* and succeeding cases, the Supreme Court has never explicitly considered this issue. But, just as there is no established guarantee of the right to masturbate, there are likewise no laws (that we know of) criminalizing this activity, except when it violates public indecency statutes or is coerced by a third party. There *are*, however, laws regulating the accouterments of masturbation, particularly pornography, which is used by men, mainly, to enhance sexual arousal and facilitate masturbation; and "sex toys," such as vibrators, dildos, and anal plugs, which are used by women, and to a lesser extent by men, for sexual self-stimulation.[29]

Currently, regulation of pornography hinges on the concept of obscenity as defined in *Miller v. California* (see above). *Miller* was the culmination of a long line of contentious court decisions stretching back to the 1930s.[30] The principal focus of the debate over pornography centers on the "value" of pornographic material and the "ideas" it conveys. Conspicuously absent from these debates is any discussion of the *purpose* of pornography—namely, to enhance male sexual arousal during masturbation.[31] Like the emperor without his clothes, pornography is rarely acknowledged as fodder for male masturbation. Yet, when viewed historically, masturbation and pornography clearly were conflated. Anthony Comstock, the turn-of-the-century anti-obscenity zealot, viewed masturbation as the cause of numerous ills, both social and physical. In Comstock's opinion, "pornography's most deadly effects are felt by the victims in the habit of secret vices."[32] As we conjectured in our book, *With Pleasure: Thoughts on the Nature of Human Sexuality,*

> The ultimate goal of antiobscenity campaigns [is] the prevention of masturbation. However, masturbation is extraordinarily difficult to detect, and hence to control, because it is an extremely clandestine activity. A direct attack against the evils of masturbation is therefore unfeasible. This being the case, Comstock and like-minded antiobscenity crusaders instead attacked the "scourge" that provokes, accompanies, and reinforces the sin of masturbation—namely, pornography.[33]

Recent events in Alabama demonstrate that the attack on masturbation has not abated but has merely taken more subtle form. Masturbating while watching a pornographic video is not illegal in Alabama, nor is masturbating with the help of a vibrator or dildo. But *selling* a vibrator or dildo *is* illegal in Alabama and in several other states.[34] The Alabama law prohibiting the sale of "sex toys," "sexual aids," or as the court would later refer to them, "sexual devices," reads in relevant part: "It shall be unlawful for any person to knowingly distribute . . . any device designed or marketed as useful primarily for the stimulation of human genital organs."[35] Violation of this law is punishable by a fine of up to $10,000 and a term of up to one year in the county jail or one year of hard labor.

In 1999, one year after the statute was enacted, the American Civil Liberties Union challenged it in federal court on behalf of six women: one who operated a "sex boutique," one who sold sex aids at Tupperware-style parties, and four who made use of the devices in question. In their brief, the women asserted that the "dildo law" was an invasion of their right to privacy and personal autonomy that was not justified by an appropriately narrow, compelling state interest in the regulation of sexual devices. The U.S. District Court for the Northern District of Alabama, which heard the initial complaint, considered three potential state interests: "Banning the public display of obscene material, banning 'the commerce of sexual stimulation and auto-eroticism, for its own sake, unrelated to marriage, procreation, or familial relationships,' and banning the commerce in obscene material."[36] In each instance the district court concluded that the law did not rationally advance the state's ostensible objective. The court therefore found in the women's favor because the law bore no "rational relation to a legitimate state interest." However, the court rejected their assertion that the law violated their constitutional right to privacy ("this court refuses to extend the fundamental right of privacy to protect plaintiffs' interest"), despite acknowledging that the devices in question may have therapeutic and medical use for individuals afflicted with sexual dysfunction.

The State of Alabama appealed the district court opinion to the Eleventh Circuit Court of Appeals, which reversed the earlier decision that the statute lacked a rational basis, declaring that "the State's interest in public morality is a legitimate interest rationally served by the statute."[37] Apparently, the Court found persuasive Alabama's argument that "a ban on the sale of sexual devices and related orgasm stimulating paraphernalia is rationally related to a legitimate legislative interest in discouraging prurient interests in autonomous sex." Making procurement of sexual devices more difficult, the court asserted, would discourage "the pursuit of orgasms by artificial means for their own sake," which, Alabama argued, "is detrimental to the health and morality of the State."[38]

Further, in upholding the law "on its face," the circuit court dusted off a compelling, if well-worn, justification: protecting the moral purity of minors. Although no evidence was presented that the devices in question were accessible to minors, the court concluded that "Application of Alabama's statute to those who sell sexual devices to minors, to such extent that those devices are deemed harmful to minors, would not violate any fundamental rights. The statute has possible constitutional applications and therefore is not facially unconstitutional."

The circuit court's decision that the Alabama dildo law was not facially unconstitutional because "it may constitutionally be applied to those who sell to minors sexual devices which are deemed harmful to minors" (not that any such devices *have* been shown to be harmful to minors) echoes the concerns of Section 223 of the Communications Act, restricting dial-a-porn access to adults. Certainly, the protection of children, whether our own or those of others, is a hard priority to ignore.[39] However, sensible legislation and regulatory actions also should respect adults' right to self-satisfaction—whether by hand or by vibrator—as well as their right to listen to, read, or watch pornography.

SEX: INDECENT OR OBSCENE?

Obviously, dial-a-porn raises important issues about the right of Americans to hear sexually charged speech. Less obvious are the lessons to be gleaned from dial-a-porn regarding the regulation of sexuality in general. Dial-a-porn teaches us that indecency is inextricably tied to consent. The concept of "indecency" allows the government to prosecute otherwise protected speech under certain circumstances, such as when it violates Section 223's rules forbidding dial-a-porn access by minors. The concept of "consent" determines when an indecent communication may be called a crime. As operationalized by the FCC, indecent speech is legal, provided that the listener is over eighteen years of age and is listening by consent. Minimal age and consent are verified, ostensibly, by requiring the use of a credit card or a valid identification code.

Thus, the Right of Access to dial-a-porn and other indecent speech is protected provided that consent is given. We believe that this standard is germane to sexual expression under both the First and Ninth Amendments. Sexual behavior is no less amenable than dial-a-porn to a right of access governed by issues of indecency and consent. Because persons under eighteen are generally incapable of giving legal consent (as Section 223 explicitly recognizes), sexual interactions should be reserved for consenting adults,[40] as is access to indecent speech or communications (e.g., pornographic magazines or videos). If, however, sexual acts (or speech, stimuli, etc.) are regarded as obscene, consent and access are irrelevant, because obscenity has no constitutional protection, as we discuss in chapter 7.

Taking the analogy a step further, we reach the issue of how one might divide sexual *behavior* into categories of indecent and obscene. We note as an initial matter that the dividing line between indecency and obscenity is slippery at best. Recall from our discussion of *Pacifica* that "indecent" and "obscene" have in certain contexts been construed to mean the same thing. Although the *Pacifica* case aimed to distinguish between the two, the speech in question (Carlin's discourse on the seven dirty words) was not erotic in nature and did not appeal to the "prurient interest," one of the three prongs of *Miller*'s obscenity definition. Where speech is erotically charged, as is the case for dial-a-porn, the line between indecency and obscenity is most ambiguous. Section 223 made use of the concept of consent to build a boundary between the two. We would do the same for sexual behavior itself. Thus, as with dial-a-porn, consent would be the ruling motif (see chapter 7). Of course, precisely defining these concepts and gaining legal credence are two separate matters.

As a first step, we want to emphasize that we strongly believe that it is a mistake to label constitutionally protected sex, let alone speech, as indecent. "Indecent" is a pejorative label, intended to malign the activity, despite constitutional protection. Indecent speech is speech that is improper and immodest, and therefore "bad." If one merely wanted to distinguish speech that is inappropriate for children, the "adult" designation would suffice (as in "adult videos" or "adult entertainment"). Further, although the Constitution protects indecent speech, indecency borders on obscenity, which is, by definition, illegal.

Overlooking the subjective implications of the labels "indecent" and "obscene" and focusing instead on the critical distinction between these adjectives, we find that indecent speech, however offensive, is constitutionally protected, whereas obscene speech is not. Suppose, then, that we extend this distinction to sexual behavior itself. Some behaviors would thereby be legally protected, though many people might find them personally objectionable, while other behaviors would lack such protection. By convention, the two classes of behaviors could provisionally be labeled as "sanctioned" and "unsanctioned." The goal of such a division would be to create behavioral categories that are analogous, if not logically equivalent, to "indecent" and "obscene" speech, but void of the extraneous implications associated with these terms.

Presuming that a compelling rationale existed for dividing sexual behaviors into sanctioned and unsanctioned categories, a major obstacle would still remain: namely, establishing a legally defensible system for drawing the line. That is, by what principle should sexual behaviors (as opposed to sexual speech) be categorized? Distinguishing normative from non-normative behaviors clearly will not do. The Constitution protects many non-normative attitudes and behaviors. Indeed, by design, the Constitution is meant to act as a bulwark, sheltering the rights of minorities against tyranny by the majority. If the sanctioned/unsanctioned dichotomy is to have any value, it must be based on objective standards that respect personal liberty and individual choice while minimizing potential harms.

As we reviewed in chapters 3 and 4, the Supreme Court has been reluctant to extend sexual rights beyond the confines of the marital relationship, and even within that relationship, the freedom to engage in nonreproductive behaviors, such as oral or anal sex, is not necessarily respected by the states, many of which criminalize these activities.[41] By and large, then, in the view of the Court and many of the states, only heterosexual intercourse merits serious constitutional protection. Nonreproductive sexual behavior—especially sodomy—and nonmarital or extramarital sexual relationships (fornication and adultery, respectively) are considered "obscene" and are therefore illegal. We would eliminate this sexual prejudice by appeal to the Ninth Amendment, which, as we demonstrated in chapter 4, was intended to protect behaviors of an essentially private character that do no tangible harm to the public welfare.

To safeguard the rights of sexual minorities (and members of the supposed majority who, like many Americans, nevertheless engage in taboo activities now and again), Ninth Amendment protections must encompass a broad array of sexual behaviors. Does this mean that all private sexual behaviors would be sanctioned under our scheme? If not, how would sanctioned and unsanctioned behaviors be distinguished? To us, the dividing line is obvious. The distinguishing criterion is informed consent, which subsumes issues of age, competence, and potential for harm. Consensual sex is normative at best and indecent at worst, but is (or should be) protected in any case, hence "sanctioned." In contrast, nonconsensual sex is coercive and harmful, and therefore should not be protected regardless of the particular behaviors involved.

The capacity to provide informed consent requires that one possess the maturity and intelligence required for adequate forethought, which is legally presumed to mitigate harm. In the absence of consent, harm (physical, psychological, or both) is a likely consequence. For example, adult-child sex is criminalized because children are incapable of providing legal consent (the assumption being that, because of their youth, they are emotionally—or intellectually—incompetent to grasp the full meaning and future implications of their decisions), and because the potential for harm is great.

Justified concerns over informed consent are reflected in many existing sexual behavior regulations. Rape, sexual abuse of children, exhibitionism, and so forth are illegal because they are nonconsensual and potentially harmful. These behavioral interactions include a clearly recognizable "perpetrator" as well as an equally recognizable "victim." Several of these acts are violent as well, but it is not the violence per se that makes them illegal; rather, it is the lack of consent. Many people incorporate violent elements, such as whipping or spanking, into their consensual sex lives; such behavior is indecent or atypical, and perhaps not to everyone's tastes, but nonetheless it is—or should be—within the sphere of protected behavior. Likewise, although some people may find non-missionary position intercourse offensive, it is protected, we believe, by the Ninth Amendment's unenumerated right to sexual expression.

Thus, if we were to draw the line between sanctioned and unsanctioned sex, our conceptual rule would be informed consent. Consensual sex would be analogous to indecent speech and nonconsensual sex would correspond to obscene speech. (Notably, even consensual heterosexual intercourse would fall in the "indecent" category, to protect the sensibilities of those who find *this* behavior distasteful.) Our classification scheme is consistent with the Miller guidelines. Under a *Miller*-type standard, consensual sex would be not obscene, but merely indecent, for it has "serious value" (see chapter 7). This value finds form in Justice Harry Blackmun's dissent in *Bowers v. Hardwick*, where he remarked, "The Court recognized in *Roberts* that the 'ability independently to define one's identity that is central to any concept of liberty' cannot truly be exercised in a vacuum; we all depend on the 'emotional enrichment from close ties with others.'"[42] The value of consensual intimacy is beyond question. It serves as the foundation for our closest relationships, including the reproductive relationships that sustain society, and provides happiness and pleasure to millions of Americans each day.

Having established the basic recipe, we now add the missing ingredient to our system of sexual rights: an analog to the Right of Access. Adults are permitted access to speech, indecent and otherwise, under the umbrella of the First Amendment. Indecent speech is protected because it serves a constitutional purpose by permitting exposure to ideas, political or otherwise. Presently, there is no parallel principle for sexual behavior—no general right of sexual expression. However, were such a "right of sexual access" established through the Ninth Amendment's rights retained by the people (see chapter 4), the parallels with protected speech suggest that it would operate by granting adults the right to engage in consensual sex and that any attempt to abridge this right would be required to be minimally restrictive and could be undertaken only in the service of a compelling governmental interest.

The most daunting obstacle to implementing such a scheme is overcoming the legal and historical prejudices surrounding sex. Dial-a-porn and pornographic videos have an advantage here because they fall under the protection of the First Amendment. The right to free speech and press are extraordinarily prized in our society, and as such are given great latitude as a way of ensuring that these freedoms are not encroached upon. Sex, on the other hand, as we have discussed previously, comes under the more opaque and rather confused right to privacy, or more generally, under the Fifth and Fourteenth Amendments. Without the substance of Ninth Amendment protection, sexual rights have been too narrowly defined.

As we discuss at length in chapter 3, the Supreme Court concluded in *Bowers* that states could criminalize sex between consenting adults of the same gender, despite the fact that these very same activities are permitted for heterosexuals. Justice White's commentary in this case is particularly illuminating. According to Justice White, homosexual behavior does not merit constitutional protection because it fails to satisfy the requirements of the Fourteenth Amendment's due process clause. Justice White noted that this clause protects only those rights that meet one of two tests: The right must be such that "neither liberty nor justice would exist if [it] were sacrificed," or it must be "deeply rooted in this Nation's history and tradition." Homosexual behavior fails both tests, according to Justice White, because homosexual acts were outlawed in all fifty states prior to 1961 and remain outlawed in many states even today. Thus, presumably, homosexual behavior is not deeply rooted in U.S. history and tradition, and moreover, according to Justice White, liberty can prevail without it.[43]

In our opinion, Justice White is wrong on both counts. First, blind kowtowing to historical prejudice has been rejected by the Court itself, and rightly so, on numerous occasions, from *Brown v. Board of Education*[44] (famously rejecting "separate but equal" segregation laws) to *Loving v. Virginia*[45] (invalidating a miscegenation statute). And second, there arguably is no liberty more essential to the human condition than the right to freely express one's sexuality, whether reproductively or otherwise. In *Bowers*, Justice White and the Court refused to recognize homosexuals' fundamental right to sexual intimacy, reserving the cherished right to privacy (and therefore intimacy) to heterosexuals. As we have stressed throughout this book, this position is unduly prejudicial and conceptually muddled. In concentrating on the reproductive *potential* of sex, the Court fails to appreciate the myriad meanings and multi-faceted significance of human sexual behavior. Sex serves many survival-related functions, of which reproduction is but one. It is short-sighted, and "unnatural," to focus the fundamental right of sexual expression on reproductive acts. Doing so fails to recognize the significance of sex for emotional bonding, intimacy, enhancing self-esteem, conflict resolution, and so forth.[46]

Although the ostensible concern in *Bowers* was privacy, the real issue was the power of the state to impose a vision of correct sexual behavior. Justice White, in particular, advanced a "slippery-slope" argument in which a little sodomy here and a little sodomy there would eventually lead to an entire "parade of horrors":

> And if respondent's submission is limited to the voluntary sexual conduct between consenting adults, it would be difficult, except by fiat, to limit the claimed right to homosexual conduct while leaving exposed to prosecution adultery, incest, and other sexual crimes even though they are committed in the home. We are unwilling to start down that road.[47]

This grave prediction certainly was exaggerated. Guidelines such as those presented here forge a path with conspicuous boundaries and therefore provide a means by which to keep the floodgates closed. For example, although we support constitutional protection for some forms of sexual expression (e.g., consensual fornication and sodomy), we draw the line at others, including but not limited to adult-child sex and human-animal sex ("bestiality"), since neither a child nor an animal can legally consent to sex.

What is needed, it appears, is a reconceptualization of the legal foundations of sexual regulation that recognizes the fundamental right, inherent in the Ninth Amendment, to engage in consensual reproductive and nonreproductive sexual behaviors. As we have argued, the distinction between protected and potentially criminal acts should be based on the concept of informed consent. The history of dial-a-porn regulation shows that it is possible to safeguard individual rights while simultaneously protecting others against potential harms. Provided that appropriate restrictions are respected, American adults can freely listen to sexual dialogue with constitutional approval. Soon, hopefully, they will be able to partake of the full complement of consensual sexual acts with the same protections.

6

Does Prostitution Deserve Constitutional Protection?

IN THE EARLY PART of the twentieth century, one New York physician defined a prostitute as a "woman who satisfies the physical side of the sexual desire of a man without regard as to whether the passion is associated with admiration and respect, and insists on money in payment for her efforts."[1] We will adopt a somewhat simpler definition: a prostitute is a woman (or man) who engages in the explicit exchange of sexual services for money or other remuneration. In this chapter we primarily focus on female prostitutes because they constitute the vast majority of persons who trade sex for money, and because existing legal regulations were designed with women in mind.[2] Consequently, we often eschew gender-neutral language in favor of feminine pronouns.

Prostitution assumes many forms, from the high-priced call girl who may charge several thousand dollars for a single night's pleasure to the streetwalkers who patrol Hollywood Boulevard and the women who work in the legal brothels of Nevada. But the list does not end with these familiar archetypes. Other gradations of prostitution include "hand-job whores" who offer masturbation as a complement to the usual massage parlor services,[3] lap-dancing strippers who gyrate men to orgasm,[4] "crack whores" who trade sexual favors for their drug of choice, and male "hustlers" who have sex with other men for a price.[5] Though these examples span a wide range of working conditions, sexual services, and fee scales, they have one thing in common: all these persons are in the business of selling sexual access.

Prostitution, of course, has existed throughout human history. American history is no exception. Prostitution was perhaps less common in colonial times, but it was not unknown, as evidenced by a 1673 Massachusetts ordinance that punished being "a Baud, whore, or vile person" with whipping and hard labor.[6] As America expanded in the decades to follow, so did the commercialization of sex. The burgeoning economy of the 1750s witnessed a corresponding growth in the "sinful trade":

> Along waterfront areas, where transients, vagrants, and prostitutes intermingled with sailors, servants, and slaves, taverns often served as fronts for "disorderly houses." Areas such as Philadelphia's "Hell Town" were considered "little better than Nurseries of Vice and Debauchery." In other districts, travelers might encounter prostitutes at the local tavern, an institution decried by John Adams "for extinguishing virtuous Love and changing it into filthiness and brutal Debauch."[7]

The situation was little changed through much of the nineteenth century. According to one historian, in the decade following the California gold rush, fully 20 percent of the women in the state exchanged sex for money.[8] The euphemism "hooker" was coined during this time, as prostitutes in Washington, D.C., honored Civil War General Joseph Hooker by naming the brothels lining Lafayette Square "Hooker Row."[9]

Brothels were once a ubiquitous feature of the urban landscape, operating under various shades of legality and tolerance. Now they are confined (legally, at any rate) to a handful of counties in rural Nevada, where the state law allows counties with fewer than 400,000 residents to set their own policies regarding brothel operations, subject to state licensing and health inspection requirements. Among these less populous counties, four ban prostitution outright, six prohibit it in unincorporated areas, and seven permit it throughout the county.[10] In all other Nevada counties (including Clark County, home to "sin city"——Las Vegas) and in all of the other forty-nine states, prostitution is expressly forbidden. Still, the commercial sex trade endures, more or less unabated, despite the millions of dollars spent annually to enforce antiprostitution statutes and the many thousands of prostitution-related arrests that occur monthly throughout the United States.

Is there a constitutional right to engage in prostitution? On the face of it, the idea seems ludicrous. Getting paid to have sex is rarely exalted as a cherished right deserving of constitutional protection. Nothing is at stake, it would seem, except a little money and the opportunity for quick, depersonalized sex. But this facile characterization overlooks many important issues we will discuss in the course of this chapter. Reduced to essentials, the decision to exchange sexual access for money is but one of the many choices people make about how they express themselves sexually. The choices involved are similar to those all of us face when making sexual decisions. The main difference is that for prostitutes the answers to these questions are largely divorced from the characteristics of the partner, the potentially romantic nature of the sexual relationship, and sexual desire per se. Instead, economics assume a primary role. This difference, though substantial, does not negate the critical element of choice common to the decisions that prostitutes and non-prostitutes alike make in regard to their sexuality. Consequently, we believe that the choice to engage in prostitution, like many of the sexual options we have discussed in this book, is a decision of essentially private character and personal determination, and therefore is deserving of constitutional protection under the Ninth Amendment.

As an initial matter, we grant that prostitution is an unpopular form of sexual expression. Most adults, women in particular, prefer sex within the context of an intimate relationship. The prospect of having sex with a random stranger is so repellent that financial incentives are rarely persuasive. Nevertheless, prostitution should not be condemned for its unpopularity. Imagine if the Constitution safeguarded only the most popular behavioral choices and allowed the government to restrict activities such as ice fishing, eating escargot, or keeping rats as pets. Or, to cite a more plausible example, what if only popular forms of artistic expression were granted constitutional protection? Controversial artists such as Eric Fischl, whose "pictures about desire and sexuality are both provocative and unsettling,"[11] would then be banished, rather than on prominent display in American museums. Sexual choices are certainly as fundamental to our lives as artistic expression, if not more so, and therefore these choices too should enjoy the full embrace of constitutional guarantees even if they upset the traditional moral order.

Although prostitution is an unpopular and comparatively rare occupational choice, this is not a foundation for criminalizing it. There are many occupations that require professionals to engage in behaviors most people would prefer to avoid. Janitors, sanitary engineers, migrant farm workers, and even nurses fall in this category. An even more striking example: few people would, by choice, elect to spend their days cleaning human cadavers and handling decaying flesh. Yet this is exactly what is required of one who pursues a career as a mortician, which is a legally protected occupation.

This rather contrived analogy raises a curious paradox. The mortician ultimately is elevated through professionalism. The prostitute, in contrast, is criminalized *because* of it. The mortician, of course, is respected because he or she provides an essential social service that has been necessary at all times and in all cultures. The same, however, could be said of the prostitute. She (or he) provides a critical service to those, for example, who for whatever reason are unable to procure willing sex partners. This service has existed throughout history and, in one form or another, in nearly all cultures. If sex, which the Supreme Court has described as "a great and mysterious motive force,"[12] is highly valued in our society but is unavailable to certain segments of the population, prostitution is an obvious solution—comparable to the mortician acting on behalf of families unwilling or unable personally to prepare their dead for burial.

IS PROSTITUTION OBSCENE?

No doubt many people consider the sale of sex to be an obscenity. But is it really? In the previous chapter we outlined a classification scheme for sexual activities. The distinguishing feature of "obscene" acts was the lack of consensuality. To the extent that prostitution is a freely chosen occupation, and the sex-for-cash transactions reflect informed consent, one could argue that it should not be considered obscene.

For a more "objective" standard, we can turn to the legal definition of obscenity, as codified in *Miller v. California*.[13] We realize, of course, that this standard was intended to provide a basis for distinguishing obscene from nonobscene literature, works of art, and other forms of expression potentially protected by the First Amendment. Still, the *Miller* test has been used in state courts to judge whether "sexual devices" (vibrators, dildos, and so forth—see the discussion in chapter 5) are "obscene,"[14] which suggests that it might be relevant to sexual behavior as well.

Adapting *Miller* to the present analysis, a behavior would be considered obscene if it satisfies all three of the following conditions:

(1) the "average" person applying "contemporary community standards" would find that the behavior, taken as a whole, appeals to
   prurient interest;
(2) the behavior is patently offensive sexual conduct specifically defined by the applicable state law; and
(3) the behavior, considered in all its aspects, lacks serious value.

With regard to the first prong of the *Miller* test, many might argue that
prostitution appeals to the "prurient interest."[15] Sex is not supposed to
be a commodity, to be bought and sold. Therefore, engaging in prostitution or patronizing prostitutes might be taken as evidence of a
"shameful or morbid interest in sex"[16]—that is, a prurient interest. We
contend, instead, that in most instances prostitution satisfies "normal,
healthy sexual desires."[17] The illegality and stigma attached to prostitution may make it "shameful" but the interest in sex that drives the
commercial sex industry is certainly not unhealthy

As for the second *Miller* clause, depending on the sexual service offered for sale, prostitution might or might not be "patently offensive
sexual conduct specifically defined by the applicable state law." Consensual heterosexual intercourse, with or without contraception, is protected by the Constitution and therefore is legal throughout the fifty
states. Oral or anal sex, bondage, and other activities are outlawed in
many states (though the relevant statutes are seldom enforced), but are
legal in others.[18] In those states that prohibit sodomy and other "unnatural acts," prostitution might very well satisfy the second prong of the
Miller standard. But does prostitution "considered in all its aspects, lack
serious value"? It is here, we believe, that prostitution utterly fails the
Miller test.

We have already alluded to the main value of prostitution: it provides a needed interpersonal sexual outlet for people (primarily men)
who are unable to procure consensual sexual partners. This includes
men limited by their appearance, personality, social situation, or other
circumstances.[19] The difficulty finding sex partners might only be temporary, longstanding, or permanent. In any case, prostitution offers a
solution.

Prostitution provides readily available sex that seldom discrimi-
nates by race, ethnicity, or creed, or by socially desirable qualities such
as good looks, youth, social standing, and so forth. This arrangement
obviously benefits the prostitutes, who earn money by satisfying the

need for willing sex partners, as well as their customers, who gain sexual release and some measure of sexual satisfaction. Thus, prostitution is consistent with the pursuit of happiness of both prostitutes and the men who visit them.[20] Moreover, to the (somewhat questionable) extent that the availability of commercial sex partners channels excess male sexual energy away from the wives of other men (thereby preventing adultery) or unwilling sexual partners (thereby preventing rape and sexual assault), prostitution is beneficial in a broader sense.

In short, prostitution cannot be said to "lack serious value," whether to the prostitute herself (who gains economic advantage) or to the customer (who may be unable to find willing sexual partners). Prostitution, therefore, cannot be considered "obscene" according to the modified *Miller* standards set forth above.

THE VICTORIAN DOUBLE STANDARD

In mid- to late-nineteenth-century America, a double standard dominated societal thinking on sexual matters and justified grudging acceptance of widespread prostitution. The prevailing view held that men had an entirely natural, but nearly unquenchable, thirst for sex. Women, in contrast, were thought to be unsullied by animalistic sexual desires.[21] In his influential text, *The Functions and Disorders of the Reproductive Organs*, Dr. William Acton, a noted nineteenth-century physician and sexual authority, postulated that "the majority of women (happily for them) are not very much troubled with sexual feelings of any kind."[22] The availability to men of female commercial sexual partners helped relieve women of their supposedly unwanted conjugal obligations, except when necessary for procreation. And it did so with minimal threat to the family itself (once one accepts the double standard of fidelity for wives, but not husbands). For, were prostitutes unavailable, men might instead select sexual partners from the larger pool of single and already-married women, with potentially dire consequences to the stability of the family, either their own or that of another man.[23]

Thus prostitution was accepted as a "necessary evil" that provided men with an outlet for their sexual appetites, free from romantic entanglements that could endanger the family (although, as Ben Franklin's personal history attests, this was not always the case). The famed nine-teenth-century philosopher Arthur Schopenhauer observed that "there are 80,000 prostitutes in London alone: and what are they if not sacrifices on the altar of monogamy?"[24] The benefits of prostitution were obvious: "Passionless" wives were spared the chore of pleasuring their husbands; the chastity of unmarried women was protected; and the economic and emotional stability of the family was preserved—all while men enjoyed the freedom to satisfy their carnal instincts!

This, by and large, was considered the natural order of things. In their classic book, *Intimate Matters: A History of Sexuality in America*, John D'Emilio and Estelle Freedman suggest that "Throughout most of western culture, men had enjoyed the freedom to have sexual relations with mistresses or prostitutes; since female chastity maintained honor and legitimacy within the family, only women's transgressions were severely punished."[25] In some cities, such as Philadelphia, prostitution was not considered a crime.[26] Elsewhere, the laws that existed to regulate the commercial sex trade were only sporadically enforced. Chicago, it was said, was home to more than five hundred brothels in 1860, and in New York City there were an estimated six thousand prostitutes, or one for every sixty-four men. Prostitutes catered to the growing numbers of single men in urban areas, in addition to acting as a "marital safety valve."[27] Indeed, most men in turn-of-the-century New York frequented prostitutes, averaging three visits each per week.[28]

However, men's patronage of brothels was not without disadvantages, particularly for wives. The commercial nature of the client-prostitute relationship, in which men trade cash for sexual pleasure—their own, not that of their partner—typically does not encourage creative or particularly intimate lovemaking on the man's part. Many nineteenth-century men had their first and possibly only premarital sexual experiences in local bordellos. These commercial sex encounters may have reinforced their tendencies toward sexual selfishness and inconsiderateness. Men's generally poor sexual etiquette is reflected in the historian William Shade's observation that "for women sexual intercourse in the nineteenth century was basically Hobbesian: nasty, brutish and short."[29] Therefore: "The prevailing ideal of the passionless woman who received little enjoyment from intercourse may well have reflected male sexual incompetence as much as a lack of female desire. . . . In a vicious circle, a belief in the fundamental asexuality of women also provided men of that era with an excuse for their poor sexual performance and neglect of their partners' needs."[30]

Moreover, prostitution provided a portal for the introduction of sexually transmitted diseases (STDs) into the marital relationship. This threatened not only the health of husband and wife, but also the vitality of the family, by inducing sterility in women and—especially in the case of congenital syphilis—causing deformity or even death in future offspring. Prince Morrow, a physician and the founder, in 1905, of the American Society for Sanitary and Moral Prophylaxis,[31] remarked that "social diseases" (i.e., STDs) "link the debased harlot and the virtuous wife in the kinship of a common disease."[32] In short:

> Middle-class Americans, and especially Protestant women, had many reasons to oppose prostitution. For one, all sexuality that took place outside of marriage generated deep concerns about social order. In general, the "fallen woman" symbolized the fate of the familyless individual in the anonymous city. Sexual commerce also represented the extreme case of the separation of sexuality, not only from reproduction, but also from love and intimacy. . . . Moreover, the prostitute evoked fears of disease at a time of recurrent and inexplicable cholera epidemics and a growing incidence of syphilis.[33]

Society's tacit acceptance of prostitution ended near the turn of the century with the advent of the Social Purity movement, which teamed women's groups, former abolitionists, temperance workers, and ministers in unified opposition to prostitution, intemperance, public immorality, and the double standard that held women to an ideal of purity even as men enjoyed considerable latitude to gratify their sensual nature, principally with prostitutes.[34] The Victorian belief in female sexual disinterest was (at least partially) repudiated in favor of a single standard of moral purity and continence for both men and women that stressed romantic love within marriage. The demise of the double standard signaled the death of the "family stability" justification for prostitution, but not the death of prostitution itself, of course; prostitution was simply driven underground, or into geographically circumscribed "red light" districts.[35]

SECONDARY EFFECTS

Against the backdrop of widespread social reform at the end of the nineteenth century, many states and municipalities passed laws prohibiting prostitution, or more rigorously enforced existing laws. Then, as now, the principal underlying concerns about prostitution—beyond the obvious moral question—were the threat of sexually transmitted diseases and the overall impact of prostitution on the social order. The criminalization of prostitution is motivated and justified on the grounds that the "secondary effects" supposedly associated with prostitution, such as fostering crime and spreading STDs, outweigh the potential benefits of prostitution and the curtailment of individual liberty such criminalization would entail. These ancillary, material harms have historically played a larger role than perceived moral harms in antiprostitution legislation.[36]

At the close of the nineteenth century and into the twentieth, social hygiene/social purity reformers seized upon prostitution as the root cause of the proliferation of sexually transmitted diseases: "All other modes of propagation are almost nil."[37] Lacking effective means of preventing the transmission of STDs (thick rubber condoms were available but were seldom used), prostitutes became hubs in disease transmission networks. There was little sympathy for the victims of STDs, whether prostitute or client. Sexually transmitted diseases (or "venereal diseases," as these maladies were known until very recently) were simply the price men paid for their immoral escapades with prostitutes. Wives and children, in contrast, were cast in the role of victim in the STD tableau:

> Prostitution is pregnant with disease, a disease infecting not only the guilty, but contaminating the innocent wife and child in the home with sickening certainty almost inconceivable; a disease to be feared as a leprous plague; a disease scattering misery broadcast, and leaving in its wake sterility, insanity, paralysis, and the blinded eyes of little babies, the twisted limbs of deformed children, degradation, physical rot and moral decay.[38]

Fears of casual (i.e., nonsexual) transmission through shared eating utensils, drinking cups, and so forth were widespread; once venereal disease had entered the home, it was believed, all were susceptible. To protect the "innocent," legislative reform was undertaken to punish the guilty—that is, the prostitutes themselves.

The ensuing century witnessed marked advancements in our understanding of the transmission, treatment, and *prevention* of STDs. Sexually transmitted diseases, by and large, are now classed as preventable diseases, condoms being the first line of defense.[39] But to be successful, prevention requires a conscious effort. Where prevention fails, prompt diagnosis and treatment can limit further transmission of disease and ensure its containment.

The present-day evidence linking prostitution to the spread of STDs is inconclusive. Because STDs represent an occupational liability that can limit a prostitute's ability to support herself, prostitutes are generally motivated to protect themselves against STDs through the use of condoms and other safe sex strategies. Several studies indicate very high rates of condom use with customers, but much less condom use with non-paying partners.[40] Convergent testimony is provided by the clients of prostitutes, who report higher rates of condom use during sexual encounters with prostitutes than with other (nonprostitute) partners.[41] Nevertheless, relatively high STD rates have been reported among prostitutes in several studies.[42] However, it is not clear whether these infections were acquired "on the job," or as a consequence of unprotected sexual relations with non-paying partners, or as a result of using contaminated syringes when injecting drugs. The very low STD incidence observed among Nevada's legal prostitutes (see below) suggests that, *under controlled conditions*, the potential for STD transmission is not significant. Moreover, there is no convincing evidence that prostitution has been a significant factor in the spread of HIV (human immunodeficiency virus) in the United States.[43] Sylvia Law, a professor of law, medicine, and psychiatry at New York University, estimates that "the two percent of men who contract HIV through heterosexual contact probably contract it from wives and lovers, rather than from commercial sex workers."[44]

Meanwhile, some of the *highest* STD rates have been detected in precisely those individuals *least* likely to patronize prostitutes—sexually active young men and women.[45] Each year, nearly one out of every four sexually active teenagers acquires an STD.[46] Teenagers account for approximately 25 percent of the 12 million new STD cases each year, and approximately two-thirds of people who acquire STDs in the United States are younger than twenty-five.[47] These frightening statistics led the Institute of Medicine to conclude that "adolescents (10–19 years of age) and young adults (20–24 years of age) are the age groups at greatest risk for acquiring an STD."[48] Unlike prostitutes, who tend to be older or more sophisticated about sexual matters, sexually experimenting young people are seldom as cautious as they should be about sex, particularly in their use of condoms.[49] Thus, criminalizing prostitution as a strategy to reduce the proliferation of sexually transmitted diseases is unduly discriminatory, poorly targeted, and largely ineffective. If the goal is to reduce the incidence of STDs, a more effective strategy would be to implement pervasive and rigorously monitored public health measures with *appropriate* target populations, such as sexually active adolescents and young adults.

Prostitution is often accused of promoting criminal activity (other than prostitution itself), from sex crimes and drug-related offenses to organized crime.[50] Although prostitution may be *associated* with increased crime, there is little evidence that prostitution, per se, is *responsible* for this increase.[51] Rather, it is the criminalization of prostitution that inadvertently creates detrimental consequences. Indeed, prostitutes themselves are often the victims of violent crime. According to Law,

> Many studies of women who work the street report that eighty percent have been physically assaulted during the course of their work. Women who provide commercial sex are often the victims of rape. They are murdered, perhaps at a rate forty times the national average. Police systematically ignore commercial sex workers' complaints about violence and fail to investigate even murder. . . . Customers, pimps, police and other men inflict these harms on women.[52]

In contrast, in countries where prostitution is legal, such as West Germany and the Netherlands, prostitutes' comparatively high visibility discourages the commission of crime in the first instance and, if crime does occur, their eyewitness accounts can assist law enforcement in the detection and subsequent prosecution of criminals.[53]

Substantial time, energy, and money is expended in the enforcement of prostitution statutes in the United States. According to Julie Pearl, in 1986, "police in Boston, Cleveland, and Houston arrested twice as many people for prostitution as they did for all homicides, rapes, robberies, and assaults combined."[54] She estimates that, in one year alone, sixteen of the largest U.S. cities spent more than $120 million waging a futile battle against prostitution while "an unacceptably large amount of assaultive crime [went] undeterred and unpunished."[55] The "clean-up" of New York's Times Square in 1978–1979, for example, succeeded in doubling the arrest rate, but at a considerable societal cost, as reflected in the concomitant 40 percent increase in rape, robbery, burglary, and felonious assault complaints.[56]

Although it certainly is reasonable for legislators to take into account the secondary effects of prostitution, it is important to emphasize that even if the argument were more persuasive, there would still be viable alternatives to an outright prohibition of prostitution. As David J. Richards, a noted legal scholar, suggests: "If there are crimes associated with prostitution, they are more rationally attacked by decriminalization and by criminal statutes directed at the evils themselves, not by overbroad statues which actually encourage what they claim to combat."[57] As discussed above, the criminalization of prostitution is itself responsible for many of the crimes charged against it, and the redirection of funds away from violent crime further exacerbates the situation. Criminalization also encourages conditions unfavorable (or less favorable) to the practice of safer sex, thereby contributing to the spread of STDs.

Decriminalization coupled with strict regulation of prostitution would permit regular monitoring and treatment of incident STDs, so as to prevent their further dissemination, as well as the institution of "100% condom" rules requiring all male patrons to wear a condom and other procedures to reduce the threat of STD transmission. In Nevada's legal brothels, prostitutes thoroughly examine customers' genitals for any indication of disease, such as lesions, cuts, and open sores, and refuse sex to customers who fail this inspection.[58] Prior to sex, customers are required to wash themselves with an antiseptic solution and water and to don a condom.[59] The prostitutes undergo monthly HIV testing and regular medical examinations for syphilis, gonorrhea, herpes, and venereal warts.[60] Women who test positive for one or more non-HIV STDs are provided appropriate treatment and are forbidden to work until the STD has resolved. The incidence of STDs among these women is extremely low. At one brothel, more than 7,000 STD tests were conducted between 1982 and 1989, yielding only two cases of syphilis and nineteen cases of gonorrhea.[61] Through June 1993, more than 20,000 HIV tests had been conducted among Nevada's brothel workers, with no positive test results.[62] In sum, the evidence from Nevada suggests that decriminalization, in tandem with legal regulatory schemes, would better protect the health and safety of *both* prostitutes and their customers.

If decriminalization is a politically intractable option, as is likely in many communities across the nation, the alleged secondary effects of prostitution could be limited by restricting commercial sexual activities to specially zoned areas, similar to the treatment generally accorded nude dancing and the theatrical exhibition of adult movies.[63] Like prostitution, nude dancing and adult movies are disdained for their perceived contravention of sexual morals, yet are legally restricted based on their supposed secondary effects, rather than on moral grounds. Nude dancing and adult movies are presumed to claim a measure of First Amendment protection, limiting the power of government to proscribe these activities. Similarly, if there is a Ninth Amendment right to engage in prostitution, thereby precluding the states from banning it entirely, then to the extent that secondary effects are demonstrable, the zoning approach used to regulate nude dancing and adult theaters might provide a workable strategy for managing prostitution as well.

Amsterdam, Copenhagen, and several other European cities rely on zoning restrictions to regulate the extent of sexual commerce within their borders. A similar solution was adopted in turn-of-the-century America in response to growing concerns about the proliferation of prostitution in urban areas in the late nineteenth and early twentieth centuries. Rather than attempting to completely eradicate prostitution, "municipal governments anxious to segregate vice activities officially designated such discrete areas [i.e., red light districts] so as not to offend the moral sensibilities of those respectable citizens who wished to avoid this commerce."[64] A red light district where prostitutes openly solicited customers could be found in virtually every major American city. A 1912 study indicated that New York was home to 1,800 houses of ill repute; Philadelphia had 372, Baltimore had more than 300, and the small Wisconsin burg of Watertown had 19.[65]

One of the most notorious of the red light districts that flourished at the beginning of the twentieth century was New Orleans's "Storyville." This impoverished twenty-four-block area of decrepit homes and businesses became the officially recognized center of local sexual commerce as the result of an 1897 municipal ordinance. Interestingly, the ordinance that created Storyville

[d]id not, in fact, decree that prostitution would be legal within its boundaries. To do so would have meant certain defeat of the measure. Instead, the ordinance decreed in no uncertain terms that prostitution would be *illegal beyond Storyville's boundaries*. Because the ordinance said nothing, one way or the other, about the legality of prostitution *inside* of Storyville, Storyville became a land of legal limbo for prostitution. Because prostitution already existed there, it was simply allowed to continue because *there was no law on the books against it*.[66]

Like red light districts throughout the nation, Storyville fell victim to the social purity crusades of the 1910s and officially "closed" in 1917. During this decade, many states enacted "red light abatement" laws that allowed private citizens to file complaints against houses of prostitution, leading to investigations and, where indicated, the sealing of buildings used for commercial sex.[67] By 1917, thirty-two states had red light abatement laws, and by 1920, "the red-light district had passed into history; the system of commercialized prostitution that reigned in American cities for almost half a century was destroyed."[68] But, of course, prostitution did not cease with the closure of the red light districts; it simply became more clandestine, and less safe, with pimps and others replacing brothel madams, and cheap hotels, parked cars, and back alleys replacing the comfort and relative security of the bordello.

PROTECTING WOMEN FROM THEMSELVES

The criminalization of prostitution historically has targeted female sex workers over and above their male customers.[69] Toward the end of the nineteenth century, when laws against prostitution were first put into real effect, procuring prostitutes was not a punishable offense.[70] At the time, law enforcement's handling of sexually transmitted diseases also singled out women. When STDs flared up, female prostitutes but not their male customers were tested and blamed.[71] These patterns of disparate treatment have persisted. Even today, most states impose more serious penalties on sexual sellers than on buyers.[72]

Historically, prostitution laws were meant not only to punish women's sexual transgressions, but to protect the supposedly "weaker sex." Prostitutes routinely were characterized as degraded, fallen women incapable of protecting or saving themselves. Men were to blame for their debased condition: "It cannot be concealed that the treachery of man, betraying the interests of . . . woman, is one of the principal causes, which furnishes the victims of licentiousness. Few, very few . . . have sought their wretched calling."[73] In this particular melodrama, the government assumes the role of savior and ignores evidence that it is restraining women from making autonomous economic choices. By claiming that women were "forced" to be prostitutes (but not forced into sweatshops, for example), criminalization "protects" women from *themselves* by preventing them from making foolish choices about their sexuality. The fallacy of this thinking was clear, if repressed, even in the nineteenth century. Thus, "it was extremely difficult to persuade inmates of brothels to forsake their road to ruin."[74] D'Emilio and Freedman relate that "Most prostitutes did not think of themselves as fallen women, nor did they aspire to middle-class moral standards. Rather, they often resisted reformers' attempts to make them leave the city, take up sewing, or become domestic servants."[75]

A common theme underlying antiprostitution reformers' efforts, whether in the nineteenth, twentieth, or twenty-first century, is that women are incapable of making informed, rational choices and managing their sexual and economic lives. This belief in the frailty and incompetence of women was strikingly evident in the 1908 case of *Muller v. Oregon. Muller*, which concerned a state statute that limited the work hours of women to ten per day, occurred during an era when statutes that adjusted the balance of power in employment situations were generally struck down. However, the Supreme Court's decision in *Muller* went against this trend in order to protect the weaker sex. In defense of its decision, the Court explained:

> History discloses the fact that woman has always been dependent upon man. He established his control at the outset by superior physical strength, and this control in various forms, with diminishing intensity, has continued to the present. . . . Though limitations upon personal and contractual rights may be removed by legislation, there is that in her disposition and habits of life which will operate against a full assertion of those rights. . . . She is properly placed in a class by herself, and legislation designed for her protection may be sustained, even when like legislation is not necessary for men and could not be sustained. It is impossible to close one's eyes to the fact that she still looks to her brother and depends upon him. Even though all

restrictions on political, personal and contractual rights were taken away, and she stood, so far as statutes are concerned, upon an absolutely equal plane with him, it would still be true that she is so constituted that she will rest upon and look to him for protection; that her physical structure and a proper discharge of her maternal functions—having in view not merely her own health, but the well-being of the race—justify legislation to protect her from the greed as well as the passion of man.[76]

The commonplace image of the helpless woman in need of rescue was further reflected in the "white slave" hysteria that gripped the nation about the time of the *Muller* decision. This social panic was fueled by antiprostitution groups who distributed sensational (and occasionally titillating) tracts describing a widespread and highly organized commerce in female flesh. In these frightening tales, "The procurer, a dark and sinister alien-looking figure, stalked the countryside in search of unsuspecting village girls. . . . Winning their confidence with pledges of love or promises of employment, these pimps seduced unsuspecting women to abandon their homes and follow them to the city."[77] Once there, the girls were met with all manner of horrors, which the antiprostitution tracts described in lurid detail. Despite the lack of concrete evidence that any such trade in young female flesh actually existed, in 1910 Congress passed the Mann Act (or White Slave Traffic Act), which made it illegal to transport a woman across state lines for "immoral purposes." Women were thus protected from despicable men who might otherwise entice them into lives of debauchery and debasement.

The "prostitute as victim" stereotype, which persists to this day, denies women potential agency to *choose* to become prostitutes, just as they choose to initiate other sexual relationships. In his 1858 survey of New York City prostitutes, William Sanger unearthed a surprising (and widely discounted) statistic: more than one-fourth of the women he interviewed said they had voluntarily become prostitutes "in order to gratify the sexual passions."[78] Similarly, many contemporary prostitutes report experiencing considerable satisfaction from their chosen profession; they appear to enjoy their work and believe they are providing an important social service.[79] Some prostitutes derive sexual pleasure from their encounters with customers,[80] while others gain emotional fulfillment from enriching the lives of their paying clientele.[81] But for many if not most commercial sex workers, the main incentive is money, pure and simple.[82] They may find the work distasteful or even repugnant, but prostitution is one of the highest-paying jobs available to persons with limited education and skills, and therefore is an attractive economic option for many women and men.

THE SEXUAL MARKETPLACE

When viewed impartially, prostitution can in most instances be reduced to a personal, economic choice to trade sex for money. Of course, the exchange of money for sex is hardly limited to prostitution. The implicit exchange of monetary equivalents for sexual access—whether dinner and a movie, a diamond ring, or crack cocaine—is a sizable and commonplace exception to the "free" exchange of sexual favors. Gift-giving is an important component of courtship rituals the world over, and in many cultures this practice amounts to an implicit barter of sex for other goods. It is only for the purposes of criminalization, regulation, or denunciation that we need distinguish such culturally normative conduct from "prostitution." But the existence of these practices makes it difficult to delineate the boundaries of "prostitution" cross-culturally: "Gift giving or even cash payment for sexual intercourse cannot be used as criteria to define prostitution, for these occur in courtship or even in marital situations."[83]

Marx and Engels, in their description of marriage as "legalized prostitution," give voice to the popular sentiment that, ultimately, a tacit exchange of sex for money is inherent in a great variety of relationships.[84] Indeed, two leaders of the American suffrage movement, Susan B. Anthony and Elizabeth Cady Stanton, argued that in marriage as well as in prostitution women exchanged sex for economic support.[85] The difference between prostitution and marriage, suggests feminist-anarchist Emma Goldman, is simply whether a woman "sells herself to one man . . . or to many men."[86] Although the economic transactions inherent in dating and marital relationships are usually more subtle than expressly charging for sex, these relationships nonetheless suggest that sexual access is a negotiable commodity, with a steady supply of buyers and sellers. Prostitutes are merely a small subset of the sexual "sellers" who have chosen to avoid the usual channels of courtship in favor of setting a specific price for a specific sexual act.

Should the government be allowed to restrict freedom of choice in our sexual barter system? By analogy, what if the government began compelling people to follow a strict, federally sanctioned diet? Regulating what we are allowed to eat would provoke outrage and would be viewed as an affront to the principle of individual self-determination. The same, we argue, is true of mandating marriage, procreation, or even intimacy as the defining feature of sexuality. This, too, "fails to satisfy the ethical and constitutional requirement that legally enforceable moral ideas be grounded in equal concern and respect for autonomy and facts capable of interpersonal validation."[87] Consequently, we believe that the marital-procreative model of sex cannot justifiably be used to criminalize prostitution.

Most women who engage in prostitution do so because their vocational options are restricted, either by skill base, employment opportunities, or other factors.[88] For individuals with limited skills and few assets, prostitution is often a better economic solution than its alternatives. As such, it is an autonomous act, consistent with economic liberty. Prostitution may be an unpopular career choice, but it is not injurious to others, and it can be well suited to the limited options available to persons who find themselves in a difficult economic situation. Viewed objectively, prostitution is just "another occupation with its own rewards and liabilities, and prostitutes choose or accept theirs as much as anyone chooses a trade or profession."[89]

Although prostitution is challenging work, it is not inherently less inspirational or satisfying than working at a low-paying factory job or toiling in a coal mine, and the pay is much better. "Is it any wonder," asked the Chicago Vice Commission early in the twentieth century, "that a tempted girl who receives only six dollars per week working with her hands sells her body for twenty-five dollars per week when she learns there is a demand for it and men are willing to pay the price?"[90] Martha Nussbaum, professor of law and ethics at the University of Chicago, offers the following comparison of prostitutes and factory workers:

> Both face health risks, but the health risk in prostitution can be very much reduced by legalization and regulation, whereas the particular type of work the factory worker is performing carries a high risk of nerve damage in the hands, a fact about it that appears unlikely to

change. The prostitute may well have better working hours and conditions than the factory worker. . . . She has a degree of choice about which clients she accepts and what activities she performs, whereas the factory worker has no choices but must perform the same motions again and again for years.[91]

There is no objective reason to legally constrain individuals (particularly women) from making economic choices about constitutionally protected behaviors. As Richards concludes: "In a society committed to equal concern and respect for autonomy, people are entitled to make choices for themselves as to trade-offs between alienation, social service, and remuneration. We certainly can criticize these decisions, but we do not regard criminalization as an appropriate expression of our condemnations."[92]

Indeed, the Supreme Court has defended as fundamental the right to engage in one's chosen occupation (*Schware v. Board of Bar Examiners of New Mexico*, 1957). Rudolph Schware was denied admission to the bar of New Mexico based on his "questionable" moral character, as supposedly evidenced by his former membership in a communist organization. In reversing the bar's decision, the Court took great pains to describe Schware as the product of economic impoverishment. In the words of the Court:

> The record of the formal hearing shows the following facts relevant to Schware's moral character. He was born in a poor section of New York City in 1914 and grew up in a neighborhood inhabited primarily by recent immigrants. His father was an immigrant and like many of his neighbors had a difficult time providing for his family. Schware took a job when he was nine years old and throughout the remainder of school worked to help provide necessary income for his family. After 1929, the economic condition of the Schware family and their neighbors, as well as millions of others, was greatly worsened. Schware was then at a formative stage in high school. He was interested in and enthusiastic for socialism and trade-unionism as was his father. In 1932, despairing at what he considered lack of vigor in the socialist movement at a time when the country was in the depths of the great depression, he joined the Young Communist League. At this time he was 18 years old and in the final year of high school. From the time he left

school until 1940 Schware, like many others, was periodically unemployed. He worked at a great variety of temporary and ill-paying jobs. In 1933, he found work in a glove factory.[93]

Schware's life choices, including his choice to affiliate himself with communism, were reasonable responses to his economic situation and did not reflect any immorality. Rather, immorality lay in the state's denial of his occupational aspirations. The Court stated the applicable rule of law as follows: "A State cannot exclude a person from the practice of law *or from any other occupation* in a manner or for reasons that contravene the Due Process or Equal Protection Clause of the Fourteenth Amendment."[94] Although *Schware* referenced the Fourteenth Amendment, its natural rights analysis (in giving substance to the "liberty" of the due process clause) is consistent with our Ninth Amendment argument, and its relevance to the case of prostitution seems transparent.

A final perspective to consider is that of the prostitute's customer, or "john." From his vantage point, there may be little difference between paying for sex and doing what's necessary to procure "freely given" sex. Notice that sex rarely is truly "free." Courtship can be a surprisingly expensive avocation. If obtaining sex is the only objective, paying for a prostitute's services may be more cost-effective, both monetarily and timewise.[95]

The prostitute is the consummate capitalist, supplying a service to meet a demand. Ultimately, it is the customers (primarily men), who are willing to pay money for sexual favors, that create this profession. If male customers stopped buying sexual services, prostitution would no longer exist. As Adam Smith noted centuries ago, it is the *buyer*, not the seller, who ultimately sets the price. This is basic supply-and-demand economics. Why not let the market determine whether a prostitute is financially successful? If customers are unwilling to buy her wares, or to pay enough to make her chosen profession profitable, she eventually will go out of business.

MONOPOLIZING SEX

The American legal system includes numerous laws and regulations that directly affect the manner in which markets operate. Monopolization is a case in point. The laws prohibiting monopolies are designed to penalize individuals or companies who control a product to such an extent that they exclude competition or free trade in that product. Two conditions must be met in order for monopolization to rise to the level of a criminal offense: the corporate entity must actually possess monopoly power in the relevant market; and it must exhibit willful maintenance of that power.

Notice that the purpose of monopoly law is to exclude a particular barrier to the free trade market. Laws against prostitution, in contrast, *protect* the virtual monopoly on sexual access otherwise enjoyed by marital and similarly committed relationships. (There is still that pesky issue of "promiscuous" women, however.) These laws target an otherwise legally protected behavior (consensual sexual intercourse), distinguishing them, for example, from laws designed to prohibit the sale of illegal drugs. This restriction of free sexual trade is paradoxical in a capitalist society that permits commerce in all kinds of services (e.g., handling the dead) and dubious products (e.g., sea monkeys, penis enlargers, miracle weight-loss potions).

Perhaps lawmakers also fear, at some level, that the legalization of prostitution would encourage countless women to begin charging for sex. According to this "logic," if some women were allowed to engage in sexual commerce, most women would follow suit. However, evidence from countries where prostitution is permitted indicates otherwise. Prostitution is not a popular option for a number of reasons. First, most women prefer to have sex with partners of their own choosing, in the context of an intimate relationship. The cultural ideal of love, romance, marriage, and family is deeply rooted in our society, as are traditional preferences for monogamy and sexual fidelity. Prostitution represents a decision to sacrifice one or more of these ideals, primarily for monetary gain. Because prostitutes flaunt cultural standards of morality, they inhabit the fringes of "decent" society. Being called a "whore" is not a compliment. Prostitutes also risk physical harm from clients, even in controlled working environments. And, although legalization would substantially reduce the threat of STD infection (as illustrated by Nevada's legal brothels), prostitutes would still face greater STD risks than other women. Finally, according to evolutionary theorists, millennia of evolution has created female psychologies that predispose women to "shun men who emit cues that signal that they are pursuing a short-term, rather than long-term, mating strategy."[96]

Clearly, then, it is largely inconceivable that, were prostitution legalized, women would flock to the trade.

On the other hand, although a considerable number of men likely would avail themselves of commercial sex opportunities if prostitution were legalized, not all men would do so, and few men would do so to the exclusion of (unpaid) romantic relationships. In his groundbreaking study of the sexual behavior of American men, circa 1940, pioneering sex researcher Alfred Kinsey estimated that 69 percent of the adult male population had visited a prostitute at one time or another.[97] However, patronizing prostitutes has become less acceptable than it was during the lifetimes of the men Kinsey interviewed (some of whom were born prior to the start of the twentieth century). Recent estimates suggest that approximately 15 to 20 percent of North American men have at some time paid to have illicit sex with a prostitute.[98] These estimates provide a lower bound on the proportion of men who would conceivably patronize prostitutes were the trade legalized.

Men seek the company of prostitutes for various reasons. In a British sample of 134 customers, the following were the main reasons given for patronizing prostitutes:

(1) *Partner variety.* It is characteristic of men to seek, or at the very least be interested in, having sex with a variety of partners.

(2) *Specific sexual acts.* Many of the men were unable to convince their usual partners to perform certain acts, primarily oral sex.

(3) *Specific physical characteristics.* Prostitution accorded men the opportunity to have sex with women whose bodies or ethnic background were in accord with their preferences.

(4) *Anonymous and casual sex.* Some of the men were attracted to the very fact that the contact was free of emotional bonds or other types of commitment.

(5) *Illicit excitement.* Some men were attracted by the fact that the contact was "illicit" and illegal. That is, the "adventure" itself was erotically exciting.[99]

In short, prostitutes provide men with something they are unable (or unwilling) to procure elsewhere, whether variety in acts or partners, excitement, or particular physical characteristics, such as attractiveness. The "demand" for these qualities cannot be eliminated simply by suppressing the "supply." As we argue in our book, *With Pleasure: Thoughts on the Nature of Human Sexuality*,

> Obviously, the market value of prostitution is enhanced in proportion to its ability to serve as a reasonable substitute for an unavailable commodity in the sexual marketplace. If oral-genital sex, for example, is unavailable or highly restricted in the "free" sexual market (including marriage), then the unsatisfied demand will inflate the worth of this practice in the commercial sex marketplace. Indeed, this appeared to be the case for fellatio, circa 1970: "Every married guy who comes in here wants to stick it in my mouth because their wives won't let them." Thus, in some sense, prostitution provides a natural counterweight to society's repression of sex. Where religious strictures or other forms of repression dominate, prostitution can be expected to flourish.[100]

Still, not *all* men would become "johns" if the opportunity arose. Men, too, value sexual and emotional intimacy of the type unavailable in commercial sexual encounters. The main reason men patronize prostitutes is sex, pure and simple. Contrary to the fairytale portrayal in *Pretty Woman*, these men are not buying a relationship, they are buying sex. In contrast, intimate (noncommercial) relationships offer numerous emotional, psychological, and practical benefits in addition to the physical experience of sexual pleasure that cannot be duplicated by transitory dalliances with paid partners. Few men, we would venture, would completely sacrifice the potential for love and shared intimacy with a partner of their choosing for a life of fleeting sexual gratification with paid partners. Moreover, the history of prostitution in America suggests that the existence of widespread commercial sex is not incompatible with commitment, marriage, and family—for example, average family size is now much smaller than it was in the late nineteenth and early twentieth centuries. It seems rather unlikely, therefore, that commercial sex could ever replace close, intimate relationships as the central organizing feature of our socio-sexual system.

MORALS, MARKETS, AND MADISON'S NINTH

There is scant evidence linking prostitution to increased crime or the spread of sexually transmitted diseases in contemporary America. Furthermore, to the extent that harmful secondary effects can be demonstrated, they appear mainly to be a direct consequence of the illegality of prostitution, rather than of prostitution per se. Secondary effects could be better dealt with by decriminalizing and regulating prostitution, as is done in Nevada and many European cities. Zoning laws could be used to restrict prostitution to particular circumscribed areas, and health codes could be enforced to ensure consistent condom use in all commercial sex encounters, coupled with periodic physical examinations and STD testing.

But, if the secondary effects of prostitution are negligible, or at least circumventable, why is commercial sex still vigorously condemned? The answer, to put it simply, is that prostitution rubs people the wrong way. The Supreme Court admitted as much when in 1908 it argued that prostitution is hostile to the "idea of the family":

> [Prostitution] refers to women who for hire or without hire offer their bodies to indiscriminate intercourse with men. The lives and example of such persons are in hostility to "the idea of the family, as consisting in and springing from the union of life of one man and one woman in the holy estate of matrimony; the sure foundation of all that is stable and noble in our civilization, the best guaranty [sic] of that reverent morality which is the source of all beneficent progress in social and political improvement."[101]

But why should marital fidelity, or the family, be the foundation for *any* American sex law? Ben Franklin *started* his family with a prostitute, and America profited as a consequence (one of their offspring went on to become the governor of New Jersey). And how do we explain the following disparity: prostitution is criminalized in *every* state of the union, including parts of Nevada, but adultery is not treated so harshly. It seems disingenuous (to say the least) to tolerate adultery despite the turmoil that it creates while punishing prostitution on grounds that the latter threatens monogamy and the family. If prostitution can wreak havoc with a person's life, adultery can certainly inflict as much damage (if not more) on persons, marriages, and families. In fact, adultery is *always* a threat to marriage because, by definition, it always involves (at least) one married partner. Nevertheless, adultery is generally regarded as a more pardonable sin than prostitution and is rarely if ever punished as a crime.

That the American populace espouses devotion to family and the "holy" state of matrimony is certainly understandable, considering our Judeo-Christian heritage. On the other hand, there is no justifiable reason that this ideology should be the legal foundation for appropriate sexual conduct. Ben Franklin made this point in 1747 in his satire, *The Speech of Polly Baker,* in which Miss Baker defends herself against prosecution for having given birth to a "bastard child":

> You believe I have offended heaven and must suffer eternal fire. Will not that be sufficient? What need is there, then, of your additional fines and whipping? Can it be a crime (in the nature of things I mean) to add to the number of the King's subjects, in a new country that really wants people? I own it, I should think it a praiseworthy, rather than punishable action . . . and therefore ought, in my humble opinion, instead of a whipping, to have a statue erected in my memory.[102]

America may be a Christian nation at heart, but Christianity is not the only valid basis for judging the morality of people's conduct. Many cultures and religions celebrate diverse forms of sexual relations (e.g., Hinduism, Shintoism) and consider them essential to healthy development.[103] Yet, such evidence is conveniently ignored by the American judicial system in the service of an implicit endorsement of early Judeo-Christian notions about sex, and marriage, and the proper role of women in society.

Once we dispense with the subjective, moralistic condemnation of prostitution, little basis remains for prohibiting commercial sexual activities. Enforcing prostitution statutes costs American taxpayers hundreds of millions of dollars each year and diverts already strained law enforcement resources away from serious crimes, such as assault, rape, murder, and robbery. Whatever revulsion some Americans might feel at the notion of trading sexual access for cash, prostitution is not a pressing social concern. In one national poll, fewer than half of adult respondents agreed with the statement "prostitutes do more harm than good."[104] Moreover, in a nationwide survey commissioned by the U.S. Justice Department in which respondents were asked to rank the severity of various "offenses," prostitution ranked 174th out of 204 and patronizing a prostitute ranked even lower.[105] Neither offense was considered as serious as cheating on one's taxes or calling in a false fire alarm.[106] In light of public sentiment and the high cost of enforcing prostitution laws, Pearl wonders "whether we can afford to keep it illegal."[107]

Beyond the economic costs (including foregone tax revenues that would otherwise accrue if prostitution were legalized) are the substantial costs to our personal freedoms. We have argued throughout this book that the Ninth Amendment protects our freedom to make fundamental choices about how we express ourselves sexually, including the choice to reproduce or not and choices to engage in non-normative sexual conduct. If the First Amendment's free speech clause can be stretched to cover pornography, then surely the Ninth Amendment's rights retained by the people can encompass an essentially personal, private behavior that differs from traditional courtship rituals mainly by asking a specific price for a specific sexual act. There is no objective legal basis for criminalizing autonomous economic choices involving constitutionally protected sexual behaviors. Instead, it is more consistent with the spirit of the choices and rights protected by the Constitution to extend these rights to encompass the decision to charge a price for sex. As long as the behavior itself is legal and the harm to society minimal, economic considerations cannot be dispositive. Why should an explicit financial relationship (e.g., $50 for oral sex) be criminal when the implicit financial relationship (e.g., oral sex in exchange for free rent) is fully legal? (This situation is reminiscent of the paradox in *Roe v. Wade*, where it was legal in Texas to self-abort but not to have a physician perform an abortion.)

By and large, it is women, not men, who control sexual access in human societies.[108] Women should have the right to initiate sex for romantic, experimental, or commercial reasons. To deny them the freedom to choose to have sex for economic reasons obstructs an arena in which women have power and unduly limits their economic options. Clearly, there are many male customers out there. But it is women, mainly, who are in the position to demand a price for sexual access. The criminalization of prostitution in America is an unjustified restraint of free trade that adversely and prejudicially affects women.

One of our founding fathers, Alexander Hamilton, repeatedly paid the price to continue his extramarital affair (see chapter 1). He concluded the affair when he could no longer afford it, which is how markets operate. If customers like Alexander Hamilton and millions of other American men are willing to pay for sexual access, there is no objective legal rationale for denying them the opportunity to do so.

Ultimately, if we can charge a price for disposing of the dead, it seems reasonable to be able to charge a price for providing sexual pleasure to the living.

7

Child Pornography

Black, White, and Gray

THE DECEIT, COERCION, and harm implicit in pornographic images of children evokes nearly universal condemnation. Child pornography is particularly horrifying not only because it documents the criminal sexual abuse of a child, but because this enduring record of abuse violates the child's right to future privacy and because such pornography often is used as a tool to perpetuate the sexual exploitation of children.[1]

Not surprisingly, there are few advocates of child pornography. Save the discrete musings of individual pedophiles, or of pedophile organizations such as the North American Man-Boy Love Association, few clamor to this cause. Clearly, child pornography is, and should be, *ganz verboten*. But while it is easy to condemn child pornography, it is much more difficult to identify possible instances of child pornography *as* child pornography.

Take the case of *U.S. v. Knox*, which was first argued before the Third Circuit Court of Appeals in August 1992.[2] Stephen Knox was a graduate student at Pennsylvania State University in whose possession were found three films of very young girls dancing around in bathing suits, leotards, and similarly "revealing" attire. Although none of the girls were naked, "crotch shots" were prominently featured in all three films, which had titles like "Little Girl Bottoms." Because of the camera's insistent focus on the girls' (clothed) genital regions, the films were deemed to have included "lascivious exhibition of the genitals or pubic area" and Knox was convicted of child pornography.

When Knox filed an appeal seeking to overturn his conviction, arguing, among other things, that the absence of nudity invalidated the "lascivious exhibition" finding, the Justice Department concurred. The Chief Supreme Court Advocate, Solicitor General Drew S. Days III, filed a brief in support of Knox's appeal, indicating that child pornography statutes apply only to nudity or to genitals whose contours are evident through clothing.[3]

In response to the Solicitor General's report, the Supreme Court returned the case to the Court of Appeals for reconsideration. The Third Circuit considered but rejected the Solicitor General's position, maintaining that the federal child pornography statute contained no nudity or discernibility requirement. Undaunted, Knox turned again to the Supreme Court. By this time, however, due to pressure from Congress and the president, the Justice Department had reversed itself. In a letter from President Bill Clinton to Attorney General Janet Reno, the beleaguered new president, flexing before swine (i.e., child pornographers), stated, "I find all forms of child pornography offensive and harmful, as I know you do, and I want the federal government to lead aggressively in the attack against the scourge of child pornography."[4] In the end, the Supreme Court declined to hear Knox's final appeal, and his conviction stood firm.

Despite President Clinton's fulminations against "all forms of child pornography," the cultural and judicial boundaries of "child pornography" are often fuzzy. Child pornography resists easy categorization. Seldom is it a black-and-white issue. Instead, child pornography all too frequently populates the gray areas of human sexual deviance and criminal regulation. In *Knox*, for example, there was no nudity, and the Justice Department initially agreed with Knox's position until it was cowed into submission.

Before delving into the many shades of gray, let us first address the "black and white," the easily identifiable regions of child pornography, since their standing under the First and Ninth Amendments is negligible. We will define these uncontested areas as images that portray a child engaging in overt sexual interactions, including self-stimulation (masturbation), and images that clearly depict a child's genitals in a sexually provocative way. In contrast to mere nudity, examples of provocative sexual poses would include: legs spread apart to better reveal the genitalia, with accompanying hand placement and facial gestures to connote sexual interest; holding the labia open to exhibit the vaginal opening; and so forth. Obviously, many more examples could be presented. The point is simply to introduce the areas of child pornography about which there is little debate and for which there are no constitutional protections.

But what of the "gray areas" of child pornography? For instance, is nudity required for an image to be pornographic, as Knox suggested, or is a sexually suggestive pose enough? Are the Calvin Klein ads of 1995—in which young-looking models posed, fully clothed but with various items of underwear showing—instances of child pornography? Conversely, is *every* photo of a naked child pornographic? Should child pornography laws forbid a loving parent from making a video of her naked two-year-old splashing around the bathtub? Satisfactory answers to these and related questions are critical to the criminal prosecution of child pornographers and to the protection of individuals who are unjustly accused. The question that continues to plague the courts is how to make the definition of "child pornography" potent enough to protect against the truly heinous, but not so powerful that it unduly encroaches upon civil liberties.

Existing child pornography statues have failed in this attempt, as a result of myriad definitional difficulties, which we will review in detail. But this need not imply that attempts to regulate and abolish child pornography are futile. Instead, the solution proposed herein—which, we believe, is maximally consistent with First and Ninth Amendment rights—is to enact and enforce rigorous requirements of informed consent for the production and distribution of the sexualized images of children. In this way, the law can protect children from possible harms associated with such imagery without having to invoke the definitional morass of constructs such as "lewd" and "lascivious." An additional benefit to this approach is that consent is a well-developed legal concept, with well-established precedents and broad applicability. Moreover, because children are *incapable* of consenting to having their sexualized images recorded, consent becomes an issue of parental responsibility. The net effect of this shift in focus to issues of informed consent, we believe, would be to consistently and effectively criminalize most, if not all, instances of child pornography while excluding benign cases from the reach of the law.

Our proposal to use informed consent as a governing standard for regulating the gray areas of child pornography advances the larger objectives of this book—namely, to secure a foundation for sexual rights based on the Ninth Amendment. Previous chapters have offered the thesis that Americans have a fundamental right to make reproductive and nonreproductive decisions and to express themselves sexually. In chapters 4 and 5 we qualified this sexual right by introducing informed consent as a major constraint on our sexual freedoms. The present chapter elaborates the rationale and application of consent-based sexual rights limitations by considering the concrete example of child pornography. Although the issues underlying this constraint are not predicated upon accepting our arguments about the Ninth Amendment, the material presented here elucidates an obvious limit on the broad interpretation of choices relevant to reproduction and human sexuality. As we discussed in chapter 5, many men masturbate to pornography, and we believe they have a constitutionally protected right to do so. But what if the pornography in question depicts a child having sex with an adult? We argue here that consent is as material to the production and use of sexual images as it is to behaviors with sexual partners. Thus, child pornography is illegal, and Americans have no "right" to it, because children cannot consent to it.[5]

PROTECTING KIDS

The Protection of Children against Sexual Exploitation Act, enacted by Congress in 1977, was the initial template for America's child pornography laws. Over the years it has undergone some revision,[6] but the substance remains intact. Among the notables, the knowing production, distribution, sale, or possession of visual depictions of minors engaged in "sexually explicit conduct" are outlawed by the Act. Initially, the phrase "sexually explicit conduct" was defined as actual or simulated: (1) sexual intercourse (including genital-genital, oral-genital, anal-genital, and oral-anal acts, whether between persons of the same or the opposite sex); (2) bestiality; (3) masturbation; (4) sadistic or masochistic behaviors; or (5) "lewd" exhibition of the genitals or pubic area of any person (including adults in the presence of children). However, in the 1984 revision of the Act,[7] "lewd" exhibition of the genitals or pubic area" became "lascivious exhibition of the genitals or pubic area."[8] Although a seemingly frivolous semantic alteration, this linguistic modification was justified by the following logic: "'Lewd' has in the past been equated with 'obscene'; this change is thus intended to make it clear that an exhibition of a child's genitals does not have to meet the obscenity standard to be unlawful."[9]

The Child Protection Act's deliberate use of "lascivious" in place of "lewd" was in response to the Supreme Court's landmark opinion in

New York v. Ferber.[10] In this 1982 case, the Supreme Court concluded that pornographic depictions of children lack First Amendment protection even if the depictions are not "obscene." Unlike obscenity laws, which aim to protect "the sensibilities of unwilling recipients,"[11] child pornography laws are designed to protect children from exploitation and abuse.[12] Therefore, standards for adjudicating obscenity (e.g., "community standards," "redeeming value," and "prurient interest") have no relevance in determining what constitutes child pornography:

> The question under the *Miller* test of whether a work, taken as a whole, appeals to the prurient interest of the average person bears no connection to the issue of whether a child has been physically or psychologically harmed in the production of the work. Similarly, a sexually explicit depiction need not be "patently offensive" in order to have required the sexual exploitation of a child for its production. . . . It is irrelevant to the child [who has been abused] whether or not the material . . . has a literary, artistic, political or social value. . . . It would be equally unrealistic to equate a community's toleration for sexually oriented material with the permissible scope of legislation aimed at protecting children from sexual exploitation.[13]

Thus, *New York v. Ferber* empowered legislatures to prohibit sexually explicit depictions of minors as a means of preventing child sexual abuse. If a child is harmed by pornography, the context is immaterial.

LASCIVIOUSNESS

Given the *Ferber* mandate to protect children, the critical question becomes: Which images are sexually exploitative or abusive of children? The issue, once again, ranges from the black and white to the many shades of gray. Most people would agree that the behaviors described as "sexually explicit conduct" in the first four clauses of the Child Protection Act (including intercourse, bestiality, masturbation, and sadomasochism) are unquestionably exploitative and harmful. But what of the fifth clause of the Child Protection Act? Is the "lascivious exhibition of the genitals or pubic area" necessarily exploitative? On the face of it, it certainly *sounds* exploitative. Yet, when the actual meaning of this clause is carefully scrutinized and possible misinterpretations are considered, its problematic nature becomes evident. Indeed, upon close examination, the "lascivious exhibition" question reveals itself as a prototypical example of the murky "gray" area of child pornography.

Take, for instance, the definition of "lascivious." According to *The Oxford Dictionary of Current English*, "lascivious" means "lustful or inciting to lust" and "lewd" means "lascivious or obscene." The definitional morass is obvious. "Lascivious" is clearly a synonym for "lewd," which Congress has already deemed problematic. If "lascivious" is synonymous with "lewd," and if "lewd" is equated with "obscene," then "lascivious" may also be equated with "obscene," and the definitional difficulties begin anew. Indeed, in *Hamling v. United States* the Supreme Court equated the meanings of a list of "generic" descriptors in a congressional statute, including, among others, "obscene," "lewd," and "lascivious."[14] And in *United States v. Wiegand*, a case we review below, the Ninth Circuit Court of Appeals asserted that "'Lascivious' is no different in its meaning than 'lewd.'"[15]

Worse yet is the definition's introduction of the concept of "lust," which *The Oxford Dictionary* defines as "strong sexual desire." Presumably, one could argue that most nude images of children are void of lust because children—especially young children—are incapable of exhibiting, or even experiencing, "strong sexual desire." But does the absence of lust in images of children render them nonpornographic? The second part of the definition of "lascivious," which focuses on the power to *excite* lustful thoughts, seems to expand the definition of child pornography to include anything and everything that might appeal to a pedophile. Under this standard, the infamous Coppertone ad that showed a dog pulling at a young girl's bathing suit bottom is evidently pornographic, as is any commercial photograph that displays a child in underwear. Thus, whether "lust," "lewd," or "lascivious" is at issue, the legalistic terminology of child pornography statutes remains vague and problematic.

Unfortunately, case law itself is no less convoluted. Consider the case of *United States v. Dost*.[16] Robert Dost and Edward Wiegand were charged with child pornography for taking twenty-two nude photographs of two young girls. Twenty-one of the photographs were of a fourteen-year-old, posed in both supine and sitting positions, taken at the Dost residence. The other photograph depicted a ten-year-old girl at the beach. Dost posed the girls, while Wiegand took the photos.

United States v. Dost was argued before the U.S. District Court for the Southern District of California in 1986. The main consideration in this case was whether the photographs depicted minors engaging in "sexually explicit conduct," and, in particular, whether they contained a lascivious exhibition of the genitals or pubic area. This case is especially significant because it was the first attempt to articulate criteria for assessing whether an image constitutes lascivious exhibition of the genitals or pubic area. The district court concluded that the following factors should inform this determination:

(1) Whether the focal point of the visual depiction is the child's genitals or pubic area;
(2) Whether the setting of the visual depiction is sexually suggestive (i.e., in a place or pose generally associated with sexual activity);
(3) Whether the child is depicted in an unnatural pose, or in inappropriate attire, considering the age of the child;
(4) Whether the child is fully or partially clothed, or nude;
(5) Whether the visual depiction suggests sexual coyness or a willingness to engage in sexual activity;
(6) Whether the visual depiction is intended or designed to elicit a sexual response in the viewer.

Two questions arise immediately upon consideration of these factors. First, are the factors *themselves* clear enough to facilitate a reliable assessment of lascivious exhibitionism? And second, do the Dost photographs qualify as "lascivious exhibition of the genitals or pubic area" under these factors?

Consider the second question first. Having never seen the Dost photographs, we are obviously at a considerable disadvantage. However, based upon the description of the photographs contained within court records, it seems readily apparent that they were in fact "lascivious." The photos are described as follows:

> The photographs of the 14-year-old girl depict her totally nude posed in a variety of positions. Most pictures are of her reclining on some draped material, resembling a bed, with her genitals and breasts fully exposed. In most of the pictures, her legs are open and her arms are raised behind her head. In the majority of the pictures, her pubic area

is in the foreground so as to be the prominent focal point of the photo-graph. The single picture of the 10-year-old child portrays the child sit-ting on the beach . . . totally nude . . . her legs are spread apart . . . her pubic area is completely exposed, not obscured by any shadow or body part.[17]

The U.S. District Court further noted (referring to the photographs of the fourteen-year-old) that "the focal point of the photographs are the girl's well-developed genitalia; indeed, some of the poses border on the acrobatic in order to obtain an unusual perspective on her genitalia. . . . As for the suggestion of a willingness to engage in sexual activity, her open legs do imply such a willingness." Finally, referring to the photo-graph of the ten-year-old:

> What strikes the Court most strongly, however, is the unusual pose of this girl. The average 10-year-old child sitting on the beach, especially when unclothed, does not sit with her legs positioned in such a man-ner. . . . This unnatural pose combined with the picture's emphasis on the girl's genitalia leads the Court to conclude that it too constitutes a "lascivious exhibition of the genitals."[18]

From this description it seems clear that Dost and Wiegand created "lascivious" photographs of minors—thereby sacrificing all claims to First and Ninth Amendment protection. However, even though the Dost photographs are clearly lascivious, the criteria introduced to make a determination of the "lascivious exhibition of the genitals or pubic area" remain problematic. For example, in Dost the court also stated:

> Of course, a visual depiction need not involve all of these factors to be a "lascivious exhibition of the genitals or pubic area." The determina-tion will have to be made based on the overall content of the visual de-piction, taking into account the age of the minor.[19]

Can this be interpreted as meaning that satisfying only one or a few Dost factors could be sufficient to render an image pornographic? For instance, if the image is designed to arouse a pedophile (Dost factor #6), is it thereby child pornography? Similarly, when evaluating the image of a child, what constitutes "sexual coyness or a willingness to engage in sexual activity"? If her legs are spread and her genitals exposed, the conclusion seems obvious. Yet, what if she is merely scantily attired? Does a photograph of a scantily-clad fourteen-year-old girl connote sexual coyness? Is the Louis Malle film *Pretty Baby* (starring Brooke Shields) an instance of artistic child pornography, due to its great appeal to pedophiles? Finally, even the most obvious of the *Dost* factors—"whether the focal point of the visual depiction is on the child's genitalia or pubic area"—has already proven problematic. As discussed earlier, *United States v. Knox* struggled with the question of whether photographs that focus on the genitalia require nudity, or evidence of the contour of the genitals, to be judged pornographic.

Wiegand's 1987 appeal from his conviction in the *Dost* case, *United States v. Wiegand*, covers related territory. For example, *Wiegand* asked whether child pornography, treated as a commodity, is sufficiently identifiable to form the object of a search warrant. The Ninth Circuit Court of Appeals concluded in the affirmative, stating:

> Little was left to the imagination, and nothing to the discretion, of the searches as to what they were to look for and carry off. They were restricted to film depicting explicit acts of sexual conduct—explicitly described in the warrant—by children under the age of 18.[20]

Again, this conclusion seems obvious, and relatively straightforward, until it is recalled that the "lascivious exhibition of the genitals and pubic area" is part of the definition of explicit sexual conduct. (One might also question how the federal agents were expected to judge the ages of the girls in the films.) This ambiguous clause, as demonstrated throughout this chapter, leaves quite a bit to the imagination and discretion of the viewer.

Wiegand also revisited a very controversial aspect of the *New York v. Ferber* case. Although in *Ferber* the Supreme Court concluded that child pornography does not merit First Amendment protection, the Court also noted—though it is rarely mentioned—that "a tiny fraction" of images portraying sexual acts involving children *might* fall within the auspices of the First Amendment.[21] When introduced in *Wiegand*, this commentary was offered not in Wiegand's defense, but in reference to the search warrant:

> A warrant to search for film portraying the sexual exploitation of children is not defective because the possibility exists that a tiny fraction

of the material seized might be found to fall within the exception acknowledged by *Ferber*. In the protection of children otherwise privileged expressions may be affected.[22]

Wiegand not only substantiated the surpassing interest of government in protecting children, but verified in a clear voice that such protection is intrinsic to child pornography laws:

> The crime punished by the statutes against the sexual exploitation of children, however, does not consist in the cravings of the person posing the child or in the cravings of his audience. Private fantasies are not within the statute's ambit. The crime is the offense against the child— the harm "to the physiological, emotional, and mental health" of the child.[23]

But if *Ferber* and *Wiegand* affirm the moral imperative to protect children from the myriad harms of pornography, it remains to establish the bounds of harm, particularly if we want simultaneously to preserve First and Ninth Amendment rights. In a recent case, *Ashcroft v. Free Speech Coalition*, the Supreme Court determined that "virtual" child pornography (i.e., computer-generated images of children) is not "intrinsically related" to the abuse of children, and so may not be proscribed. The Court offered the following rationale:

> While the Government asserts that the [virtual] images can lead to actual instances of child abuse, the causal link is contingent and indirect. The harm does not necessarily follow from the speech, but depends upon some unquantified potential for subsequent criminal acts. . . . The mere tendency of speech to encourage unlawful acts is not a sufficient reason for banning it.[24]

But other issues of potential harm remain. For example, is a nude photograph of a child invariably lascivious? And if not, what makes it so? This question was addressed in *United States v. Villard*.[25] In this case, Robert Villard was charged with possessing a magazine (*Beach Boys No. 2*) containing four pictures of a minor engaged in the "lascivious exhibition of the genitals or pubic area." What makes this case especially interesting is that the photographs themselves were *not* introduced as evidence. Villard's own copy of *Beach Boys No. 2* disappeared, and the government was unable to locate a duplicate. In its place the jury viewed surveillance videotapes showing Villard and a government informant named Henry Feltman looking at, and commenting upon, *Beach Boys No. 2*. Although the jury couldn't see the magazine from the videotape, it was apparent that the four photographs were contained on two opposing pages. In viewing the tapes, the jury heard the following exchange:

FELTMAN: Excellent. Oh, even better. This is what, *Beach Boys No. 2*? In Paris, huh?

VILLARD: Yeah, I went to the address, they were closed up and they didn't open until Tuesday and I left Sunday . . . or something like that.

FELTMAN: Uh huh.

VILLARD: So there was no way I could rearrange my trip even though I . . .

FELTMAN: Now what kind of store would you find these in?

VILLARD: Uhh, I bought these in a gay bookstore.

FELTMAN: O.K. Certainly un . . . got nothing on there.

VILLARD: It's done with mirrors.

FELTMAN: Huh?

VILLARD: They have mirrors.

FELTMAN: I wonder if he's asleep. He's three quarters hard. Maybe he sleeps in the buff like that. He's pretty hairy, though, God but not just much under the arm.[26]

Explaining this videotape to the jury, the government informant, Feltman, provided the following testimony:

Okay. I was looking at *Beach Boys No. 2*. The magazine was opened like this. You could see there was two photographs on each page. Like a left page and a right page. Now these pictures were all of the same boy. This boy was approximately 14, 15 years old. He was fully nude. He was lying on what appeared to be a bed or a mattress. And his eyes were closed as though he was sleeping. However, looking at the two pictures on the left page, versus the two pictures on the right page, they were very, very similar. They pretty near looked the same. This is where Bob said it looks like it was done with mirrors. This was . . . [this] page was a reflection of the left page. The right page, vice versa.

It could work either way. However, I don't believe he was asleep because there were slight variations between each photograph. The way the boy was lying there had been a little bit of movement each time. His knees were bent slightly upwards during this. . . . And he had three quarters, you know, like a three quarters erection, semi erect . . . these were close, closein [sic] type photographs showing him from his head down to approximately knee level. That they filled the photographs on each page. They filled the entire page.[27]

Villard introduces some interesting issues, besides the question of whether nudity is tantamount to lasciviousness. In particular, because the magazine itself was unavailable, the determination of lasciviousness revolved solely around Feltman's subjective impressions. Thus, this case raises the critical question of how easily "lasciviousness" can be discerned. If lasciviousness is readily discernable, like anger (for example), then the average person could, conceivably, make a reasonable determination of lasciviousness. Hence, a firsthand description by an objective viewer could provide testimony to the lasciviousness of a particular piece of evidence, even in its absence. Of course, some would question whether a government informant (such as Feltman) represents an unbiased viewer, let alone whether lasciviousness can be reliably assessed. Certainly, as the cases discussed previously suggest, the criteria for making this judgment are potentially problematic.

Moreover, because the age of the model is critical to determining whether *Beach Boys No. 2* is in fact "child" pornography, it is essential to apprehend: (1) whether Feltman can reliably assess age; (2) whether the model altered his appearance to appear younger, for example, by shaving under his arms; and (3) whether the photographs were retouched to give a more youthful appearance to the model. Unfortunately, without the photographs, these questions cannot be answered.

However, even if it could be established that the model was, in fact, under eighteen years of age, the court would still have two other issues to consider. First, can it reasonably convict Villard in the absence of the actual photographs? And if so, were the photographs, as represented by Feltman, actually lascivious?

The jury answered "yes" to both questions and convicted Villard of "transporting child pornography across state lines"—this despite the absence of the photographs and the glaring problems with Feltman's testimony. However, Villard entered a motion for judgment of acquittal, and in a surprising turn of events, the District Court granted the motion, deciding that the evidence presented was not sufficient to support a conviction.

The government appealed the case, but the Third Circuit Court of Appeals affirmed the judgment of the District Court.[28] Furthermore, the Court of Appeals adopted the *Dost* factors as a means to determine whether an exhibition is lascivious, adding that more than one (but not all) of the *Dost* factors must be present in order to demonstrate lasciviousness. The court then concluded that the pictures, as described, were *not* lascivious. This conclusion was based upon several related findings.

First, while acknowledging that the boy had a partial erection, the court emphasized that the genitals were not the focal point of the photographs (the photographs showed the boy's body from head to knees). Moreover, although the court admitted that the bed provided some evidence of lasciviousness, it was not enough to make the photographs, as a whole, conclusively lascivious. In reference to the third *Dost* factor (whether a child is depicted in an unnatural pose), the Court of Appeals ruled that "The government's assertion at oral argument that photographing a naked boy with a partial erection is unnatural is irrelevant, of course, because our focus must be on the contents of the picture itself rather than on the producer of the picture."[29] The court also asserted that nudity, in and of itself, was insufficient to brand a photo as lascivious. Additionally, the court concluded that in order to claim a visual depiction was designed to elicit a sexual response in the viewer, the prosecution must demonstrate that it was *intended* to elicit such a response, not merely that it effectively elicited that response. That is, just because Villard found the photos sexually arousing does not mean that they were intended to elicit such a response. (The court referred to the logic behind the opposite assertion—i.e., that usage determines intent—as "conclusory bootstrapping.")

Villard is significant because it established that child nudity per se is not necessarily pornographic, even if a partially erect penis is depicted. This finding is somewhat surprising; one could certainly argue that the partial erection "sexualizes" the photograph. On the other hand, one could also argue that the erection was merely a consequence of sleep (i.e., a nocturnal erection).

In *Villard* the court also elaborated upon the "focal point" issue. The mere presence of exposed genitalia does not necessarily mean that the genitals are being focused upon. Presumably, since Feltman testified that the photographs were three-quarter body shots of a supine, sleeping male, the Court of Appeals concluded that the genitals were neither exclusively highlighted nor excessively attended to and that therefore the genitals were not the focal point of the photos.

Perhaps these appellate findings were unduly influenced by the absence of the photographs themselves. Conceivably, the impact of the photographs could have been much greater had they been available for viewing, with a consequent increase in the likelihood of conviction. However, perhaps anticipating this concern, the Court of Appeals turned to the District Court's opinion in this case, which included a discussion of several allegedly comparable images of nude children. Quoting the District Court:

> When a picture does not constitute child pornography, even though it portrays nudity, it does not become child pornography because it is placed in the hands of a pedophile, or in a forum where pedophiles might enjoy it. *Faloona v. Hustler Magazine, Inc.* (nude pictures of children did not constitute child pornography when published in "legitimate" *Sex Atlas* or in "raunchy" *Hustler* magazine, because they did not depict children engaged in sexual conduct).[30]

Unfortunately, this returns us to an earlier difficulty—namely, providing an adequate definition of sexual conduct. Overt sexual acts, including masturbation, undoubtedly constitute "sexual conduct," whereas mere nudity, at least in accordance with *Villard* and *Faloona*, does not. The sticking point, to reiterate, is the lascivious display of the genitals. But when does nudity become lascivious? In line with *Villard*, the depiction of a partial erection is not necessarily lascivious, but according to *Dost*, the opposite is apparently true of photographs showing a young girl whose legs are spread apart. Is there a contradiction here, or possibly a gender bias in application?

In any case, it is clear that, notwithstanding the *Dost* factors, the determination as to whether a particular depiction is lascivious is not always straightforward. Does this mean that an expert witness is required to distinguish the truly lascivious (i.e., "pornographic") from less offensive depictions of children? The answer is "yes" only if lasciviousness is *not* readily apparent to the average person. After all, the expert's sole function is to aid the jury in making technical determinations. Is lasciviousness so opaque that an expert is needed?

The function of the *Dost* factors (whether the genitals are the focal point of the depiction, whether the child is unnaturally posed, etc.) is to make the assessment of lasciviousness clearer. Obviously, if lasciviousness were readily apparent to all, the *Dost* factors would be unnecessary.[31] However, the *Dost* factors are utilized in child pornography cases because, as the Court of Appeals in *Villard* noted, "'lascivious' [is] a term which is less than crystal clear."[32] But are the *Dost* factors *themselves* "crystal clear"? As intimated throughout this section, the answer is no. The *Dost* factors include many concepts (e.g., unnatural pose, sexually suggestive, focal point, sexual coyness, etc.) that demand elaboration, particularly when applied to depictions of nude children or adolescents.

For example, consider two popular photography books, Jock Sturges's *Radiant Identities* and Sally Mann's *Immediate Family*. Sturges and Mann are prominent photographers who have won international acclaim for their telling portraits. Their books are published by reputable publishers and are accessible in many mainstream bookstores. What makes these books distinctive is that they contain photographs of nude children—in Sally Mann's case, her own.

Though many Americans buy these books, it also seems safe to assume that many if not most American pedophiles possess them as well. If the images they contain appeal to pedophiles and prompt masturbatory activities, an important issue is raised: are they therefore child pornography? At least according to a broad interpretation of the *Dost* clause concerning the photographer's intent, some of these images undoubtedly are.[33] Similarly, it could be argued that the pictures are sexually suggestive or sexually coy. In sum, then, despite the acclaim these books have garnered (though not without controversy) and their wide availability, the photographs contained therein could be considered lascivious child pornography. Conversely, recognizing the artistic value of these photographs, many would argue that there is nothing lascivious or pornographic about naturalistic depictions of nude children, such as those contained in Mann's and Sturges's books. Lasciviousness, it appears, is largely in the eye of the beholder.

Nowhere was this more evident than in the case of Stephen Knox (*United States v. Knox*), to which we now return.

Recall that Knox was convicted of possessing child pornography—in the form of three films showing young girls cavorting in bathing suits, leotards, and similar attire—despite the fact that the films contained no nudity. The films did, however, contain numerous "crotch shots," which the Court deemed "lascivious exhibition of the genitals and pubic area." But were the genitals and public area really "exhibited" in the films? The dictionary defines "exhibit" as: "to present or expose to view; show; display." At the very least, then, for something to be exhibited, it must be visible. Yet neither genitals nor pubic areas were visible in Knox's films, which were nevertheless judged to be lascivious.

Even more absurd was the prosecution's interpretation of "pubic area." Presumably, the prosecution was aware of the difficulty inherent in the claim that the genitals were being exhibited, when in fact they were never in view. The upper thigh, however, was. Consequently, in one of the many bizarre twists in this case, the prosecution contended that the upper thigh was a part of the pubic area. Knox's attorneys hadn't anticipated this novel if outrageous argument and did not have an expert ready to contest it. However, when they finally obtained Dr. Todd Olsen, Director of Human Gross Anatomy at the Albert Einstein College of Medicine, to refute the prosecution's chimerical anatomy lesson, it was too late to assist Knox; the deadline for evidential testimony had passed.

The Knox case clearly demonstrates the inadequacy of child pornography laws based upon the "lascivious exhibition of the genitals and pubic area." It borders on the ludicrous to claim that something is being exhibited if that something is shielded from view. A covered crotch shot is not the same as the genitals; the upper thigh is certainly not the pubic area. And while existing criminal statutes do not demand nudity as a prerequisite for the lascivious exhibition of the genitals, it stands to reason that to be exhibited they must be visible, lascivious or not. Obviously, "flashing" and "mooning" would have very different meanings if the flasher or mooner were wearing a bathing suit or leotard. The latter, it seems, is closer to "I see London, I see France, I see (so and so's) underpants"—not his or her genitals.

HARM

Clearly, lasciviousness is too ambiguous a concept to provide an adequate foundation for the edifice of modern child pornography statutes. On the other hand, there seems to be a broad consensus among professionals that participating in pornographic activities can harm children psychologically, emotionally, and sometimes physically. This, coupled with *Ferber*'s emphasis on the protection of children as the primary goal of anti–child pornography legislation, suggests an alternate tack: why not explicitly harness "harm" to serve as the cornerstone of child pornography laws?

Unfortunately, the concept of harm is itself problematic. Remember that the main complication in applying the definition of "sexual conduct" adopted by the Child Protection Act arises not from the first four prongs of the definition, but from the fifth prong as it relates to lasciviousness. Although it is relatively simple to demonstrate that exploitation and harm occur to children who are victims of child pornography that contains explicit sexual conduct as defined by the first four prongs, the fifth prong is, once again a different matter. What's the harm, one wonders, in a little lascivious display?

Consider the case of *United States v. Wolf*.[34] On a cold December evening in 1987, William Wolf went Christmas shopping accompanied by two friends and their two children, one of them a five-year-old girl. After shopping, the entire group returned to Wolf's apartment. Later, when it was time to leave, Wolf asked the young girl's parents if she could spend the night at his apartment. The parents assented, and the five-year-old slept over.

Early the next morning, while the young girl was asleep on his waterbed, Wolf took photographs of her. Either he raised her nightgown and spread her legs apart, or this had occurred naturally during her sleep. In either case, her legs were spread, and because she was not wearing any underwear, her genitals were exposed. Indeed, the primary focus of the photographs was the girl's genitals, as her head was barely visible in the photos.

In a prototypical act of criminal stupidity, Wolf mailed the undeveloped film to an out-of-state company for processing, including in the package two five-dollar bills and a hand-printed note that read: "Send to W.J.W., 2421 North Sterling, Apartment 112-W, Oklahoma City, Oklahoma." Naturally, the photography lab suspected that the nude child was a minor and contacted the FBI. Wolf eventually admitted taking the photographs.

Although the photographs were deemed lascivious, the question remains: was this experience harmful to the child? Let us presume, for rhetorical purposes, that neither the sleeping child nor her parents ever learned of the photographs. Let us also presume that the photographs were not for distribution, were developed by Wolf himself (rather than an outside photo lab), and were to remain solely in his possession. Now, given these hypothetical conditions, was the girl harmed by having had her picture taken? And if not, would the absence of harm constitute a reasonable defense in a case such as Wolf's?

These considerations bear a superficial resemblance to the intractable philosophical dilemma of whether a tree falling in the woods, without anyone hearing it, actually makes a sound. Although it is relatively obvious that in many instances participation in explicitly sexual conduct is harmful to children, it is not difficult to create scenarios where harm may be absent, particularly with regard to nude photographs. Is a nude photograph of a sexually experienced seventeen-year-old harmful and exploitative? Are Sally Mann's photos of her own children exploitative? Or, consistent with *Wolf*, is a nude photograph of a sleeping child harmful even if the child is unaware that he or she has been photographed and the photograph itself is never distributed? It seems quite clear that these and similar questions are, at the very least, debatable. The concept of harm, like lasciviousness, is much too vague to provide a practicable basis for child pornography statutes.

INFORMED CONSENT

Lasciviousness is exceedingly vague, and harm, in many instances, depends upon the context. Neither, therefore, provides the bedrock upon which enforceable child pornography statutes can be securely erected; nor can they ensure that First and Ninth Amendment rights are not unduly violated. How, then, can child pornography be criminalized? One solution, as mentioned previously, lies in the concept of informed consent. Lasciviousness and harm may be debatable; consent, if ruled inoperative, is not.

The legalistic interpretation of informed consent surfaces in three primary contexts. In constitutional law, informed consent generally signifies that consent has been given in response to a complete explanation of the relevant issues. For instance, an individual who has been accused of committing a crime has a constitutional right to an attorney, as provided by the Sixth Amendment. However, a person can waive this right if that waiver is "knowing and intelligent"[35]—meaning that the explanation was explicit ("you have a right to counsel") and was preceded by a warning ("can be used against you"). In this circumstance, often referred to as the Miranda rule,[36] the individual who waives the right to counsel has provided informed consent to that waiver.

Informed consent also manifests itself in tort law. The primary aim of the law of torts is to provide individuals with compensation for harm suffered as a result of the conduct of others.[37] A fundamental question in tort law is what kinds of conduct constitute actionable wrongs (i.e., wrongs that can be sued over). This question is especially important because actionable wrongs typically imply knowledge of the potential for harm, hence a "duty" either to abstain from the potentially harmful conduct or to obtain informed consent from those who are thereby placed in jeopardy. Doctors, for example, exercise their duty by obtaining the patient's consent prior to performing an invasive or risky procedure. In so doing the exact nature and risks of the proposed medical procedure are explained to the patient, who may then elect or refuse the procedure. Obtaining informed consent not only protects the patient from potentially harmful outcomes, but also (partially) protects the doctor from possible legal actions should the patient be harmed (or die) as a direct consequence of the medical procedure or complications arising therefrom.

Finally, informed consent has relevance to criminal law, and in particular to consensual sexual relations. Rape, sexual harassment, and so forth are crimes perpetrated in the absence of consent; indeed, the lack of consent is the defining characteristic of these crimes.

Informed consent is defined by the California Penal Code (section 261.1) as "positive cooperation in act or attitude pursuant to an exercise of free will. The person must act freely and voluntarily and have knowledge of the nature of the act or transaction involved." Thus, when applied to sexual conduct, the criteria for informed consent adopted within criminal law involve two critical aspects: the ability to understand the nature and consequences of the sexual act, and evidence of a freely chosen decision to engage in sexual relations. Thus, informed consent, whether explicit or implied, is only relevant to sexual relations with individuals who are *capable* of consenting.[38] Sexual relations involving a child or a mentally, psychologically, or emotionally challenged person raise the concern as to whether such a person even has the capacity to provide informed consent.

The issue of informed consent is especially complicated with regard to the sexual rights of developmentally disabled people.[39] Developmentally disabled adults have a right to privacy, and hence, a right to sexual relations. Furthermore, their bodies are developmentally competent and motivated for sex. Yet, in many cases, intellectual and cognitive limitations diminish their ability to provide informed consent and make them vulnerable to sexual abuse. The trick, therefore, is to provide developmentally disabled people with sufficiently detailed sex education that they understand the nature and consequences of sex, thereby both enhancing their sexual freedoms and protecting them from sexual coercion and abuse.

On the other hand, where children are concerned, the consent issue appears relatively straightforward. Quite simply, children do not have the intellectual and cognitive capabilities, nor the physical maturity, to provide informed consent to sexual relations with adults. They can neither understand the nature and consequences of sex nor fully appreciate their right to bodily integrity—in particular, their right to refuse sex with an adult. Thus, children cannot give informed consent, and as a result, sex between an adult and a child is a crime.

In a consent-based framework, the actionable concern becomes the *potential* for harm, rather than any actual harm itself. Occasionally, sexually abused children say that they enjoyed the contact, or, when grown up, say that such contact was beneficial. Although there are numerous explanations for why such children (or adults) deny the harmfulness of the experience,[40] the concept of informed consent renders these explanations moot. By law, a child cannot give informed consent to sex with an adult, and transgressions should be punished accordingly.

A similar argument is applicable to child pornography. Children cannot provide informed consent to having their sexualized images recorded because they cannot fully appreciate the present and future potential for harm posed by such actions, including such broad implications as: (1) how they might be later perceived by peers and colleagues; (2) how family and friends might respond; and (3) how they themselves might later react (i.e., as adults) to both the use (e.g., as masturbatory prompts) and persistence of such imagery. Even the rudiments of human sexuality are a mystery to most children, much less the notion that some people (primarily men) become sexually excited and masturbate to orgasm upon viewing photographs of nude children. Nor can children comprehend the permanence lent to such images by modern computers and digital storage media, and in particular by the Internet. It is almost a certainty that where nude photos lurk in the background of a famous politician or celebrity, they will be exposed. For these and other reasons, children are incapable of providing informed consent, and this, ultimately, is why child pornography is a crime—and why First and Ninth Amendment rights of access are denied child pornography.

In contrast, adults *can* provide informed consent in matters pertaining to their own bodies. Thus, participation in pornography—posing for photos, appearing in adult films and videos, nude dancing, and so forth—is within the individual sphere of determination for adults but not for children. For consenting adults, society permits adult participation in pornography regardless of how society might pathologize such behaviors. If the sexual depictions or performances are not obscene (e.g., as determined by *Miller*), then there are no legal consequences to the actors, models, or producers. The case of children is obviously different. As summarized by the court in *Wiegand*,

> Human dignity is offended by the pornographer. American law does not protect all human dignity; legally, an adult can consent to its diminishment. When a child is made the target of the pornographer-photographer, the statute will not suffer the insult to the human spirit, that the child should be treated as a thing.[41]

We must, however, admit the possibility that in limited instances the "pornographer-photographer" will not have treated the child as a thing; Sally Mann's artistically executed photos of her children provide one example. Since a child cannot consent to participate in nude or sexually explicit depictions, do these pictures constitute child pornography? The answer, from our vantage point, is no.

As is the case for many other spheres of parental decision making, it seems reasonable to suppose that parents should have the right to provide consent in lieu of their children. Parents can provide consent for their children to undergo potentially fatal medical procedures, and conversely can deny their children needed medical attention. Parents can also involve their children in dangerous religious rites such as snake-handling, can usurp their rights to a standard education, and so on. If parents are already accorded the right to provide consent for their children in such diverse and legally complex arenas, why should posing for nude photos be any different? To deny parents this authority would contradict the fundamental legal basis for the parent-child relationship established in *Meyer v. Nebraska*,[42] in which the Supreme Court ruled that the Fourteenth Amendment protects parents' rights to "establish a home and bring up children," and subsequently reinforced in *Prince v. Massachusetts*, when the Court announced that "the custody, care, and nurture of the child reside first in the parents."[43] Thus, we propose only that the laws concerning the sexual imagery of children be brought into line with existing standards for other areas of parental responsibility and authority. The guiding principle in all cases is whether parents have acted in the best interests of the children—whether the activity in question is sex, surgery, or snake-handling.

A CONSENT-BASED FRAMEWORK

The critical issue for a consent-based framework, or any other child pornography standard, is to establish criteria that balance our compelling interest in protecting children from harm with our respect for the rights of parents (e.g., to videotape their children cavorting nude) and the First and Ninth Amendment rights of others to view sexualized materials that are not classified as child pornography.

In a consent-based framework, parental consent would be required for all sexually explicit and nude materials (where "sexually explicit" is defined parallel to the first four prongs of the Child Protection Act), and all materials whose focal point is the genitals. Where questions arise regarding whether a particular image is or is not "sexually explicit," or does or does not focus on the genitals, prudence dictates that consent be obtained. In all instances, a record of parental consent would be required when the images were first produced (parents and legal guardians would be exempted from this requirement) and whenever they were subsequently distributed. Consent would thus act similarly to the FCC's operationalization of Section 223 of the Communications Act (see chapter 5): by providing evidence of compliance with the intent behind the criminalization of child pornography—namely, protecting children from potential harms associated with sexual coercion and exploitation—parents and others would be shielded from unwarranted persecution.

In the absence of explicit consent and in the case of questionable images, the judicable issue would be whether the image has inflicted foreseeable harm, or could foreseeably harm the child in any way. Although this could lead to the perceived anomaly that in certain cases the same image if distributed could be adjudged differently (on the issue of harm) than had it been maintained for private use, this result would be compatible with related case law.

Recall that in *Stanley v. Georgia* (discussed in chapter 3), the Supreme Court established that adults may possess obscene material (with the exception of child pornography) in the privacy of their homes.[44] This was an intriguing finding, as statutes regularly proscribe commercial sales of obscene materials. The majority opinion in *Stanley* reaffirmed the legality of these statutes, which originally were upheld in *Roth v. United States*.[45] Thus, in *Stanley* the Court created a constitutional right to *possess* obscenity, while maintaining that no constitutional right exists to *obtain* obscene materials. The Court made this point quite explicit in a later case, *United States v. 12,200 Ft. Reels of Super 8 MM Film*: "the protected right to possess obscene material in the privacy of one's home does not give rise to a correlative right to have someone sell or give it to others."[46]

As with the differential treatment accorded the supply versus private possession of obscenity, for borderline or nonconsensual images, the fact that they were supplied to others or intended for distribution may be dispositive. The Supreme Court in *Ashcroft* declares why this should be so: "Like a defamatory statement, each new publication of the speech [or child pornography] can cause new injury to the child's reputation and emotional well-being."[47]

We now consider how our framework would apply to specific instances of sexual/nude imagery of children. To the extent that parental consent is provided, most "innocent" nude images would appear to present few legal difficulties. This category includes nude photographs parents take of their children (e.g., the classically embarrassing bearskin rug photo); artistic nudes of the Sally Mann variety; and "lifestyle nudes" emanating from nudist and other belief systems in which nudity is accepted as a natural physical state. Certainly, the privacy guarantees derived from the Fourteenth Amendment suggest that parents have a right to take nude photographs of their children, presuming that they are not for distribution, and providing that they do not contain actual sex. The main consideration, as suggested above, is whether or not the creation and possible distribution of the images in question represents a form of parental neglect or abuse. That is, has the parent harmed (or abused, exploited, neglected, etc.) the child, or created the foreseeable potential for harm, by consenting to the production and distribution of a nude image?

In the case of artistic or nudist photographs one could certainly argue that aesthetic and lifestyle considerations mitigate concerns about underlying intent and potential harms. Nudity, it can be argued, is more "natural" than wearing clothing, and parents certainly should not be penalized for recording this "natural state of affairs." The same would be true for the anthropologist who creates a photographic record of his or her research. Nevertheless, in these and in all other instances, the ultimate determination of whether a parent has harmed his or her child by consenting to sexual imagery resides within the court's legitimate purview.

Because harms may not materialize until years after an image was produced, children should have recourse to challenging parental decisions within some reasonable window (e.g., ten or twenty years) following the attainment of legal majority. Allowing for this possibility would give further pause to parents who might otherwise provide consent without considering the long-term consequences for their children of participating in sexual imagery, artistic or otherwise.

Consider, for example, the cover photograph of Jock Sturges's 1994 book, *Radiant Identities*. The photograph, titled "Misty Dawn," shows an attractive twelve(?)-year-old girl, nude to the waist, with upstretched arms holding a rope. It is a beautiful and provocative photograph. However, it is also conceivable that this girl, as she matures into a woman, may no longer appreciate having her nude image displayed on the cover of this book, aesthetic considerations notwithstanding. There are undoubtedly many women who regret having appeared nude in *Playboy* magazine, even though they were adults when they made that choice. A child model is another matter, because he or she is incapable of providing informed consent and must abide by the decisions of her parental guardians. The question is whether her guardians acted in her best interests, or whether they created foreseeable harm.

The same criterion of demonstrated neglect or foreseeable harm would apply to less innocent instances of sexual imagery, such as those intended to invoke arousal in certain individuals. Few people would argue that children are left unharmed by being depicted in overtly sexual conduct or in sexually provocative situations and poses, regardless of parental consent, and therefore images of this type generally would be prohibited. But, again, decisions as to harm and neglect would need to be made on a case-by-case basis. Convictions would ensue whenever it is believed that children have been psychologically, emotionally, or otherwise damaged by their participation in the production or the subsequent distribution of erotic imagery.

There are a number of advantages to basing child pornography statutes on the concept of consent. First and foremost, it would criminalize the production and distribution of all pornographic images of children for which parental consent was not obtained. Pornography itself could be defined according to an objective, physical standard, without descending into the subjective abyss of "lasciviousness" and similarly vague terms. The standard we propose would recognize as pornography all sexually explicit and nude images, and all materials whose focal point is the genitals, and would legitimate production, possession, and distribution only under strict requirements of informed consent and absence of harm. This approach is amenable to the discourse of First and Ninth Amendment rights, whereby reproductively relevant choices (e.g., oral sex, contraception, etc.), for example, are dependent upon informed consent. Lasciviousness, in contrast, is not easily integrated into the larger discourse.

Of course, one could argue that the crime of child pornography is so heinous and so readily apparent as to obviate the entire issue of consent. But child pornography is not all black and white. The law as currently constituted leaves many issues unaddressed, especially in the gray areas surrounding the lascivious display of the genitals. In *United States v. Knox*, for example, a zoom lens was used to create a continuous stream of crotch shots of young girls dancing and playing in leotards. Was this or was this not a lascivious display of genitals? In *Knox*, mightn't it have been easier to question whether the girls' parents provided informed consent to the zoomed crotch shots? Presumably, the parents were unaware of the nature of the photos. In fact, neither the girls nor their parents consented to participate in a "crotch shot" film, the production of which would therefore be criminal under consent-based child pornography statutes.

Similarly, we could reexamine each of the cases introduced in this chapter and question whether informed consent was provided. Doing so avoids the myriad definitional problems of lasciviousness and associated interpretive difficulties, such as whether nudity is necessary to make a photograph sexual. If informed consent is required, these concerns no longer matter. Consent is binary—either it was provided, or it was not. There is no gray, only black and white.[48]

VOLITION AND CONSENT

We first introduced the theory that drives the perspective of this chapter—specifically, that sexual rights should be dependent upon informed consent—in our book, *With Pleasure: Thoughts on the Nature of Human Sexuality*.[49] *With Pleasure* emphasizes that humans are designed to pursue sexual pleasure no less than reproduction, but it also stresses the necessity to restrain and regulate violent and nonvolitional sexual acts. Unlike violent sexual acts, such as rape, nonvolitional acts tend to be covert and are therefore more difficult to prosecute. For instance, sexual harassment, though not violent, is still nonvolitional. Sexual harassment is emotionally disturbing because it is unwanted and is void of consent. Child pornography falls in the same category, whether it is patently abusive (e.g., adult-child intercourse), or debatably sexual (e.g., lascivious, coy, etc.). In either case, children cannot act with volition. They cannot make informed choices about sexual imagery, and therefore they cannot provide informed consent.

The question of consent is fundamental to the concept of law, its application, and its effectiveness.[50] This is especially true of the Ninth Amendment. One cannot choose appropriate forms of sexual expression if one is incapable of informed consent. On the other hand, laws are implemented and obeyed because society consents to their underlying rationale and recognizes the importance of maintaining order. That is, laws function only when granted the implicit consent of the society that created them. Moreover, the issue of consent is made explicit in many laws, especially those related to sexual conduct. Sexual intercourse without consent is rape; proffering repeated unwanted (i.e., unconsented to) sexual advances is sexual harassment; and so on. Similarly, we believe, the acts depicted in pornography also require consent, regardless of whether the model is an adult or a child. The difference between the two situations is that children are incapable of granting such consent. However, parents can provide their consent in lieu of their children's, as they do in other areas of parental responsibility. The two issues are then: (1) was parental consent granted, and (2) in providing consent, has the parent injured, neglected, or abused the child?

Requiring consent seems a somewhat more parsimonious way of prohibiting child pornography and of making such regulations consistent with the legal regulation of sex in general and Ninth Amendment sexual decision making in particular. What's more, as advocated previously in *With Pleasure*, although we believe nonconsensual sex should be prohibited to protect against possible harms, we also believe that all consensual sexual relations between adults (including oral, anal, and homosexual practices) should be decriminalized.[51]

In summation, we urge that the statutes relevant to the sexual exploitation of children be changed to define, and address the absence of, informed consent. This proposal would require a thorough revision of prevailing child pornography statutes, but the end result would be more encompassing and enforceable than existing statutes. Thus, in the rhetoric of politics, we're very tough on child pornography—despite being "loose" with the Ninth Amendment. However, this toughness does not stem directly from issues of harm (which obviously are important), or the condemnation of sex (which is more problematic, particularly where questions of "lasciviousness" and "lust" are concerned), but from a serious concern about children's rights and their inability to provide informed consent. If they can't legally consent to it, they can't do it—it's that simple.

8

The Past and Future of the Ninth Amendment

WE BEGIN THIS FINAL CHAPTER with three simple questions. First, how many fornicators are reading this book? Second, are there any sodomites among you? What about adulterers?

An affirmative answer to any one of these questions could potentially result in a criminal conviction. For example, if you live in the state of Arizona or Illinois and are unmarried and cohabiting with your lover, you are (potentially) committing the crime of fornication: "A person who lives in a state of open and notorious cohabitation is guilty of a misdemeanor" (Arizona); "It is a misdemeanor to engage in sexual intercourse with a person to whom the offender is not married if the behavior is open and notorious" (Illinois). Similarly, if you live in Washington, D.C., or Idaho and engage in oral or anal sex, you may have committed a felony crime: "It is a felony to take the sexual organ of another person into one's mouth or anus or to place one's sexual organ in the mouth or anus of another or to have carnal copulation in an opening of the body other than the sexual parts with another person" (Washington, D.C.); "The infamous crime against nature is a felony" (Idaho). Finally, if you are married but are having sexual relations with an unmarried person, you are guilty of a felony offense in the states of Massachusetts and Michigan: "Adultery, a felony, occurs when a married person has sexual intercourse with a person who is not his or her spouse, both are guilty of adultery where either one or both is married" (Massachusetts); "Adultery is sexual intercourse between two persons either of whom is married to a third party. Adultery is a felony" (Michigan). The worst-case scenario, it seems, is the married person who has oral sex with someone other than his or her lawful spouse: two felony complaints and a misdemeanor could result.

Most readers undoubtedly are amused by this discussion. Although these examples are real criminal statutes, they are rarely enforced.[1] Moreover, in the twenty-first century, most Americans would be surprised at the existence of such laws. Or, if they knew about them, they would disregard them anyway. Clearly these laws, like municipal ordinances against spitting in public or swearing in the company of women, were made to be broken.

Not all sex laws in America warrant disregard, however. Some, in fact, are *meant* to be enforced and *should* be enforced. Laws forbidding child sexual abuse, rape, and child pornography clearly fall within this category. In contrast to the "crimes" of fornication, sodomy, and adultery, sexual assault and sexual exploitation of children are reprehensible because they force a victim into sexual conduct absent informed consent. Lack of consent is a critical defining characteristic of true sex crimes, as we have emphasized repeatedly, particularly with regard to child pornography.

But consensual sex should *not* be criminalized, no matter how bizarre, immoral, or distasteful society at large may find it. If a man is willing to pay $50 for fellatio, and another person would rather perform oral sex on this stranger than let her or his children go hungry, then society should have no power to interfere with this exchange. Ours is a nation founded on elaborate notions of liberty and the pursuit of happiness in all its aspects, including the pursuit of sensual and economic satisfaction.

In this book we have argued that consensual sexual expression is a fundamental right consistent with the natural rights philosophy that deeply influenced the founding fathers—the philosophy that forms the basis of our fundamental precepts of liberty, humanity, and social justice. Sexual freedom is cut from the same cloth as the freedom of expression (First Amendment), the right to bear arms (Second Amendment), and the other rights guaranteed to all Americans by the first eight amendments of the Bill of Rights. But it is not included among these amendments. Instead it is one of the unenumerated rights captured by James Madison's Ninth Amendment, which protects those fundamental rights not explicitly listed elsewhere in the Constitution.

In this book we have suggested a theoretical rationale for recreating sex laws in America, based on the Ninth Amendment's protection of unenumerated rights, which are "retained by the people." We also have provided an initial vision of how such a recreation might proceed. We have emphasized the importance of nonreproductive sexual behavior and demonstrated how prejudice and bigotry arising from the unique moral traditions of our society have blinded us to an acceptance of sexual freedom as a fundamental right. But the Constitution, and the American legal system founded thereupon, cannot abide unjust prejudice. Regulations against aspects of moral conduct cannot be sustained lacking a demonstrable state interest. No such interest exists in the case of the "victimless" crimes of prostitution, sodomy, masturbating to pornography, and so on. As long as these are consensual acts, there is no victim, there is no crime, and there is no persuasive state interest in regulating them; there is only the desire to enforce a narrow view of moral conduct that prejudicially favors the tenets of Christian ideology over other, equally valid religious and moral conceptions of right and wrong.

During the nearly two hundred years between ratification of the Bill of Rights and *Griswold v. Connecticut*, the Ninth Amendment was the "Forgotten Amendment" in American jurisprudence, ignored or rendered impotent through misunderstanding of its true intent and a persistent fear that giving substance to the amendment would precipitate a flood of claims to dubious rights that would be upheld, or not, based solely on the whims of the judiciary (Raoul Berger has likened the Ninth Amendment to "a bottomless well in which the judiciary can dip for the formation of undreamed of 'rights' in their limitless discretion"[2]). However, in light of the history reviewed in chapter 2, which clearly demonstrates the critical role of Madison's Ninth and Tenth Amendments in securing ratification of the Constitution, it is disheartening, to say the least, that the Ninth has been largely ineffectual in guaranteeing those *natural* rights the framers of the Constitution meant it to protect.

Two analogies, presented below, may help clarify why and how this sorry state of affairs came into being. The first addresses the disparity between Madison's Ninth Amendment and the Court's interpretation thereof; the second suggests how Madison's exquisite blueprint for protecting unenumerated rights could have devolved into a practically meaningless waste of parchment.

SET THEORY

The Court has very narrowly interpreted the intent of the Constitution, expanding rights one at a time, with the Bill of Rights as a foundation. Despite the recognition of a small number of implied rights, such as the right to privacy, the Court has generally adopted an incremental approach, building upon already recognized rights in a limited, finite manner. To the extent that rights and powers are complementary,[3] by permitting only finite protections, the Court has permitted infinite encroachments upon individual liberties. To better understand this, we turn to the mathematical formalism known as "set theory."

Set theory provides a mathematical framework for studying *sets* (or collections) of objects. Although intuitive notions of what sets are and how they combine almost certainly predate written history, the eclectic eighteenth-century mathematician Georg Cantor is usually credited with developing set theory in its modern form. Today, set theory is widely appreciated as a profoundly beautiful expression of order, stretching from everyday counting numbers to an infinitude of infinities.

Any well-defined collection of objects can form a set. For example, the set of whole numbers that are greater than zero and less than ten is denoted as {1,2,3,4,5,6,7,8,9}.[4] Often, however, mathematicians are more concerned with one or more *subsets* of a larger set, rather than with the larger set as a whole. Suppose, for instance, that S is the set of numbers greater than zero and less than ten. One subset of S is the set of whole numbers greater than zero and less than 4. Call this subset T. Thus, T equals {1,2,3}.

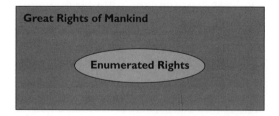

FIGURE 1. The Bill of Rights was meant to secure all the Great Rights of Humankind. The first eight amendments protect the enumerated rights, shown in the center. The remaining rights (the complement of the set of enumerated rights, comprising the region outside the central ovoid) are protected by the Ninth Amendment to the Constitution.

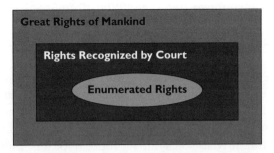

FIGURE 2. The rights recognized by the Court form a subset of the Great Rights of Humankind.

Having defined a subset *T*, it is natural to look at the subset of *S* that is left over after the elements of *T* are removed—that is, the members of *S* that are *not* in *T*. This set is called the *complement* of *T*, relative to *S*. For example, the *complement* of *T* = {1,2,3}, relative to *S* = {1,2,3,4,5,6,7,8,9}, is the set {4,5,6,7,8,9}. It is important to emphasize that the complement of a given set (such as *T*) can only be defined relative to a particular, specified larger set (such as *S*). Whenever mathematicians speak about a set's complement, the larger set—which is sometimes known as the universe—is either specified explicitly or understood implicitly.

Conceptually, the first eight amendments of the Bill of Rights define a certain set, *B*, of protected rights. This set contains the right to free speech, the right to assemble peaceably, the right to avoid self-incrimination, and so forth. Madison and the other framers of the Constitution recognized that *B* was but a subset of a much larger universe, understood to consist of the "great rights" or "natural rights" of humankind. Linguistically, it is clear that the complement of *B*, relative to this larger universe, is the set of natural rights that are *not* enumerated in the first eight amendments. Figure 1 illustrates this relationship. These are the rights the Ninth Amendment was intended to protect. Together, the first eight amendments, supplemented by the Ninth, secure all of the "Great Rights of Humankind," whether enumerated or not.

Importantly, the Court recognizes only a finite subset of the set of Great Rights, as illustrated in figure 2. The complement of this set comprises those natural rights protected by the Constitution (as envisioned by Madison and the other framers) but *not* recognized by the Court. Because these rights are not recognized as falling within the sphere of constitutional guarantees, the possibility of governmental encroachment is increased. Thus, in practice, our rights have diminished while the government's power has swelled. Is this what the founding fathers intended?

History suggests not. The Ninth Amendment was meant to protect *all* the Great Rights of Humankind (not just a subset thereof), while the Tenth Amendment reserved to the people, or to the states acting as their agents, those powers not expressly granted to the federal government in the Constitution. Madison's initial proposal for the Ninth and Tenth Amendments stated:

> The exceptions here or elsewhere in the Constitution, made in favor of particular rights, shall not be so construed as to diminish the just importance of other rights retained by the people, or as to enlarge the powers delegated by the Constitution; but either as actual limitations of such powers, or as inserted merely for greater caution.[5]

Thus, as originally proposed, rights were meant to be expansive and powers restricted. By eschewing the Ninth Amendment, the Court has essentially reversed the intended positions of rights and powers, sacrificing individual liberty and the pursuit of happiness in favor of unwarranted governmental interference.

CONSTITUTIONAL BIOLOGY

The preceding discussion raises several closely related questions: How could we have arrived at such a state of affairs, given the magnificent blueprint for government provided by the U.S. Constitution? How did we lose rights that the Ninth Amendment implicitly affirms? And why does the "practice" of Ninth Amendment jurisprudence deviate from the "theory"?

Although there are many possible answers to these difficult questions, we will start with a simple metaphorical hypothesis. First we need to review the biological concept of a genotype, which is the genetic blueprint for the construction of a human being or other living organism. The genotype encodes all the potential characteristics of the organism, but it does not determine them. Rather, the characteristics that are realized in the mature organism—the "phenotype" of the organism—are shaped by the genotype's interactions with its external environment.[6] Identical corn seeds can produce vastly different plants as a function of soil, sun, and water; that is, identical genotypes can lead to divergent phenotypes. In sum, the genotype is the genetic constitution of an organism, whereas the phenotype is the physical realization that results from the interaction of the genotype with the environment.

Similarly, the Constitution provides the "genotype" for our government. The Constitution's genotype was fixed in the 1790s with the ratification of the Bill of Rights. The genotype consists of the procedures, laws, and directives encoded in the seven articles and ten amendments that make up the Constitution and the Bill of Rights. The Constitution's phenotype, in contrast, is not fixed, but has evolved and developed as a consequence of interactions with the specific proximal environment dictated by America's unfolding social, economic, and political history, as well as through interpretation by the courts.

The debate over slavery can be used to illustrate the distinction between the Constitution's genotype and its phenotype. Despite appeals to the natural rights of humankind, as reflected in the Declaration of Independence ("all men are created equal"), slavery was legal before, during, and long after the Constitution was ratified. The injustice and hypocrisy of African slavery persisted even in the face of powerful appeals to end the horrors of this noxious practice. Thomas Paine's (1775) widely distributed essay on slavery in America argued that

> Christians are taught to account all men their neighbours; and love their neighbours as themselves; and do to all men as they would be done by; to do good to all men; and man-stealing is ranked with enormous crimes. Is the barbarous enslaving [of] our inoffensive neighbours, and treating them like wild beasts subdued by force, reconcilable with all these divine precepts? Is this doing to them as we would desire they should do to us? If they could carry off and enslave some thousands of us, would we think it just?—One would almost wish they could for once; it might convince more than reason, or the Bible.[7]

These sentiments notwithstanding, slavery persisted in America until the passage of the Thirteenth Amendment in 1865, nearly a hundred years after the constitutional convention in Philadelphia.

One way of understanding how our "beautiful" Constitution could have tolerated slavery for as long as it did is to distinguish its genotype from its phenotype. Both the spirit of the written Constitution—especially the Bill of Rights—and the founding fathers' acceptance of natural rights philosophy suggest that slavery is antithetical to the Constitution's genotype. Nevertheless, economic and social conditions in postrevolutionary America enabled slaveholders to manufacture enough support to keep slavery legal, despite a written Constitution designed to preserve the natural rights of man, including freedom from bondage. However, by the conclusion of the bloody upheaval of the Civil War, the environment had changed drastically enough to support the complete abolition of slavery. A change in the Constitution's proximal environment therefore was reflected by a change in its phenotype, bringing it closer to the ideal realization of liberty for all encapsulated in the Constitution's genotype.

In the past two hundred years the social environment also has changed sufficiently that sexual behaviors that might once have been considered obscene are now viewed as normal variations of the multifaceted human capacity for sexual expression. Indeed, it is our belief that, just as the natural right to be free from slavery was gradually embraced as the moral and economic environment shifted, it is now time to recognize another of humankind's fundamental rights, as encoded in the Constitution's genotype—namely, the right to choose freely the circumstances and manner in which we express our sexuality.

Just as fertile soil, abundant sunshine, and access to water are needed to ensure that corn seeds grow into healthy and productive plants, thereby fulfilling the promise of their genotypes, so too the proper environment is necessary to ensure that the promise of the Constitution is fully realized. Two aspects of the Constitution's proximal environment are especially critical to its health and vitality with regard to sexual rights: first, a Court that respects the inherent rights of humankind—such as the fundamental right to sexual expression—by embracing the substance of the Ninth Amendment; and second, a sexually literate populace, capable of fully appreciating the range and limitations of their sexual rights.

A CHANGING CONSTITUTION

The Constitution is a living document that grows in response to changes in the sociopolitical environment. This vitality is simultaneously the Constitution's greatest strength and the source of its most difficult challenges. The Supreme Court eloquently captured this duality in the following passage from *Weems v. United States*:

> Time works changes, brings into existence new conditions and purposes. . . . In the application of a constitution, therefore, our contemplation cannot be only of what has been but of what may be. Under any other rule a constitution would indeed be as easy of application as it would be deficient in efficacy and power. Its general principles would have little value and be converted by precedent into impotent and lifeless formulas. *Rights declared in words might be lost in reality.*[8]

Such has been the unfortunate fate of the Ninth Amendment's unenumerated rights: they have been "lost in reality" due to the reluctance of the courts to give substance to the text of this pivotal proviso. The Ninth Amendment declares not only that unenumerated rights exist, but that they are not to be disparaged. Clearly, ignoring these rights disparages them.

Unenumerated rights should not be denied simply because identifying and appropriately enforcing them is an arduous and uncertain task. Courts are called upon regularly to give definite form to indefinite constitutional provisions, as illustrated by substantive due process adjudication (see chapter 4). This is the intended role of the judiciary in constitutional law: to *interpret* and apply the Constitution in ever-changing circumstances. As Madison observed, we are not bound to follow the prejudices and foibles of the past:

> The glory of the people of America [is] that whilst they have paid a decent regard to the opinions of former times and other nations, they have not suffered a blind veneration for antiquity, for customs, or for names, to override the suggestions of their own good sense, the knowledge of their own situation, and the lessons of their own experience.[9]

Our "own good sense, the knowledge of [our] own situation, and the lessons of [our] own experience" converge to suggest that in certain realms of conduct, such as sexual expression, the freedom to exercise personal autonomy has been drawn too narrowly. Fortunately, past mistakes can be corrected by future action. Instead of adhering to outdated limitations on individual liberty, we can through careful constitutional adjudication bring the practice of law, and the protection of basic human rights, into closer alignment with the ideal of personal autonomy encoded in the Constitution's "genes." Rejuvenating the Ninth Amendment is the key to this enterprise. Courts must begin to respect both the words and the spirit of this amendment by recognizing and protecting unenumerated rights.

We believe there is a natural right to sexual expression that arises not from the American political system, nor from the Constitution, nor from the philosophical and moral underpinnings of our society, but directly from our nature as humans. However, as we explained in chapter 4, it is not necessary to accept the view that sexual expression is a natural right to recognize sexual liberty as an unenumerated right meriting Ninth Amendment protection.

Once one admits that there is a Ninth Amendment right to engage in private, consensual sexual conduct, the courts are beholden to respect and protect that right, just as they safeguard the Constitution's enumerated rights. Speaking of unenumerated rights in general, Charles Black concluded:

> The Ninth Amendment declares as a matter of law—of constitutional law, overriding all other law—that some rights are "retained by the people," and that these shall be treated on an equal footing with rights enumerated. This would have to mean that these rights "not enumerated" may serve as the substantive basis for judicial review of governmental actions.[10]

Protecting sexual rights would require a drastic reversal in juridical attitudes. Were this change effected, sexual rights would be accorded a "presumption of liberty," reversing the current situation in which restrictive legislation is granted a "presumption of constitutionality."[11] Only when the state demonstrated convincing evidence of societal harm could a sexual right legitimately be curtailed. A demonstration that legislation implements a majority preference or that it serves a rightful end would be insufficient to overcome the presumption of liberty pertaining to an unenumerated Ninth Amendment right.[12] As outlined in chapter 4, absent an "exceedingly persuasive justification,"[13] sexual rights should be innocent until proven otherwise.[14] When government intrudes into its citizens' private lives, the burden of justifying its actions should fall on the government rather than on the citizens.

Imagine that *Bowers v. Hardwick* were reargued before a newly enlightened Court that recognized sexual freedom as an unenumerated right secured by the Ninth Amendment. Michael Hardwick's behavior (having sex with another man) would be protected as a private, consensual expression of his right to sexual autonomy, unless evidence were presented that his conduct had harmed or imperiled others. Because the State of Georgia could provide no real evidence of harm and no "exceedingly persuasive justification" for intruding into Hardwick's private life, the case would be dismissed.

Under Ninth Amendment sexual rights adjudication, as envisioned here, consenting adults would be let alone to conduct their private sexual lives, to make their own choices, to find their own happiness. This is what the framers of the Constitution intended, and this is what the Constitution's genotype portends.

Change is never easy, but often it is necessary. Changing how courts view the Ninth Amendment and how they adjudicate cases involving fundamental sexual rights issues is necessary to ensure that all Americans can pursue sexual fulfillment without unwarranted intrusions by the government.

SEXUAL LITERACY

In this book we have championed the notion that sexual decision making should be included among the unenumerated rights retained by the people vis-à-vis the Ninth Amendment. We also have discussed how, in practice, these rights might be limited in certain circumstances, for example with regard to child pornography, or expanded, as in the case of "dial-a-porn" and prostitution. In this section we presume, for rhetorical purposes, that a right to sexual and reproductive decision making exists, and we ask: what does the American populace need in order to sensibly and meaningfully exercise this right? Specifically, we are concerned here with sexual education, broadly conceived. Intelligent decision making in today's complex sexual landscape requires information beyond the basic birds and bees.

In 1987, E. D. Hirsch published a book titled *Cultural Literacy* whose simple premise—that Americans are no longer culturally literate (if ever they were)—ignited an enduring controversy about the province and effectiveness of American education, formal and otherwise.[15] Hirsch decried what he perceived to be a lack of cultural literacy among the American populace. According to Hirsch, not only is cultural literacy needed to make sense of the current events reported in the daily news, it is a prerequisite for democracy. As a remedy to America's shameful deficiency in this area, he prescribed exactly what Americans need to know to ascend to the heights of cultural competency, in the form of a list—or "The List," if you prefer. To expedite America's journey to cultural literacy, Hirsch presented his version of the thinking person's list (which includes dates, names, cities, nouns, etc.), running from A (*abbreviation*) to Z (*Zurich*).

Much has been said about Hirsch and about The List. Some take umbrage at the suggestion that Americans are culturally deficient, others at Hirsch's presumptiveness in fashioning The List in his own intellectual image. Rather than enter this particular fray, however, we wish to focus narrowly on Hirsch's thesis that a modicum of knowledge ("literacy") is a prerequisite for active participation in a modern democracy, and to argue that this tenet applies to *sexual* literacy no less than to *cultural* literacy.

The question that needs to be addressed is whether American citizens can fully understand their sexual rights and appreciate the limitations imposed on those rights without being sexually literate. Although this question arises within the context of the arguments advanced elsewhere in this book—and on our interpretation of the Ninth Amendment, in particular—the answer does not *depend* upon these arguments. Regardless of the legitimacy of a constitutional right to sexual decision making, American citizens still need to make informed decisions and be able to form coherent opinions on a broad range of sex-related topics, including but not limited to: contraception, premarital sex, abortion, sexually transmitted diseases, homosexuality, prostitution, pornography, nonconsensual sex, and sexual harassment. Many of these issues are tied to constitutional questions, whether they concern the privacy (or Ninth Amendment) protections that secure a woman's right to an abortion or a married couple's right to engage in sodomy, or whether they address such fundamental questions as the applicability of First Amendment free speech guarantees to pornographic words and images. However, while there is no denying the desirability of a sexually literate populace capable of fully appreciating and actively debating the merits of the Supreme Court's decisions in *Bowers v. Hardwick* or *Roe v. Wade*, the goal of sexual literacy is not to create a nation of lawyers, but to foster a society capable of understanding and expressing their sexual rights and protecting the sexual health and well-being of themselves, their loved ones, and the country as a whole.

What sort of knowledge might a sexually literate person possess? First, there are the basic biological facts—what goes where, and how all the plumbing works. Sexual anatomy and physiology are paramount, as is information about statistical norms (what is the average age at which a girl experiences menarche? how long should a male's penis be?) and the range of diversity found within the human species. Medical issues are also important. What are the pros and cons of tubal ligation? Of circumcision? How does sex reassignment surgery work? How is HIV transmitted, and more importantly, how can it be blocked?

The second main sphere of sexual information concerns the psychological side of sex, including the manner and processes by which people develop sexual identities, sexual orientations, sexual feelings (e.g., pleasure, desire, excitement), sexual emotions (e.g., guilt, jealousy), sexual choices (e.g., when and where to masturbate, what to fantasize about, when and where to start sexual relations, whether to remain monogamous, etc.). Again, information about the normative and the not-so-normative is necessary for people to appreciate the wide variations that exist in human sexual expression and to situate themselves within this broader context. What proportion of the population is homosexual? What proportion is transsexual? Why are some men sexually aroused by women's footwear? Do most women masturbate? And so forth.

A third domain of literacy encompasses social, cultural, and political issues. What is legal, what is sanctioned, and what is deviant? Why is obscene material banned, and should it be? And what does it mean for something to be "obscene" anyway? Is marriage better conceived of as a religious institution open only to heterosexual couples or as a legal arrangement that should be available to any committed couple, regardless of gender? Can female circumcision (a.k.a. genital mutilation) be tolerated through appeals to cultural relativism? Why is it illegal to kiss a cow in Mississippi?

There are, of course, many other areas of knowledge relevant to sexual literacy, including behavioral science (does viewing pornography encourage some men to rape women?), genetics (is homosexuality inherited?), the fine arts (from the erotic decorations adorning the Attica urns to the provocative photographs of Robert Mapplethorpe), anthropology (what are the cross-cultural differences and similarities in sexual expression?), and even animal behavior (if homosexual behaviors are common in the animal world, can they still be considered "unnatural"?), to name but a few.

In his book, Hirsch used newspaper articles and famous quotes to illustrate the importance of cultural literacy. According to Hirsch, the culturally illiterate cannot fully comprehend important news. And because they cannot comprehend the news, they cannot meaningfully participate in informed political debate. The same, we will demonstrate, is true of sexual illiteracy.

Consider the following excerpt from *The Wall Street Journal*:

> RU-486, the abortion pill recommended for approval by a regulatory panel, isn't the only new abortion option for American women. Two other pharmaceutical methods for ending or preventing pregnancy may soon come into wider use—in large part because they involve drugs already on the market for other purposes.[16]

What does this say about sex? And more importantly, can this material be fully comprehended by the sexually illiterate? Certainly, it can be absorbed by persons with only a cursory knowledge of the issues, including the fact that pregnancy can be exogenously terminated. But is this enough, especially given the controversy surrounding abortion?

The topic of abortion subsumes many questions about sex. For example, how does conception occur and how can it be prevented? How does post-conception prophylaxis (e.g., the RU-486 "abortion pill") work, and how well does it work? When can it be used? Why then, but not later? If it fails, what options are there? And so on. Additional questions might concern other equally important areas of cultural and scientific competency, including issues of fetal development, religious proscriptions, legal prohibitions, and so forth.

Because abortion is an extraordinarily complex and divisive issue, some measure of sexual literacy promotes, at the very least, a better understanding of the underlying themes. *Roe v. Wade*, for example, raised a variety of biological, moral, psychological, and legal issues related to reproduction—ranging from the medical risks of abortion to the constitutional definition of "persons." Even debate over the *choice* to engage in sex found its way into *Roe*. During oral arguments before the Supreme Court, attorneys for the State of Texas implied that the issue of abortion would be moot if women were more careful about sex. Justice Potter Stewart protested, suggesting (tongue-in-cheek) that abortion would be equally moot if women were more careful about living in the state of Texas! His point was simple. Personal mistakes are ubiquitous and often unavoidable. Choices of spouses, jobs, clothing, houses, and hair color, for example, are (upon reflection) unwisely made. Thus, there was no reason to discriminate against lack of foresight in the sexual arena alone.

Sexual literacy also aids digestion of the abortion debate in all its complexity. The topic of abortion circumvents traditional partisan boundaries. Although extreme positions on abortion can be categorized according to religious and political affiliations, the middle ground is more conflicted, encompassing a wide diversity of opinion. Take, for example, second- and third-trimester abortions. Tolerance for first-trimester abortions is not necessarily related to tolerance for later-term abortions. For many people abortion ceases to be an option as the fetus grows and becomes more "human." Likewise, some people support abortion only on a "case-by-case" basis. Careful distinctions are sometimes drawn, for example, between biological reasons for having an abortion, such as the possibility of a genetic disorder, and psychological motives for seeking an abortion, such as an impending divorce or financial worries. Or the circumstances under which conception occurred might be taken into account, especially in instances of rape or date rape. There are many other points of contention—for example, concerning the proper age of consent for abortion procedures, whether consent is needed from both biological parents of underage women, and so forth—that complicate the politics and ethics of abortion, for supporters as well as opponents.

What facts should a sexually literate person know about abortion to engender better sexual decision making and facilitate informed debate? First, he or she must understand the basic meaning and the nuances associated with the term "abortion," including the fundamental fact that abortion causes the termination of a pregnancy; distinctions between "spontaneous" abortions and those that are induced exogenously; and the difference between abortion and prophylactic methods of birth control. Second, an understanding is needed of abortion procedures, both surgical and pharmacological. (Many opponents of elective abortion suggest that if people knew the "truth" about abortion, including the gory specifics of some types of abortions—especially late-term abortions—fewer women would undergo these procedures.) Third, an informed populace should be familiar with the fundamentals of fetal development in order to understand the different implications of first-, second-, and third-trimester abortions, as well as to appreciate how un–abortion-like RU-486–induced abortions really are.

The various arguments for and against abortion also must be fully articulated in any educational campaign. Ethical, moral, religious, medical, and political viewpoints must be presented thoroughly, and with balance. The complications introduced by issues such as rape, incest, and genetic testing (including the possibility such testing entails of parental "deselection" of undesirable fetal characteristics) must also be introduced, as must social issues surrounding the choice to abort, including questions of authority (e.g., is it solely the mother's choice?) and capacity (e.g., can teenagers have abortions without parental consent?). Other options must be discussed in detail—including prophylactic contraception, having and raising the child, or giving it up for adoption. Finally, the potential psychological consequences and quality of life implications, both of abortion and of these alternatives to abortion, must be fully explored.

If successful, this educational intervention would produce two main outcomes. It would increase informed decision making, and it would enhance the quality of debates about abortion. On the other hand, if education dissolved into proselytizing for one side or another, the purpose would be defeated. There are already enough pro and con groups fighting for public attention and sympathy by providing only one side of this complex issue. Education, to stay true to its aim, must inform rather than convert.

Although all Americans could benefit from a deeper understanding of this topic, abortion education must, at a minimum, reach those populations that can most directly profit from its curriculum—meaning, in large part, sexually active young adults (e.g., high school students through twenty- and thirty-somethings). The success of this educational intervention would need to be assessed periodically, to characterize the populations being reached; to evaluate its effectiveness in increasing abortion-related knowledge, both over the short term and with regard to long-term retention; and to assess its impact on live birth rates, abortion rates, adoption rates, prophylactic contraceptive use, and sexual abstinence.

This is obviously an idealized form of an educational intervention, and one that would meet with considerable religious and political opposition. We have introduced it for a simple purpose—namely, to describe sex education of the highest order and to provide an example of the kind of process that would produce sexual literacy for a concrete topic—in this case, abortion. Additionally, we want to stress that sexual literacy is both necessary and essential to critical personal choices and profound societal debate.

PORNOGRAPHIC LITERACY

Abortion is an issue many people are forced to face at some point in their lives, even if only to encourage them to remain sexually abstinent. Its potential to affect a broad cross-section of the American populace makes it an ideal springboard to advance our argument regarding the necessity of sexual literacy. But what of sexuality issues with less potential impact on the lives of the "average" American? Is an intimate knowledge of other aspects of sexuality imperative for ensuring the protection and exercise of our sexual rights? Conversely, can we understand, and participate fully, in debates provoked by sexual issues and questions in the absence of overarching sexual literacy?

Again, the answer is no. Consider, for instance, the topic of pornography. What, one may ask, could be lower, or more debased, than the manner in which sex is portrayed in pornography? If we listen to the present-day Comstockians (encompassing an uneasy coalition of the Christian Right and left-leaning antipornography feminists such as Andrea Dworkin and Catharine MacKinnon), we must conclude that nothing, in fact, is worse. Death, insanity, and rape are all proffered as direct—even inevitable—consequences of pornography. And even if we ignore the doomsday ideology expressed by present-day antipornography zealots, the long American history of censoring and criminalizing sexually explicit material (including James Joyce's *Ulysses*) provides ample evidence of the ubiquity and persistence of antipornography sentiments.[17]

But perhaps this view, which conceives of pornography as a pestilence demanding obliteration, warrants reconsideration. Perhaps there is more to pornography than meets the eye. If so, the American populace deserves to understand the substantive issues underlying the debates. For example, there is the complex question of the constitutionality of pornographic representations. Do the freedoms of speech and press protect sexual imagery? Or is this constitutionality question a judicial fluke precipitated by unscrupulous defense attorneys, forever appealing to First Amendment protections? Obviously, there are deep foundational issues of concern here—regardless of vantage point.

Pornography has been the topic of repeated public debate and—at least since 1957—of nearly continuous constitutional scrutiny. Recently, the debate has focused on the Internet, as highlighted in the following excerpt, again drawn from *The Wall Street Journal*:

> A special federal court panel here struck down congressional restrictions on indecent material on the Internet, as "unconstitutionally overbroad" because they ban protected indecent speech between adults. . . . In addition, the court said the law wouldn't be effective because it wouldn't apply to sexually explicit material sent by people outside the U.S. "As much as 30% of the sexually explicit material originates in foreign countries," the court said. "It is not obvious that the benefits thus achieved would outweigh the burden . . . imposed on the First Amendment rights of adults."[18]

What are the relevant issues here? And what do we need to comprehend in order to offer (or construct) informed opinions? First, we need some understanding of the Internet, and especially the rapidly expanding World Wide Web. Relevant questions include: Who controls the Internet? How does it work? Who has access to it? Are there ways (e.g., NetNanny) to restrict minors' access to objectionable websites? What types of erotic material are available on the Internet? And so forth. Next, we need some understanding of the Constitution, particularly the First Amendment (and, we would argue, the Ninth as well). Do the First Amendment's freedom of speech guarantees encompass pornographic imagery? Or can it be protected by some interpretation of the Ninth Amendment (as proposed herein)? Finally, we need to know something about sex and its representation in sexually explicit material and indecent speech. That is, we need to define "pornography," and to familiarize ourselves with it, in order to decide who should have access to it. Thus, comprehension of the complex issues surrounding the debate about pornography on the Internet requires literacy, sexual no less than cultural.

The central question is whether we can gainfully participate in debate about pornography without being sexually literate. Certainly, we can offer opinions. But can we fully comprehend such complex issues as legal arguments about the meaning and history of the First Amendment, the Ninth Amendment, and the legal criteria for labeling a work "obscene"? Can we offer reasoned conclusions without understanding the many varieties of contemporary pornography and their historical precedents, including the erotic arts of ancient China, India, and Greece? Does the American populace understand the distinction between pornography and obscenity? (Pornography is potentially legal, whereas obscenity, by definition, is not.) Does it appreciate the importance of debates about morality in a country void of an institutionalized religion and professing a separation of church and state? Or the reasons why the writings of D. H. Lawrence, James Joyce and Theodore Dreiser were once deemed obscene but are no longer considered so, while child pornography has been and remains obscene? Many otherwise well-informed and articulate Americans cannot discourse intelligently on these matters. Should they be in a position to decide what Americans can or can't watch on television or access on the Internet? We think not, regardless of their political vantage point. Sexual literacy is a necessary prerequisite for informed policy on sexual matters, whether the debate concerns the "morning-after abortion pill" or the contentious issue of pornography on the Internet.

SEXUAL LITERACY AND SEXUAL RIGHTS

As a final example, consider the threat of acquired immune deficiency syndrome (AIDS). Sexual literacy is crucial to understanding the social and economic consequences of the AIDS epidemic; the myriad legal debates surrounding issues of testing, partner notification, and confidentiality; and, most importantly, how to protect oneself from becoming infected with the human immunodeficiency virus that causes AIDS. Without a complete understanding of how HIV is transmitted, how to prevent it (is it safer to practice anal intercourse with a condom, or vaginal intercourse without one?), and how the virus ravages the immune systems of infected persons, how can citizens possibly comprehend the current debates about the appropriate level of funding for HIV prevention and AIDS research? How can they decide whether condoms should be distributed in local high schools? Whether surgeons, or patients, or pregnant women should be tested for HIV? Whether the federal government should be notified of all new cases of HIV, or whether the confidentiality of the individual should be protected in all instances? When it comes to AIDS, sexual literacy could save lives.

Like Hirsch's List, our list could go on and on, citing many aspects of sexual behavior that intersect with significant legal and social concerns (e.g., same-sex marriage, sexual harassment, age of consent, etc.). The point, however, is the same. Because sex is heavily scrutinized, regulated, and debated within our culture—and because sex interacts with so many fundamental constitutional questions—some measure of sexual literacy is required to participate fully and intelligently in sexuality controversies and to ensure appreciation and protection of our posited constitutionally guaranteed right to sexual expression.

Where does this leave us? We have described at length our ideas for reconstructing and safeguarding the right to sexual expression, which we believe derives from the Ninth Amendment's "rights retained by the people." With these rights comes a corresponding responsibility to ensure that they are utilized conscientiously.

How can we fight sexual illiteracy and thereby mobilize educated Americans to participate in the process by which we legally regulate sex? Is a Sexual List (like Hirsch's cultural literacy list) necessary? Would Americans buy it, and study it, if it were available? Obviously, there would be many advantages to a readily accessible Guide to Sex, or to competent and comprehensive high school and college courses designed specifically to foster sexual literacy. But many obstacles would need to be overcome, not the least of which is political opposition and the scarcity of funding to support the structures that create and nurture sexual literacy—namely, sexual research and scholarship, and the teaching of sexuality in high schools and universities.[19] Even if guides or courses were contemplated, serious questions would remain about whether they should be limited to socially relevant issues or expanded to include items beneficial to the conduct of our *personal* lives. Clearly, personal decisions regarding contraception, disease risks, pleasure, reproductive options, group status, love, and so forth all benefit from expanded sexual knowledge. Simply put, if Americans are uninformed consumers of sex, our sexual liabilities will exceed our sexual gains.

The framers of the Constitution, and James Madison in particular, displayed tremendous foresight in protecting certain rights "retained by the people," which, we have argued, include general and specific rights to sexual expression. A broad agenda of sexuality education is needed to create a sexually literate populace that can appreciate and exercise these sexual rights. Anything less would be an insult to the spirit of Mr. Madison's amendments and to the constitutional foundations of this great country.

Notes

NOTES TO CHAPTER I

1. Patterson, "The Forgotten Ninth Amendment."
2. In his concurrence in *Griswold v. Connecticut* (381 U.S. 479 [1965]), Justice Arthur Goldberg summarized, "As far as I am aware, until today this Court has referred to the Ninth Amendment only in *United Public Workers v. Mitchell*, 330 U.S. 75, 94-95; *Tennessee Electric Power Co. v. TVA*, 306 U.S. 118, 143-144; and *Ashwander v. TVA*, 297 U.S. 288, 330-331" (*Griswold* 381 U.S. 479, 491).
3. Barnett, "James Madison's Ninth Amendment."
4. Schlesinger, *The Birth of the Nation*.
5. Morris, *Alexander Hamilton and the Founding of the Nation*; Cooke, *Alexander Hamilton*.
6. Quoted in Cooke, *Alexander Hamilton*, 177.
7. Ibid., 177.
8. Ibid., 178.
9. Quoted in Morris, *Alexander Hamilton and the Founding of the Nation*, 587.
10. Quoted in Lemay, *Reappraising Benjamin Franklin*, 370.
11. Ibid.
12. D'Emilio and Freedman, *Intimate Matters: A History of Sexuality in America*, 51.
13. Stone, *The Family, Sex and Marriage in England, 1500-1800*, 539.
14. Quoted in Clark, *Benjamin Franklin: A Biography*, 57.
15. Ibid.
16. Cited in Zall, *Ben Franklin Laughing: Anecdotes from Original Sources by and about Ben Franklin*, 103.
17. Did Thomas Jefferson have a sexual relationship with Sally Hemings? Several lines of evidence suggests that he did. First, in 1873 Sally's son Madison told a newspaper reporter from the *Pike County Republican* that Jefferson was his father. Several important pieces of information emerged in that story. For example, his name and the names of his siblings were very similar to names of Jefferson's family and friends. Madison also indicated that Jefferson arranged to free all of Sally's children upon their twenty-first birthdays, which

was an exception among Jefferson's slaves. Furthermore, although Jefferson's will explicitly stipulated that Madison and his brother Eston were to be freed, all other slaves were sold or transferred upon his death. (At that time, the freeing of slave children was presumed evidence of owner parentage.) Other evidence that Jefferson did indeed have an affair with Hemings includes: John Hartwell Cocke's diary, which mentions Jefferson's "slave mistress"; the many public and private accounts of the long-term affair; the constant mention of how the children resembled Jefferson; the fact that the children were conceived only during periods when Jefferson was at Monticello, and none were conceived when he was on leave; the fact that Hemings's children were not treated as slaves; and so forth. Gordon-Reed, *Thomas Jefferson and Sally Hemings*.

18. Ibid.

19. Ibid., 246.

20. Godbeer, *Sexual Revolution in Early America*. This is not to say that in the eighteenth century the sexual abuse of slaves by their masters was entirely overlooked; it simply had not been made criminal. Thomas Paine gave voice to contemporary concerns when he appealed to God, the only authority left open to him, declaring that "[slavery opens] the way for adulteries, incests, and many shocking consequences, for all of which the guilty masters must answer to the final Judge." Paine, *Thomas Paine Reader*, 54.

21. Godbeer, *Sexual Revolution*. In an award-winning study, Eugene Genovese asserted: "Many white men who began by taking a slave girl in an act of sexual exploitation ended by loving her and the children she bore. . . . It would be hard to live with a beautiful and submissive young woman for long and to continue to consider her mere property or a mere object of sexual gratification especially since the free gift of her beauty has so much more to offer than her yielding to force" (Genovese, *Roll, Jordan, Roll*, 6-7, 415-419).

22. Godbeer, *Sexual Revolution*.

23. Quoted in Cooke, *Alexander Hamilton*, 176.

24. Early American society "tended to conceive of impotence in men as comparable to barrenness in women. . . . Sexual norms in early America not only supported this definition of impotence but also linked impotence with diminished manhood. Colonists believed that female orgasm was necessary for conception and held husbands responsible for both impregnating and giving erotic pleasure to their wives. A husband who failed at either task would likely be considered impotent." Mumford, "'Lost Manhood' Found: Male Sexual Impotence and Victorian Culture in the United States," 36.

25. Quoted in Patterson, "The Forgotten Ninth Amendment," 108.

26. Huxley, *Brave New World*.

27. Abramson and Pinkerton, *With Pleasure: Thoughts on the Nature of Human Sexuality*.

28. *Eisenstadt v. Baird*, 405 U.S. 438, 453 (1972).

29. *Griswold v. Connecticut*, 381 U.S. 479 (1965).

30. *Id*. at 499.

31. *Bowers v. Hardwick*, 487 U.S. 186 (1986).

32. *Id*. at 197.

33. According to the *Sex in America* survey, about three-quarters of all American adults admit having engaged in oral sex, and about a quarter have had anal sex (Michael et al., *Sex in America: A Definitive Survey*).

34. Quoted in Posner and Silbaugh, *A Guide to America's Sex Laws*, 70.

35. Posner and Silbaugh, *America's Sex Laws*.

36. Ibid.

37. *Bowers v. Hardwick*, 487 U.S. 186, 192 (1986).

38. Madison, *The Federalist No. 14*, in Hamilton, Madison, and Jay, *The Federalist Papers*, 72.

39. *Loving v. Virginia*, 388 U.S. 1 (1967).

40. Massey, "Federalism and Fundamental Rights: The Ninth Amendment," 326.

41. Barnett, "Implementing the Ninth Amendment," 520.

42. *Planned Parenthood of Southeastern Pennsylvania v. Casey*, 505 U.S. 833 (1992).

43. Madison, "Speech to the House Explaining His Proposed Amendments and His Notes for the Amendment Speech," 58.

44. John Hart Ely jokes that "In sophisticated legal circles mentioning the Ninth Amendment is a surefire way to get a laugh. ('What are you planning to rely on to support that argument, Lester, the Ninth Amendment?')." Ely, "The Ninth Amendment," 179.

45. *Griswold v. Connecticut*, 381 U.S. 479, 485-486 (1965).

46. *Roe v. Wade*, 410 U.S. 113 (1973).

47. *Eisenstadt v. Baird*, 405 U.S. 438 (1972).

48. *Griswold v. Connecticut*, 381 U.S. 479 (1965).

49. *Id*.

50. *Eisenstadt v. Baird*, 405 U.S. 438 (1972).

51. See, however, Justice Brennan's opinion in *Eisenstadt v. Baird*: "The marital couple is not an independent entity with a mind and heart of its own, but an association of two individuals each with a separate intellectual and emotional makeup." *Id*. at 453.

52. Abramson and Pinkerton, *A House Divided: Suspicions of Mother-Daughter Incest*.

53. *Williams v. Pryor*, U.S. Court of Appeals, 99-10798 (2001).

54. For more on the motives of men who seek the services of prostitutes, see Atchison, Fraser, and Lowman, "Men Who Buy Sex: Preliminary Findings of an Exploratory Study."

55. Adler, *A House Is Not a Home*.

56. The right to engage in heterosexual (i.e., vaginal) intercourse has been upheld by the Supreme Court in numerous cases (see, for example, *Eisenstadt v. Baird*, 405 U.S. 438 [1972] and *Planned Parenthood of Southeastern Pennsylvania v. Casey*, 505 U.S. 833). The right to engage in other forms of sexual conduct, such as anal intercourse or oral sex, has not definitively been established by the Court.

NOTES TO CHAPTER 2

1. Quoted in Cogan, *The Complete Bill of Rights: The Drafts, Debates, Sources, and Origins*, 646.

2. Quoted in Levy, *Origins of the Bill of Rights*, 13. In fact, a motion to consider a bill of rights was advanced by Massachusetts's Elbridge Gerry and seconded by Virginia's George Mason, but it was overwhelmingly defeated (Van Loan, "Natural Rights and the Ninth Amendment").

3. Cogan, *The Complete Bill of Rights*, 647-648.

4. Ibid., 654.

5. Hamilton, *The Federalist No. 84*, in Hamilton, Madison, and Jay, *The Federalist Papers*, 481-482.

6. Quoted in Caplan, "The History and Meaning of the Ninth Amendment," 259-260.

7. Cogan, *The Complete Bill of Rights*, 648.

8. Caplan, "History and Meaning of the Ninth Amendment," 276.

9. Levy, *Origins of the Bill of Rights*, 29.

10. In private, Madison referred to the task of drafting a bill of rights as "the nauseous project of amendments" (Ibid., 12).

11. Ibid., 32.

12. Quoted in Miller, *The Business of May Next: James Madison and the Founding*, 243.

13. Caplan, "History and Meaning of the Ninth Amendment," 274.

14. Levy, *Origins of the Bill of Rights*.

15. Madison, "Speech to the House," 51-52.

16. Ibid., 53-54.

17. Ibid., 55.

18. Cogan, *The Complete Bill of Rights*, 55-56.

19. Levy, *Origins of the Bill of Rights*.

20. See Barnett, "James Madison's Ninth Amendment"; Caplan, "History and Meaning of the Ninth Amendment"; Kelsey, "The Ninth Amendment of the Federal Constitution"; Redlich, "Are there 'Certain Rights . . . Retained by the People'?"

21. Letter from James Madison to George Washington, December 5, 1789; quoted in Berger, "The Ninth Amendment," 193.

22. Kelsey, "Ninth Amendment," 94.

23. Barnett, "James Madison's Ninth Amendment," 11.

24. Barnett, "James Madison's Ninth Amendment."

25. Ely, "The Ninth Amendment," 182.

26. Kelsey, "Ninth Amendment."

27. Massey, "Federalism and Fundamental Rights."

28. See, for example, Ely: "The conclusion that the Ninth Amendment was intended to signal the existence of federal constitutional rights beyond those specifically enumerated in the Constitution is the only conclusion its language seems comfortably able to support" (Ely, "The Ninth Amendment," 185). Or Justice Goldberg: "The language and history of the Ninth Amendment reveal that the Framers of the Constitution believed that there are additional fundamental rights, protected from governmental infringement, which exist alongside those fundamental rights specifically mentioned in the first eight constitutional amendments" (*Griswold v. Connecticut*, 381 U.S. 479, 488 [1965]).

29. *Marbury v. Madison*, 5 U.S. (1 Cranch) 137, 174-175 (1803).

30. Black, "On Reading and Using the Ninth Amendment," 338.

31. *Griswold v. Connecticut*, 381 U.S. 479, 491 (1965).

32. Kelsey, "Ninth Amendment," 106.

33. Ibid., 96.

34. Black, "On Reading and Using the Ninth Amendment," 338.

35. Nomination of Robert Bork to be Associate Justice of the Supreme Court of the United States: Hearing Before the Senate Committee on the Judiciary 117 (1989), 249.

36. Berger, "The Ninth Amendment."

37. Ibid., 199.

38. Berger allows for judicial enforcement of enumerated rights, relying on Madison's prediction that "independent tribunals of justice will consider themselves in a peculiar manner the guardians of *those rights*" (Berger, "The Ninth Amendment," 199), but not for protection of the unspecified rights of the Ninth Amendment. This distinction between enumerated and unenumerated rights is hardly tenable, given the Ninth Amendment's stated intent: "If the rights reserved are not to be denied or disparaged by the enumeration of other rights, but only the enumerated rights may be judicially enforced, the reserved rights necessarily shrivel" (Massey, "Federalism and Fundamental Rights," 306).

39. Berger, "The Ninth Amendment," 201.

40. Madison, "Speech to the House," 60.

41. Berger, "The Ninth Amendment," 198 (emphasis added).

42. McIntosh, "On Reading the Ninth Amendment: A Reply to Raoul Berger," 226.

43. *Griswold v. Connecticut*, 381 U.S. 479, 492 (1965).

44. The Ninth Amendment protects "other rights retained by the people,"

but elsewhere Madison refers to the "natural rights retained" by the people. Massey suggests that the Ninth Amendment was meant also to encompass rights derived from positive law (Massey, "Federalism and Fundamental Rights"). More generally, the post-colonialists wanted to secure, at a minimum, the rights they enjoyed as Englishmen. See also Kelsey, "Ninth Amendment"; Patterson, "The Forgotten Ninth Amendment."

45. John Adams, quoted in Patterson, "The Forgotten Ninth Amendment," 108.

46. Patterson, "The Forgotten Ninth Amendment," 118.

47. Levy, *Origins of the Bill of Rights*, 3.

48. Becker, *The Declaration of Independence: A Study in the History of Political Ideas*, 25. Although Jefferson was undoubtedly indebted to Locke's work, a closer analog in both structure and content to the ideas espoused in the Declaration of Independence is found in the Virginia Declaration of Rights of 1776, to which Jefferson's preamble bears a striking resemblance (Corwin, "The 'Higher Law' Background of American Constitutional Law").

49. Becker, *Declaration of Independence*, 26.

50. Ibid., 27.

51. Ibid., 32 (quoting an unnamed Cambridge University scholar).

52. Burke, quoted in Hoffman and Levack, *Burke's Politics*, xvi.

53. Levy, *Origins of the Bill of Rights*, 3.

54. Locke, *Second Treatise of Government*; Vaugh, *John Locke: Economist and Social Scientist*; Yolton, *Locke: An Introduction*.

55. Quoted in Becker, *Declaration of Independence*, 8.

56. Schlesinger, *The Birth of the Nation*.

57. Barnett, "Implementing the Ninth Amendment," 8.

58. Patterson, "The Forgotten Ninth Amendment," 122.

59. Massey, "Federalism and Fundamental Rights," 318-319.

60. Letter from James Madison to George Washington, December 5, 1789, quoted in Caplan, "History and Meaning of the Ninth Amendmment," 277.

61. Black, "On Reading and Using the Ninth Amendment," 342.

62. Ibid., *passim*.

63. Redlich, "Are There 'Certain Rights Retained . . .'"

64. McIntosh, "Reply to Raoul Berger."

65. Kelsey, "Ninth Amendment."

66. Black, "On Reading and Using the Ninth Amendment," 344.

67. *Barron v. The Mayor and City Council of Baltimore*, 32 U.S. (7 Pet) 243, 250 (1833).

68. Caplan, "History and Meaning of the Ninth Amendment"; Massey, "Federalism and Fundamental Rights"; Patterson, "The Forgotten Ninth Amendment."

69. Patterson, "The Forgotten Ninth Amendment," 114.

70. Ibid., 118. Massey makes a similar point: "Natural or fundamental ninth amendment rights are enforceable against the states because the theoretical understanding of the ninth amendment reservation . . . is to vest these rights in the people, rather than in any government" (Massey, "Federalism and Fundamental Rights," 335).

71. Redlich, "Are There 'Certain Rights Retained . . .'"; see also Berger, "The Ninth Amendment."

72. *Snyder v. Massachusetts*, 291 U.S. 97, 105 (1934).

73. Notable exceptions include the Fifth Amendment's forbiddance of criminal trials without a grand jury indictment and the Seventh Amendment's right to a jury trial in civil cases.

74. *Griswold v. Connecticut*, 381 U.S. 479, 493 (1965).

75. Caplan advances the interesting proposition that the Bill of Rights was meant to secure the rights enjoyed by citizens under their state constitutions. In his reading, the Ninth Amendment "simply provides that the individual rights contained in state law are to continue in force under the Constitution until modified or eliminated by state enactment, by federal preemption, or by judicial determination of unconstitutionality" ("History and Meaning of the Ninth Amendment," 248). Thus, "because the ninth amendment was designed not to circumscribe but to protect the enactments of the states," it is logically inconsistent "to 'incorporate' the ninth amendment through the fourteenth to apply as a prohibition against the states" (Ibid., 283-284). Therefore, the Fourteenth Amendment is superfluous with regard to the Ninth.

76. Van Loan, "Natural Rights," 177.

77. *Palko v. Connecticut*, 302 U.S. 319 (1937).

78. Barnett, "James Madison's Ninth Amendment."

79. Rationality is a standard that usually is easily met. Under rationality review the Court has gone so far as to generate reasons that *might have* justified legislative action, even when the Court had no basis to believe that the hypothesized reasons actually motivated the legislation. See, for example, *Williamson v. Lee Optical Co.*, 348 U.S. 483 (1955).

80. *Griswold v. Connecticut*, 381 U.S. 479, 501-502 (1965).

NOTES TO CHAPTER 3

1. *Griswold v. Connecticut*, 381 U.S. 479 (1965); *Roe v. Wade*, 410 U.S. 113 (1973); *Bowers v. Hardwick*, 487 U.S. 186 (1986).

2. *Poe v. Ullman*, 376 U.S. 497, 545 (1961).

3. *Griswold v. Connecticut*, 381 U.S. 479 (1965).

4. *Boyd v. United States*, 116 U.S. 616, 630 (1886).

5. *Griswold v. Connecticut*, 381 U.S. 479, 484 (1965).

6. *Id.* at 485-486.

7. *Id.* at 486.

8. *Id.* at 527.

9. *Id.* at 530.

10. O'Brien, *Storm Center: The Supreme Court in American Politics*.

11. McCorvey, *I Am Roe: My life, Roe v. Wade, and Freedom of Choice*; Shearer, "Intelligence Report."

12. Rowan television interview, "In Search of Justice." WUSA (September 14, 1987); "Janet Roe Speaks Out," *Village Voice* (April 11, 1989).

13. O'Brien, *Storm Center*.

14. Ibid., 34.

15. *Roe v. Wade*, 410 U.S. 113 (1973) was later modified by *Planned Parenthood of Southeastern Pennsylvania v. Casey*, 505 U.S. 833 (1992). *Casey* collapsed *Roe's* trimester framework and concluded that states may limit abortion only to the extent that they do not place an "undue burden" on a woman's right to choose (*Casey*, 874).

16. *Bowers v. Hardwick*, 487 U.S. 186 (1986).

17. *Id.* at 191.

18. *Id.* at 194.

19. O'Brien, *Storm Center*, 294.

20. O'Brien, *Storm Center*.

21. Ibid., 261.

22. Ibid., 261-262.

23. Ibid.

24. *Bowers v. Hardwick*, 487 U.S. 186, 199 (1986).

25. Ga. Code Ann. § 16-6-2(a) (1984).

26. *Paris Adult Theatre I v. Slaton* , 413 U.S. 49 (1973).

27. *Bowers v. Hardwick*, 487 U.S. 186, 211 (1986).

28. *Id.* at 211.

29. *Id.* at 195.

30. In his dissenting opinion in *Bowers v. Hardwick* (487 U.S. 186, 201 [1986]), Justice Blackmun noted that Hardwick's brief cited the Ninth Amendment, and Justice Goldberg's opinion in *Griswold v. Connecticut* (381 U.S. 479 [1965]) in particular, in support of his claim that the Georgia prohibition on sodomy intruded upon his right to privacy. However, Justice Blackmun did not elaborate on the implications of the Ninth Amendment for the case at hand.

31. *Whalen v. Roe*, 429 U.S. 589 (1977).

32. *New York Times v. Sullivan*, 376 U.S. 254 (1964).

33. *Rowan v. U.S. Post Office Department*, 397 U.S. 728 (1970).

34. Blackstone, *Commentaries on the Laws of England*; Samar, *The Right to Privacy: Gays, Lesbians and the Constitution*.

35. *Griswold v. Connecticut*, 381 U.S. 479, 495 (1965), quoting Justice Harlan in *Poe v. Ullman*, 367 U.S. 497, 551-552 (1961).

36. *Stanley v. Georgia*, 394 U.S. 557 (1969).

37. *Skinner v. Oklahoma*, 316 U.S. 535 (1942).

38. *Id.* at 541.

39. *Buck v. Bell*, 274 U.S. 200 (1927).

40. *Id.* at 205.

41. *Id.* at 207.

42. *Poe v. Ullman*, 376 U.S. 497, 521 (1961).

43. *Griswold v. Connecticut*, 381 U.S. 479, 530 (1965).

44. *Roe v. Wade*, 410 U.S. 113, 168 (1973).

45. *Griswold v. Connecticut*, 381 U.S. 479, 508-510 (1965).

46. *Id.* at 486.

47. Patterson, "The Forgotten Ninth Amendment."

48. Kelsey, "Ninth Amendment."

49. Patterson, "The Forgotten Ninth Amendment," 125.

50. *Griswold v. Connecticut*, 381 U.S. 479, 487 (1965).

51. *Id.* at 391.

52. *Id.* at 397.

53. Caplan, "History and Meaning of the Ninth Amendment," 245.

54. *Griswold v. Connecticut*, 381 U.S. 479, 498-499 (1965).

55. *Eisenstadt v. Baird*, 405 U.S. 438 (1972).

56. *Id.* at 443. Tellingly, the State of Massachusetts asserted "that the un-married have no right to engage in sexual intercourse and hence no health interest in contraception" (*Eisenstadt v. Baird* , 405 U.S. 438, 452 [1972]).

57. *Id.* at 453.

58. *Post v. Oklahoma*, 715 P.2d 1105, 1109 (1986).

59. Posner, *Overcoming Law*, 552.

60. Ibid.

61. Massey, "Federalism and Fundamental Rights," 322.

62. "Although [*Griswold v. Connecticut* and *Roe v. Wade*] seemed to add up to a general constitutional right to sexual freedom, the Court has not gone quite that far, as it demonstrated in 1986 [i.e., *Bowers v. Hardwick*] in upholding a ban on homosexual relations. If these cases were really about privacy, the Court would not have let the state dictate what consenting adults can in fact do in the privacy of their homes" (Lieberman, *The Evolving Constitution: How the Supreme Court Has Ruled on Issues from Abortion to Zoning*, 408).

NOTES TO CHAPTER 4

1. *Griswold v. Connecticut*, 381 U.S. 479 (1965).

2. *Poe v. Ullman*, 376 U.S. 497, 499 (1961).

3. *Griswold v. Connecticut*, 381 U.S. 479, 495 (1965).

4. In *Bowers v. Hardwick*, 487 U.S. 186 (1986), Hardwick emphasized that the Georgia sodomy statute violated his "right of intimate association" (201). Justice Blackmun agreed that in upholding Hardwick's conviction, the Court had refused to recognize "the fundamental interest all individuals have in controlling the nature of their intimate associations with others" (206).

5. *Jacobellis v. Ohio*, 378 U.S. 184, 199 (1964). When sexual rights are disentangled from the wide sweep of privacy doctrine and therefore can be seen for the fundamental rights they truly are, it should become clear that they have not only the "First and Fourteenth Amendments" in their favor, but are at heart embedded within the unenumerated rights of the Ninth Amendment.

6. *Eisenstadt v. Baird*, 405 U.S. 438, 448 (1972). *Id.* at 442 (emphasis added).

7. *Id.* at 442 (emphasis added).

8. In all, the Court found:

> If we were to conclude that the Massachusetts statute impinges upon fundamental freedoms under *Griswold,* the statutory classification [i.e., treating the married and unmarried dissimilarly] would have to be not merely *rationally related* to a valid public purpose but *necessary* to the achievement of a *compelling* state interest. But just as in *Reed v. Reed*, 404 U.S. 71 (1971), we do not have to address the statute's validity under that test because the law fails to satisfy even the more lenient equal protection standard (*Eisenstadt v. Baird*, 405 U.S. 438, 447 [1972], emphasis in original).

9. *Baird v. Eisenstadt*, 428 F.2d 1398, 1402 (1970); quoted in *Eisenstadt v. Baird*, 405 U.S. 438, 453 (1972).

10. *Eisenstadt v. Baird*, 405 U.S. 438, 453 (1972).

11. *Baird v. Eisenstadt*, 428 F.2d 1398, 1402, (1970); quoted in *Eisenstadt v. Baird*, 405 U.S. 438, 453 (1972).

12. *Romer v. Evans*, 517 U.S. 620 (1996).

13. *Id.* at 634, quoting *Department of Agriculture v. Moreno*, 413 U.S. 528 (1973); emphasis in original.

14. *Paris Adult Theater I v. Slaton*, 413 U.S. 49 (1973).

15. *Moore v. East Cleveland*, 31 U.S. 494 (1977).

16. Pollak, "Thomas I. Emerson, Lawyer and Scholar: *Ipse Custodiet Custodes.*"

17. *Moore v. East Cleveland*, 31 U.S. 494, 503 (1977).

18. According to G. Wills, Jefferson viewed "the pursuit of happiness" as a barometer of government's success: a government is successful to the extent that its constituents are "happy" (Wills, *Inventing America: Jefferson's Declaration of Independence*).

19. Quoted in Wills, *Inventing America*, 248.

20. Ibid., 250.

21. Massey, "Federalism and Fundamental Rights."

22. Quoted in Cogan, *The Complete Bill of Rights*, 637-638.

23. Ibid., 635.

24. The legal scholar Edward Corwin traced the origin of this preoccupation with happiness to Blackstone's fundamental rule of natural law: "man should pursue his own true and substantial happiness" (Corwin, "The 'Higher-Law' Background of American Constitutional Law").

25. Kelsey, "Ninth Amendment," 98-99.

26. Levy, *Origins of the Bill of Rights*. Madison, introducing his proposed amendments before Congress, also spoke of "pre-existing rights of nature" (Van Loan, "Natural Rights").

27. Levy, *Origins of the Bill of Rights*, 249.

28. Corwin, "'Higher-Law' Background of American Constitutional Law," 104.

29. Inwood and Gerson, *The Epicurus Reader*.

30. Quoted in Ryan, *John Stuart Mill and Jeremy Bentham: Utilitarianism and Other Essays*, 278.

31. Dawkins, *The Selfish Gene*.

32. Abramson and Pinkerton, *With Pleasure*.

33. Ibid., 6-7.

34. *Olmstead v. United States*, 277 U.S. 438, 478 (1928).

35. Meyers, *The Mind of the Founder: Sources of the Political Thought of James Madison*.

36. Ibid., 187.

37. Ibid., 186.

38. Sherman, "Roger Sherman's Draft of the Bill of Rights," 351.

39. Levy, *Origins of the Bill of Rights*, 232.

40. Kelsey, "Ninth Amendment," 97.

41. Abramson and Pinkerton, *With Pleasure*.

42. Schlesinger, *The Birth of the Nation*.

43. Posner and Silbaugh, *A Guide to America's Sex Laws*.

44. Patterson, "The Forgotten Ninth Amendment," 123. Charles Black concurs:

Some pause might be given if we found a real consensus uniting the *major pars* of the relevant eighteenth-century people, that some identifiable claim to a "right" was *not* to be looked on as guarded by the Ninth Amendment. But this would be a pause only. "Due process" is an evolving concept; "cruel and unusual punishment" is an evolving concept; the language of the Ninth Amendment seems even more apt than these to be mentioning an evolving set of rights, not bounded even by a negative eighteenth-century judgment based on eighteenth-century evaluations and social facts as then seen ("On Reading and Using the Ninth Amendment," 341-342).

45. Abramson and Pinkerton, *With Pleasure*.

46. Massey, "Federalism and Fundamental Rights," 331.

47. *Bowers v. Hardwick*, 487 U.S. 186 (1986).

48. For instance, mountain gorillas are known to engage in male-male sex, and bonobos in female-female sex. Chimpanzees sometimes participate in group sex "orgies" (see de Waal, *Peacemaking among Primates*).

49. *Eisenstadt v. Baird*, 405 U.S. 438, 453 (1972).

50. Levy, *Origins of the Bill of Rights*, 250.

51. Black, "On Reading and Using the Ninth Amendment," 339.

52. Ibid., 344-345.

53. Redlich, "Are there 'Certain Rights Retained . . . ,'" 147.

54. *Olmstead v. United States*, 277 U.S. 438 (1928).

55. Barnett, "James Madison's Ninth Amendment," 41.

56. Ibid.

57. Ibid., 43.

58. See, for example, *United States v. Virginia*, 518 U.S. 515 (1996), in which the Court held that the Virginia Military Institute, in operating a male-only military academy, violated the Equal Protection Clause. The Court concluded that gender-based classifications "may not be used . . . to create or perpetuate the legal, social, and economic inferiority of women" (534).

59. Notice that, were government held to such a standard with regard to other potential Ninth Amendment rights of personal autonomy (such as the "right" to use drugs, or the right *not* to wear a motorcycle helmet or seat belt), it would be able to meet its burden by reference to *actual* social costs.

60. See Redlich, "Are there 'Certain Rights Retained . . . ,'" 146. See also Barnett, "James Madison's Ninth Amendment."

61. Locke, *Two Treatises of Government*, 184.

62. Massey, "Federalism and Fundamental Rights," 344.

63. *Jacobellis v. Ohio*, 378 U.S. 184, 199 (1964).

64. *Bowers v. Hardwick*, 487 U.S. 186, 211-212 (1986).

65. Hart, "Immorality and Treason," 225.

66. *Bowers v. Hardwick*, 487 U.S. 186, 212 (1986).

67. Letter from James Madison to Thomas Jefferson, October 17, 1788 (quoted in Niles, "Ninth Amendment Adjudication," 118).

68. Tribe and Dorf, *On Reading the Constitution*, 110.

69. Abramson, *Sarah: A Sexual Biography*; Abramson, Okami, and Pinkerton, *The Sexual World*.

70. Abramson et al., "Proof Positive: Pornography in a Day Care Center"; Abramson and Pinkerton, *A House Divided*.

71. Madison, "Speech to the House," 58.

72. Massey, "Federalism and Fundamental Rights," 342.

73. *Gertz v. Robert Welch, Inc.*, 418 U.S. 323, 351 (1974).

74. *Curtis Publishing Co. v. Butts*, 388 U.S. 130 (1967), decided together with *Associated Press v. Walker*, 388 U.S. 130 (1967), extending *New York Times v. Sullivan*, 376 U.S. 254 (1964) from public "officials" to public "figures."

75. *Gertz v. Robert Welch, Inc.*, 418 U.S. 323 (1974).

76. *Dun & Bradstreet, Inc. v. Greenmoss Builders, Inc.*, 472 U.S. 749 (1985).

77. For further evidence of the Court's reticence to label people as public figures, see also *Time, Inc. v. Firestone*, 424 U.S. 448 (1976).

78. See *Gertz v. Robert Welch, Inc.*, 418 U.S. 323, 341 (1974); *Dun & Bradstreet, Inc. v. Greenmoss Builders, Inc.*, 472 U.S. 749, 759 (1985), quoting *Rosenblatt v. Bauer*, 383 U.S. 75, 92 (1966).

79. *Chaplinsky v. New Hampshire*, 315 U.S. 568 (1942).

80. *Cohen v. California*, 403 U.S. 15, 25 (1971).

81. *Ohralik v. Ohio State Bar Association*, 436 U.S. 447, 456 (1978), emphasis added.

82. *Miller v. California*, 413 U.S. 15 (1973).

83. "[B]ut I know [obscenity] when I see it," he added. *Jacobellis v. Ohio*, 378 U.S. 184, 197 (1964).

84. Black, "On Reading and Using the Ninth Amendment," 339.

85. *Bowers v. Hardwick*, 487 U.S. 186, 194 (1986).

86. In Judge Robert Bork's opinion, the Ninth Amendment "says 'Congress shall make no' and then there is an inkblot, and you can't read the rest of it, and that is the only copy you have" (Nomination of Robert Bork to be Associate Justice of the Supreme Court of the United States: Hearing Before the Senate Committee on the Judiciary 117 [1989], 249).

87. *Bowers v. Hardwick*, 487 U.S. 186, 191 (1986).

88. Ely, "The Ninth Amendment," 248 n. 52.

89. *Griswold v. Connecticut*, 381 U.S. 479, 501 (1965).

90. Niles, "Ninth Amendment Adjudication," 85.

91. *Griswold v. Connecticut*, 381 U.S. 479, 487 (1965), quoting *Snyder v. Massachusetts*, 291 U.S. 97, 105 (1934).

92. Ely, "The Ninth Amendment," 41.

NOTES TO CHAPTER 5

1. Pinkerton et al., "Factors Associated with Masturbation in a Collegiate Sample."

2. Ibid.

3. Pavelka, "Sexual Nature: What Can We Learn from a Cross-Species Perspective?"

4. Abramson, "The Relationship of the Frequency of Masturbation to Several Aspects of Personality and Behavior"; Abramson, "The Development of a Measure of Negative Attitudes toward Masturbation"; LoPiccolo and Lobitz, "The Role of Masturbation in the Treatment of Orgasmic Dysfunction"; Pavelka, "Sexual Nature."

5. Pavelka, "Sexual Nature."

6. Although one person can masturbate another, in this chapter masturbation is understood to mean sexual stimulation of one's own person, regardless of whether the stimulation is of a genital, anal, or other variety. For an extensive discussion of the many sociocultural and psychological issues associated with masturbation, see Abramson and Pinkerton, *With Pleasure.*

7. Kalven, "The Metaphysics of the Law of Obscenity," 4.

8. *Miller v. California*, 413 U.S. 15 (1973).

9. The three-pronged *Miller* obscenity definition, though problematic, is a definition nonetheless. Limitations of the *Miller* guidelines are discussed in Abramson and Pinkerton, *With Pleasure.*

10. *Red Lion Broadcasting Co. v. Federal Communications Commission*, 395 U.S. 367 (1969).

11. *FCC v. Pacifica Foundation*, 438 U.S. 726 (1978).

12. *Red Lion Broadcasting Co. v. Federal Communications Commission*, 395 U.S., 388, 389 (1969).

13. *Id.* at 389.

14. In addition to the original seven "dirty words," Carlin later added three more words that you can't say on television: "fart, turd and twat." *Carlin Communications, Inc. v. FCC*, 749 F.2d 113 (2d Cir. 1984).

15. *FCC v. Pacifica Foundation*, 438 U.S. 726 (1978).

16. *Id.* at 749.

17. *Id.* at 750-751.

18. 56 F.C.C.2d at 98, cited in *FCC v. Pacifica Foundation*, 438 U.S. 726, 732 (1978).

19. *FCC v. Pacifica Foundation*, 438 U.S. 726, 770 (1978).

20. Prior to the *Ulysses* cases of the mid-1930s (*United States v. One Book Entitled* Ulysses, 72 F.2d 705, 707 (C. A. 2d Cir. 1934)), obscenity was defined by its "tendency . . . to deprave and corrupt those whose minds are open to such immoral influence," such as children and supposedly weak-minded women

(*Queen v. Hicklin*, L.R. 3 Q.B. 360, 371 [1868]). Thereafter, obscenity was judged according to the dominant effect of a work, taken in artistic and thematic context, on the "average" reader or viewer (see Abramson and Pinkerton, *With Pleasure*; Lockhart and McClure, "Literature, the Law of Obscenity, and the Constitution").

21. 18 U.S.C. § 1461.

22. In contrast to users of broadcast media, it is highly unlikely that a telephone or computer user would happen upon pornographic sexual content by accident. Rather, in both instances, "a series of affirmative steps is required to access specific material" (*Reno v. American Civil Liberties Union*, 521 U.S. 844, 867 [1997]). This ignores, of course, the unfortunate proliferation of "spam" email, some of which may contain sexually explicit content. To our knowledge, there is no telephonic equivalent of pornographic spam.

23. Ironically, the FCC may be responsible for the continuing existence of dial-a-porn. It was the FCC's order to AT&T to divest itself of information services (e.g., dial-a-prayer, dial-a-joke) that created independent, competing service providers and set the stage for the proliferation of the dial-a-porn industry. Left to the regulatory discretion of an AT&T monopoly, dial-a-porn may have had little chance of survival. However, with competing providers vying to establish a competitive niche in the newly fractionated telecommunications industry, dial-a-porn was able to sustain itself.

24. Notice of Inquiry on Dial-a-Porn Regulations, 48 Fed. Reg. 43, 349, 1983; Krattenmaker, *Cable's Free Speech Issue*, 3 *Cable T.V. Law & Finance*, September 1984, 8.

25. *Carlin Communications, Inc. v. FCC*, 749 F.2d 113 (2d Cir. 1984).

26. For a thorough review of the legal issues surrounding dial-a-porn regulation, see E. J. Mann's excellent commentary, "Telephones, Sex and the First Amendment."

27. 47 U.S.C. 223. In light of dial-a-porn's implicit association with masturbation, it is not surprising that no politician has ever stepped forward to defend *adults'* Right of Access to dial-a-porn. Instead, the opposite has occurred, with politicians tripping over each other in an effort to condemn what they ostensibly perceive as a vile interloper of telephone sanctity.

28. *Carlin Communications, Inc. v. FCC*, 749 F.2d 113, 123 (2d Cir. 1984).

29. In the *Sex in America* survey (Michael et al.) conducted in 1992, about half as many women as men admitted having purchased an X-rated movie or video in the preceding twelve months. Surprisingly, equal numbers of women and men reported purchasing a vibrator or dildo.

In addition to their solo use as masturbatory aids, these devices are integrated into foreplay (and "other play") by many couples. Vibrators and dildos also have legitimate medical applications in the treatment of anorgasmia (lack of or difficulty in reaching orgasm) and female urinary incontinence.

30. deGrazio, *Girls Lean Back Everywhere: The Law on Obscenity and the Assault on Genius*; Hixson, *Pornography and the Justices: The Intractable Obscenity Problem*.

31. The writings of Catharine MacKinnon are an obvious exception, since masturbation is a focal point of her discussions on pornography. She views male masturbation to pornography as being an accomplice to rape. In her book, *Only Words*, she contends that men who masturbate to heterosexual pornography are in effect celebrating the rape of a pornographic actress, and thereby promoting the degradation of all women.

32. Anthony Comstock, quoted in Richards, "Free Speech and Obscenity Law: Toward a Moral Theory of the First Amendment," 58.

33. Abramson and Pinkerton, *With Pleasure*, 176.

34. The following states had laws prohibiting the sale of sexual devices as of this writing: Alabama, Colorado, Georgia, Kansas, Louisiana, Mississippi, Texas, and Virginia. However, the Supreme Courts of Colorado and Kansas have invalidated their laws as overly broad and impinging on the right to privacy (*State of Louisiana v. Christine Brennan*, Supreme Court of Louisiana, 99-KA-2291 [2000]).

35. Alabama Code 13A-12-200.2.

36. *Williams v. Pryor*, U.S. Court of Appeals, 99-10798 (2001).

37. *Id.*

38. In January 2002, John Rogers, a state legislator from Birmingham, Alabama, introduced a bill to void the state's "dildo law." Interestingly, Senate Majority Leader Tom Butler, who authored the dildo law, denied accusations that he was trying to legislate bedroom activities by noting that these devices could still be obtained from mail-order firms or through the Internet (C. Redden, "Bill Would Repeal Ban of Vibrators," *Decatur Daily News*, January 23, 2002). It is difficult to reconcile this statement with the law's asserted purpose—namely, to discourage "prurient interests in autonomous sex."

39. The protection of minors is curiously selective in the activities it targets. Openly displaying sexual devices and men's magazines is *verboten*, due to fears that minors might be corrupted through exposure to these materials. Yet alcohol producers are free to portray the joys of drinking on television; and, despite the tougher restrictions imposed on cigarette advertising in recent years, these ads remain readily accessible to minors.

40. This is not to say that persons under the age of eighteen should have no access to sexual activity. Although states would have the power to restrict sexual access to adolescents under a consent-based scheme, it would be ridiculous and unwise for a state to prosecute a teenage boy for masturbation, or even a seventeen-year-old girl for having sex with her seventeen-year-old boyfriend. Such prohibitions would be very difficult to enforce and would divert resources from other areas. In chapter 6 we demonstrate that the war against prostitution

drew resources away from the prevention and prosecution of assaultive crime (e.g., homicides, rapes, and robberies). A similar argument could be made here—namely, that in the grand scheme of things a good portion of adolescent sexual activity is relatively harmless, especially if adolescents are well educated in safe sex practices, a tack we encourage in chapter 8. In the final analysis, however, each state would be empowered to restrict the sexual activities of its minors as it saw fit, subject to restrictions of its own, such as the consent of parents to state prosecutions of their children (recall that the Fourteenth Amendment empowers parents with "the custody, care and nurture of the child"—*Prince v. Massachusetts*, 321 U.S. 158, 166 [1944]), or, in situations where parental consent is obtained, the provision of individualized judicial hearings in which the adolescent(s) in question would have an opportunity to persuade a court of their maturity, similar to the hearings currently required in cases of underage girls who wish an abortion.

41. Posner and Silbaugh, *America's Sex Laws*.

42. *Bowers v. Hardwick*, 487 U.S. 186 (1986); *Roberts v. United States Jaycees*, 468 U.S. 609, 619 (1984).

43. *Bowers v. Hardwick*, 487 U.S. 186 (1986). See also Dworkin, "Sex, Death and the Courts."

44. *Brown v. Board of Education*, 347 U.S. 483 (1954).

45. *Loving v. Virginia*, 388 U.S. 1 (1967).

46. Abramson and Pinkerton, *With Pleasure*.

47. *Bowers v. Hardwick*, 487 U.S. 186, 195-196 (1986).

NOTES TO CHAPTER 6

1. Connelly, *The Response to Prostitution in the Progressive Era*, 18.

2. Gilfoyle, *City of Eros: New York Prostitution, and the Commercialization of Sex, 1790-1920.*

3. Bryant and Palmer, "Massage Parlors and 'Hand Whores': Some Sociological Observations."

4. Lewis, "Lap Dancing: Personal and Legal Implications for Exotic Dancers."

5. Reiss, "The Social Integration of Queers and Peers"; West, "Male Homosexual Prostitution in England."

6. D'Emilio and Freedman, *Intimate Matters: A History of Sexuality in America*, 50.

7. Ibid.

8. Ibid., *passim*.

9. Ibid.

10. Law, "Commercial Sex: Beyond Decriminalization."

11. Zemel, "Private Pleasures: Fischl's Monotypes."

12. *Roth v. United States*, 354 U.S. 476 (1957).

13. *Miller v. California*, 413 U.S. 15 (1973).

14. See, for example, the Supreme Court of Louisiana's decision in *Louisiana v. Christine D. Brennan*: "While acknowledging *Miller*'s limitation to a First Amendment context, we are nevertheless guided by these principles in our determination of whether the devises at issue are indeed obscene or garner constitutional protection" Supreme Court of Louisiana, 99-KA-2291 [2000].

15. The *Oxford Dictionary of Current English* definition of "prurient" reads: "having or encouraging unhealthy sexual curiosity." The Supreme Court has defined "prurient" similarly, excluding from its parameters those materials that arouse "only normal, healthy sexual desires" (*Brockett v. Spokane Arcades, Inc.*, 472 U.S. 491, 498 [1985]).

16. *Brockett v. Spokane Arcades, Inc.*, 472 U.S. 491, 504 (1985).

17. *Id.* at 498.

18. Posner and Silbaugh, *A Guide to America's Sex Laws*.

19. Atchison, Fraser, and Lowman, "Men Who Buy Sex."

20. Annie Sprinkle, a self-billed "Notorious Prostitute/Porn Star turned Sex Guru Performance Artist," lists the following customer-oriented benefits among her "Forty Reasons Whores are My Heroines": "Whores teach people how to be better lovers. . . . Whores make lonely people less lonely. . . . Whores teach people how to have safer sex. . . . Whores relieve millions of people of unwanted stress and tension. . . . Whores heal. . . . Whores help people explore their sexual desires. . . . Whores help the handicapped" (Sprinkle, "Forty Reasons," 114-115).

21. See Brandt, "AIDS in Historical Perspective: Four Lessons from the History of Sexually Transmitted Diseases"; Burnham, "The Progressive Era Revolution in American Attitudes toward Sex"; D'Emilio and Freedman, *Intimate Matters*.

22. Acton, *The Functions and Disorders of the Reproductive Organs*.

23. The Roman poet and satirist Horace advised that "young men, when their veins are full of gross lust," should avail themselves of the prostitutes' services, "rather than grind some husband's private mill" (quoted in Taylor, *Sex in History*, 238).

24. Quoted in Richards, "Commercial Sex and the Rights of the Person: A Moral Argument for the Decriminalization of Prostitution," 1244.

25. D'Emilio and Freedman, *Intimate Matters*, 140.

26. Ibid., *passim*.

27. Ibid.

28. Kern, *An Ordered Love: Sex Roles and Sexuality in Victorian Utopias—the Shakers, the Mormons, and the Oneida Community*.

29. Shade, "'A Mental Passion': Female Sexuality in Victorian America," 17.

30. Abramson and Pinkerton, *With Pleasure*, 122. See also Gordon, *Woman's Body, Woman's Right: A Social History of Birth Control in America*.

31. The goal of the American Society for Sanitary and Moral Prophylaxis was "to limit the spread of diseases which have their origin in the Social Evil [i.e., prostitution]" (Burnham, "The Progressive Era Revolution," 896).

32. Brandt, *No Magic Bullet: A Social History of Venereal Disease in the United States*, 32.

33. D'Emilio and Freedman, *Intimate Matters*, 141.

34. Ibid.

35. This cursory review does a certain injustice to the complex history of prostitution in America. See D'Emilio and Freedman, *Intimate Matters*, for a thorough treatment of this issue.

36. Pearl, "The Highest Paying Customers: America's Cities and the Costs of Prostitution Control."

37. Dr. Ludwig Weiss, quoted in Brandt, *No Magic Bullet*, 31.

38. Report of the Chicago Vice Commission, quoted in Brandt, *No Magic Bullet*, 32.

39. Pinkerton and Abramson, "Condoms and the Prevention of AIDS."

40. Campbell, "Prostitution, AIDS and Preventive Health Behavior"; McKeganey, "Prostitution and HIV: What Do We Know and Where Might Research be Targeted in the Future?"

41. Atchison, Fraser, and Lowman, "Men Who Buy Sex."

42. McKeganey, "Prostitution and HIV."

43. Lyons and Fahrner, "HIV in Women in the Sex Industry and/or Injection Drug Users."

44. Law, "Commercial Sex," 546.

45. For a review of evidence and a discussion as to why young men are infrequent patrons of prostitutes, see Decker, *Prostitution: Regulation and Control*, 18-19, 217.

46. Alan Guttmacher Institute, *Testing Positive: Sexually Transmitted Disease and the Public Health Response*.

47. Institute of Medicine, *The Hidden Epidemic: Confronting Sexually Transmitted Diseases*.

48. Institute of Medicine, *The Hidden Epidemic*, 36.

49. Ibid., *passim*.

50. Decker states: "There is no shortage of persons who allege prostitution is intrinsically wound up in organized crime syndicate operations. " He concedes, however, that only "scattered evidence" exists that organized crime is involved in prostitution (*Prostitution: Regulation and Control*, 335-336).

51. See, for example, Chamallas, who cites a Boston study finding no strong evidence that prostitution causes robbery, other serious crimes, drug addiction, or neighborhood deterioration. Chamallas, "Consent, Equality, and the Legal Control of Sexual Conduct," 212 n.

52. Law, "Commercial Sex," 533.

53. Richards, "Commercial Sex and the Rights of the Person."

54. Pearl, "Highest Paying Customers," 769-770.

55. Ibid., 85.

56. Ibid., *passim.*

57. Richards, "Commercial Sex and the Rights of the Person," 1217.

58. Campbell, "Prostitution, AIDS and Preventive Health Behavior."

59. Ibid.

60. Albert et al., "Condom Use among Female Commercial Sex Workers in Nevada's Legal Brothels."

61. Ibid. Significantly, this low STD acquisition rate was reported *prior* to the implementation of Nevada's mandatory condom use law.

62. Ibid. In Nevada it is a felony to work as a prostitute after receiving a positive HIV test result.

63. See, for example, *Renton v. Playtime Theatres, Inc.*, 475 U.S. 41 (1986), in which the Court upheld a zoning scheme for adult theaters but would not have approved a total ban; see also *Erie v. Pap's A.M.*, 529 U.S. 277 (2000), upholding a city ordinance that required all nude dancers to wear "pasties" and "G-strings."

64. Brandt, *No Magic Bullet*, 32.

65. D'Emilio and Freedman, *Intimate Matters.*

66. Quoted in Abramson, Okami, and Pinkerton, *The Sexual World*, emphasis in original.

67. D'Emilio and Freedman, *Intimate Matters.*

68. Ibid., 213.

69. Gilfoyle, *City of Eros.*

70. See, for example, Lefler, "Shining the Spotlight on Johns: Moving toward Equal Treatment of Male Customers and Female Prostitutes"; Kandel, "Whores in Court: Judicial Processing of Prostitutes in the Boston Municipal Court in 1990."

71. Lefler, "Shining the Spotlight"; Kandel, "Whores in Court."

72. Law, "Commercial Sex."

73. D'Emilio and Freedman, *Intimate Matters*, 143 (quoting a nineteenth-century prostitution reformer).

74. Ibid., 144 (quoting a Boston moral reformer).

75. Ibid., 144.

76. *Muller v. Oregon*, 208 U.S. 412, 421-422 (1908).

77. D'Emilio and Freedman, *Intimate Matters*, 208.

78. Sanger, *The History of Prostitution: Its Extent, Causes and Effects Throughout the World*; see also Kushner, "Nineteenth-century Sexuality and the 'Sexual Revolution' of the Progressive Era."

79. See discussion in Abramson, Okami, and Pinkerton, *The Sexual World*.

80. Savitz and Rosen, "The Sexuality of Prostitutes."

81. Plachy and Ridgeway, *Red Light: Inside the Sex Industry*.

82. Ibid.

83. Symons, *The Evolution of Human Sexuality*, 257, quoting Gebhardt, "The Anthropological Study of Sexual Behavior."

84. Engels, *The Origin of the Family, Private Property, and the State*.

85. D'Emilio and Freedman, *Intimate Matters*.

86. Quoted in Abramson, Okami, and Pinkerton, *The Sexual World*.

87. Richards, "Commercial Sex and the Rights of the Person," 1239.

88. In the nineteenth century, "Low wages and poor working conditions practically forced women into prostitution." Kushner, "Nineteenth-Century Sexuality," 40.

89. Bullough and Bullough, "Female Prostitution: Current Research and Changing Interpretations," 35.

90. Quoted in Brandt, *No Magic Bullet*, 34.

91. Nussbaum, "Whether from Reason or Prejudice," 701.

92. Richards, "Commercial Sex and the Rights of the Person," 1259.

93. *Schware v. Board of Bar Examiners of New Mexico*, 353 U.S. 232, 236 (1957).

94. *Id*. at 238-239, emphasis added.

95. One man's response when asked why he visits prostitutes: "Hey, it's usually cheaper than getting sex 'for free'!" Quoted in Abramson, Okami, and Pinkerton, *The Sexual World*.

96. Buss, "Sexual Strategies Theory: Historical Origins and Current Status," 25.

97. Kinsey, Pomeroy, and Martin, *Sexual Behavior in the Human Male*.

98. Michael et al., *Sex in America*; Monto, "Why Men Seek Out Prostitutes"; Weitzer, "The Politics of Prostitution in America."

99. Abramson, Okami, and Pinkerton, *The Sexual World*, summarizing McKeganey and Barnard, *Sex Work on the Streets: Prostitutes and Their Clients*. See also Atchison, Fraser, and Lowman, "Men Who Buy Sex."

100. Abramson and Pinkerton, *With Pleasure*, 80.

101. *United States v. Bitty*, 208 U.S. 393, 401 (1908).

102. Franklin, "The Speech of Miss Polly Baker."

103. Abramson, Okami, and Pinkerton, *The Sexual World*.

104. Comment, *The Victim as Criminal: A Consideration of California's Prostitution Law*, 64 *California Law Review* 1235, 1250 (1976), citing 1973 Harris poll.

105. Bureau of Justice Statistics, U.S. Department of Justice, *The National Survey of Crime Severity*, NCJ-96017 (1985).

106. Pearl, "The Highest Paying Customers."

107. Ibid., 789.

108. Peplau, Rubin, and Hill, "Sexual Intimacy in Dating Relationships."

NOTES TO CHAPTER 7

1. The existence of child pornography helps perpetuate child pornography by normalizing it. Pedophiles may leave pornographic material lying around, or directly show it to potential victims, as a way of mainstreaming it—as in, "if it's on TV, it must be okay; if it's in magazines it must be okay; and if it's in photo albums, it must be okay."

2. *United States v S. A. Knox*, 32 F. 733 (3rd Cir. 1994).

3. Ibid.

4. Ibid.

5. A First Amendment analysis would operate similarly. There is no right to produce or have access to sexual images created without consent.

6. For example, the 1977 Protection of Children against Sexual Exploitation Act punished the knowing possession of three or more videotapes containing visual depictions of a minor engaged in sexually explicit conduct (Protection of Children Against Sexual Exploitation: Hearings before the Sub-comm. to Investigate Juvenile Delinquency of the Senate Comm. on the Judiciary, 95th Congress, 1st Sess. 77-78 [1977]); the current standard is "1 or more" (18 USCS § 2252). Also, in 1996 the Child Protection Act was amended to include computer-generated images that *appear* to depict minors but do not exploit real children (18 USCS § 2256[8][B]). In 2002, this provision was found unconstitutional (*Ashcroft v. Free Speech Coalition*, 122 S. Ct. 1389 [2002]).

7. Child Protection Act of 1984, Pub. L. No. 98-292, 98 Stat. 206.

8. This remains the standard at this writing.

9. 130 Congressional Record S3510, S3511 (daily ed. March 30, 1984) (statement of Rep. Specter). Congress also stated at this time: "1) child pornography has developed into a highly organized, multi-million-dollar industry which operates on a nationwide order; 2) thousands of children including large numbers of runaway and homeless youth are exploited in the production and distribution of pornographic materials; and 3) the use of children as subjects of pornographic materials is harmful to the physiological, emotional and mental health of the individual child and to society."

10. *New York v. Ferber*, 458 U.S. 747 (1982).

11. *Miller v. California*, 413 U.S. 15, 18-19 (1973).

12. *New York v. Ferber*, 458 U.S. 458 U.S. 747, 757 (1982).

13. *Id.* at 761.

14. *Hamling v. United States*, 418 U.S. 87, 114 (1974).

15. *United States v. Wiegand*, 812 F.2d 1239, 1243 (9th Cir. 1987).

16. *United States v. Dost*, 636 F.Supp. 833 (S.D.Cal. 1986).

17. The 1984 Child Protection Act defines a "child" as a person under eighteen years of age (18 USCS § 2256[1]).

18. *United States v. Dost*, 636 F.Supp. 833 (S.D.Cal. 1986). One might question how the Court knew that "the average 10-year-old child sitting on the beach, especially when unclothed, does not sit with her legs positioned in such a manner."

19. *United States v. Dost*, 636 F. Supp. 833 (S.D.Cal. 1986).

20. *United States v. Wiegand*, 812 F.2d, 1239, 1243 (9th Cir. 1987).

21. *New York v. Ferber*, 458 U.S. 747, 773 (1982).

22. *United States v. Wiegand*, 812 F.2d, 1239, 1243 (9th Cir. 1987).

23. *Id.* at 1245.

24. *Ashcroft v. Free Speech Coalition*, 122 S. Ct. 1389 (2002).

25. *United States v. Villard*, 885 F.2d 117 (3rd Cir. 1989).

26. *United States v. Villard*, 885 F.2d 117, 119 (3rd Cir. 1989).

27. *Id.* at 807.

28. *United States v. Villard*, 885 F.2d 117 (3rd Cir. 1989).

29. *Id.* at 124.

30. *United States v. Villard*, 885 F.2d 117, 125 (3rd Cir. 1989), quoting *United States v. Villard*, 700 F. Supp. 803, 812 (D.N.J. 1988), citing Faloona v. Hustler Magazine, Inc., 607 F. Supp. 1341 (N.D.Tex. 1985).

31. The presiding judge in *United States v. Arvin*, in contrast, insisted that "lasciviousness" is a "commonsensical term," and that a jury is "fully capable of making its own determination on the issue of 'lasciviousness'" (900 F.2d 1385, 1390 [9th Cir. 1990]).

32. *United States v. Villard*, 885 F.2d 117, 123 (3rd Cir. 1989).

33. Or perhaps even according to some interpretations of *Mishkin v. New York* (383 U.S. 502 [1966]), where obscenity can be found, even if imagery appeals only to a "deviant" group. Pedophiles obviously would fit into this category.

34. *United States v. Wolf*, 890 F.2d 241 (10th Cir. 1989).

35. Dix, "Waiver in Criminal Procedure: A Brief for a More Careful Analysis."

36. *Miranda v. Arizona*, 384 U.S. 436 (1966).

37. Hart, *The Concept of Law*.

38. Richard Posner uses the term "effective consent" when applied to such individuals. See Posner, *Sex and Reason*.

39. See the following for a full review of the issues: Abramson, Parker, and Weisberg, "Sexual Expression of Mentally Retarded People: Educational and Legal Implications"; Parker and Abramson, "The Law Hath Not Been Dead: Protecting Adults with Mental Retardation from Sexual Abuse and Violation of their Sexual Freedom."

40. See Abramson, *Sarah: A Sexual Biography*, for an illustration of how traumatic experiences of childhood sexual abuse can be internalized and eventually overcome. In a relatively small proportion of cases, adults who, as children, were involved in a sexual relationship with an adult continue to perceive that relationship in a positive light (McConaghy, "Paedophilia: A Review of the Evidence"; Rind, Bauserman, and Tromovitch, "Interpretation of Research on Sexual Abuse of Boys").

41. *United States v. Wiegand*, 812 F.2d, 1239, 1245 (9th Cir. 1987).

42. *Meyer v. Nebraska*, 262 U.S. 390, 399 (1923).

43. *Prince v. Massachusetts*, 321 U.S. 158, 166 (1944).

44. *Stanley v. Georgia*, 394 U.S. 557 (1969).

45. *Roth v. United States*, 354 U.S. 476 (1975).

46. *United States v. 12,200 Ft. Reels of Super 8 MM Film*, 413 U.S. 123, 126 (1973).

47. *Ashcroft v. Free Speech Coalition*, 122 S. Ct. 1389, 1404 (2002).

48. Admittedly, even under a consent-based standard, on the margin some pictures will bleed into gray areas. However, under our proposed standard, in line with the underlying intent of child pornography laws, those issues will be determined by recourse to foreseeable harm, rather than to "lasciviousness," the latter by its nature inviting bypass of a consideration of harm in favor of emotional and self-righteous judgment.

49. Abramson and Pinkerton, *With Pleasure*.

50. Bickel, *The Morality of Consent*.

51. Several states have revised statutes to decriminalize private, consensual, adult sexual conduct, starting with Illinois in 1961, and more recently including Montana (1997) and Georgia (1998). See Sgalla McClure, "A Case for Same-Sex Marriage: A Look at Changes around the Globe and in the United States, including *Baker v. Vermont*."

NOTES TO CHAPTER 8

1. Posner and Silbaugh, *A Guide to America's Sex Laws*.

2. Berger, "The Ninth Amendment," 192.

3. As Madison expressed it: "If a line can be drawn between the powers granted and the rights retained, it would seem to be the same thing, whether the latter be secured by declaring that they shall not be abridged, or that the former shall not be extended." Letter from James Madison to George Washington, December 5, 1789, quoted in Berger, "The Ninth Amendment," 193.

4. This formalism provides a theoretical basis for arithmetic. Zero is defined as the empty set containing no elements. The number one is defined as the

set containing only the number zero; the number two as the set containing zero and one, and so on.

5. Madison, "Speech to the House," 53-54.

6. Abramson and Pinkerton, *A House Divided: Suspicions of Mother-Daughter Incest.*

7. Paine, *The Thomas Paine Reader*, 54.

8. *Weems v. United States*, 214 U.S. 349, 373 (1910), quoted in *Olmstead v. United States*, 277 U.S. 438, 472-473 (1928), emphasis added.

9. Madison, *The Federalist No. 14*, in Hamilton, Madison, and Jay, *Federalist Papers*, 72.

10. Black, "On Reading and Using the Ninth Amendment," 338. See also Massey, "Federalism and Fundamental Rights: The Ninth Amendment."

11. See Barnett's discussion of the "presumption of liberty" in "James Madison's Ninth Amendment."

12. Barnett, "James Madison's Ninth Amendment"; Redlich, "Are There 'Certain Rights Retained. . . .'"

13. *United States v. Virginia*, 518 U.S. 515 (1996).

14. "The presumption of innocence, although not articulated in the Constitution, is a basic component of a fair trial under our system of criminal justice." *Estelle, Corrections Director v. Williams*, 425 U.S. 501, 503 (1976).

15. Hirsch, *Cultural Literacy: What Every American Needs to Know.*

16. *Wall Street Journal*, July 22, 1996.

17. Abramson and Pinkerton, *With Pleasure.*

18. *Wall Street Journal*, July 30, 1996.

19. Abramson, "Sexual Science: Emerging Discipline or Oxymoron?"

References

Abramson, P. R. "The Relationship of the Frequency of Masturbation to Several Aspects of Personality and Behavior." *The Journal of Sex Research* 9 (1973): 132-42.

——"The Development of a Measure of Negative Attitudes toward Masturbation." *Journal of Consulting and Clinical Psychology* 43 (1975): 485-90.

——*Sarah: A Sexual Biography*. Albany: SUNY Press, 1984.

——"Sexual Science: Emerging Discipline or Oxymoron?" *The Journal of Sex Research* 27 (1990): 147-65.

Abramson, P. R., M. Y. Cloud, R. Keese, and J. Girardi. "Proof Positive: Pornography in a Day Care Center." *Sexual Abuse: A Journal of Research and Treatment* 9 (1997): 75-86.

Abramson, P. R., P. Okami, and S. D. Pinkerton. *The Sexual World*. New York: W. W. Norton, 2004.

Abramson, P. R., T. Parker, and S. Weisberg. "Sexual Expression of Mentally Retarded People: Educational and Legal Implications." *American Journal of Mental Retardation* 93 (1988): 328-34.

Abramson, P. R., and S. D. Pinkerton. *A House Divided: Suspicions of Mother-Daughter Incest*. New York: W. W. Norton, 2000.

——*With Pleasure: Thoughts on the Nature of Human Sexuality*. New York: Oxford University Press, 1995.

Acton, W. *The Functions and Disorders of the Reproductive Organs*. London: Churchill, 1857.

Adler, P. *A House Is Not a Home*. New York: Rinehart, 1953.

Alan Guttmacher Institute. *Testing Positive: Sexually Transmitted Disease and the Public Health Response*. New York: The Alan Guttmacher Institute, 1993.

Albert, A. E., D. L. Warner, R. A. Hatcher, J. Trussell, and C. Bennett. "Condom Use among Female Commercial Sex Workers in Nevada's Legal Brothels." *American Journal of Public Health* 85 (1995): 1514-20.

Atchison, C., L. Fraser, and J. Lowman. "Men Who Buy Sex: Preliminary Findings of an Exploratory Study." In *Prostitution: On Whores, Hustlers, and Johns*, edited by J. E. Elias, V. L. Bullough, V. Elias, and G. Brewer. Amherst, N.Y.: Prometheus Books, 1998.

Barnett, R. E. "James Madison's Ninth Amendment." In *The Rights Retained by the People: The History and Meaning of the Ninth Amendment*, edited by R. E. Barnett. Fairfax, Va.: George Mason University Press, 1989.

——"Implementing the Ninth Amendment." In *The Rights Retained by the People: The History and Meaning of the Ninth Amendment*, vol. 2, edited by R. E. Barnett. Fairfax, Va.: George Mason University Press, 1993.

Becker, C. L. *The Declaration of Independence: A Study in the History of Political Ideas*. New York: Random House, 1942.

Berger, R. "The Ninth Amendment." In *The Rights Retained by the People: The History and Meaning of the Ninth Amendment*, edited by R. E. Barnett. Fairfax, Va.: George Mason University Press, 1989.

Bickel, A. M. *The Morality of Consent*. New Haven, Conn.: Yale University Press, 1975.

Black, C. L. "On Reading and Using the Ninth Amendment." In *The Rights Retained by the People: The History and Meaning of the Ninth Amendment*, edited by R. E. Barnett. Fairfax, Va.: George Mason University Press, 1989.

Blackstone, W. *Commentaries on the Laws of England*. Chicago: University of Chicago Press, 1979.

Brandt, A. M. *No Magic Bullet: A Social History of Venereal Disease in the United States*. New York: Oxford University Press, 1985.

——"AIDS in Historical Perspective: Four Lessons from the History of Sexually Transmitted Diseases." *American Journal of Public Health* 78 (1988): 367-71.

Bryant, C. D., and C. E. Palmer. "Massage Parlors and 'Hand Whores': Some Sociological Observations." *The Journal of Sex Research* 11 (1975): 227-41.

Bullough, B. L., and V. L. Bullough. "Female Prostitution: Current Research and Changing Interpretations." In *Prostitution: On Whores, Hustlers, and Johns*, edited by J. E. Elias, V. L. Bullough, V. Elias, and G. Brewer. New York: Prometheus Books, 1998.

Burnham, J. C. "The Progressive Era Revolution in American Attitudes toward Sex." *The Journal of American History* 59 (1973): 885-908.

Buss, D. M. "Sexual Strategies Theory: Historical Origins and Current Status." *The Journal of Sex Research* 35 (1998): 19-31.

Campbell, C. A. "Prostitution, AIDS and Preventive Health Behavior." *Social Science and Medicine* 32 (1991): 1367-78.

Caplan, R. L. "The History and Meaning of the Ninth Amendment." In *The Rights Retained by the People: The History and Meaning of the Ninth Amendment*, edited by R. E. Barnett. Fairfax, Va.: George Mason University Press, 1989.

Chamallas, M. "Consent, Equality, and the Legal Control of Sexual Conduct." *Southern California Law Review* 61 (1988): 777-862.

Clark, R. W. *Benjamin Franklin: A Biography*. New York: Random House, 1983.

Cogan, N. H. *The Complete Bill of Rights: The Drafts, Debates, Sources, and Origins*. New York: Oxford University Press, 1997.

Connelly, M. T. *The Response to Prostitution in the Progressive Era*. Chapel Hill: University of North Carolina Press, 1980.

Cooke, J. E. *Alexander Hamilton*. New York: Charles Scribner's Sons, 1982.

Corwin, E. S. "The 'Higher Law' Background of American Constitutional Law." In *The Rights Retained by the People: The History and Meaning of the Ninth Amendment*, edited by R. E. Barnett. Fairfax, Va.: George Mason University Press, 1989.

Dawkins, R. *The Selfish Gene*. Oxford: Oxford University Press, 1976.

Decker, J. F. *Prostitution: Regulation and Control*. Littleton, Colo.: F. B. Rothman, 1979.

D'Emilio, J., and E. B. Freedman. *Intimate Matters: A History of Sexuality in America*. New York: Harper and Row, 1988.

deGrazio, E. *Girls Lean Back Everywhere: The Law on Obscenity and the Assault on Genius*. New York: Vantage, 1992.

de Waal, F.B.M. *Peacemaking among Primates*. Cambridge: Harvard University Press, 1989.

Dix, J. "Waiver in Criminal Procedure: A Brief for a More Careful Analysis." *Texas Law Review* 55 (1977): 193-268.

Dworkin, R. "Sex, Death and the Courts." *New York Review of Books* 43 (1996): 44-50.

Ely, J. H. "The Ninth Amendment." In *The Rights Retained by the People: The History and Meaning of the Ninth Amendment*, edited by R. E. Barnett. Fairfax, Va.: George Mason University Press, 1989.

Engels, F. *The Origin of the Family, Private Property, and the State*. New York: International Publishers, 1942.

Franklin, B. "The Speech of Miss Polly Baker." *Maryland Gazette*, 11 August 1747.

Gebhardt, P. H. "The Anthropological Study of Sexual Behavior." In *Human Sexual Behavior*, edited by D. S. Marshall and R. C. Suggs. New York: Basic Books, 1971.

Genovese, E. *Roll, Jordan, Roll: The World the Slaves Made*. New York: Harper, 1974.

Gilfoyle, T. J. *City of Eros: New York Prostitution and the Commercialization of Sex, 1790-1920*. New York: W. W. Norton, 1992.

Godbeer, R. *Sexual Revolution in Early America*. Baltimore, Md.: Johns Hopkins University Press, 2002.

Gordon, L. *Woman's Body, Woman's Right: A Social History of Birth Control in America*. New York: Grossman, 1976.

Gordon-Reed, A. *Thomas Jefferson and Sally Hemings: An American Controversy*. Charlottesville: University Press of Virginia, 1997.

Hamilton, A., J. Madison, and J. Jay. *The Federalist Papers*. New York: Mentor Books, 1999.

Hart, H.L.A. "Immorality and Treason." Reprinted in *The Law as Literature*, edited by L. Blom-Cooper. London: The Bodley Head, 1961.

——*The Concept of Law*. Oxford: Oxford University Press, 1961.

Hirsch, E. D. *Cultural Literacy: What Every American Needs to Know*. New York: Random House, 1987.

Hixson, R. F. *Pornography and the Justices: The Intractable Obscenity Problem*. Carbondale: Southern Illinois University Press, 1996.

Hoffman, J. S., and P. Levack, eds. *Burke's Politics*. New York: Knopf, 1970.

Huxley, A. *Brave New World*. New York: Harper Collins, 1932.

Institute of Medicine. *The Hidden Epidemic: Confronting Sexually Transmitted Diseases*. Washington, D.C.: National Academy Press, 1997.

Inwood, B., and L. P. Gerson, trans. *The Epicurus Reader*. Cambridge, Mass.: Hackett Publishing, 1994.

Kalven, H. Jr. "The Metaphysics of the Law of Obscenity." *Supreme Court Review* 1 (1960): 1-45.

Kandel, M. "Whores in Court: Judicial Processing of Prostitutes in the Boston Municipal Court in 1990." *Yale Journal of Law and Feminism* 4 (1992): 329-52.

Kelsey, K. H. "The Ninth Amendment of the Federal Constitution." In *The Rights Retained by the People: The History and Meaning of the Ninth Amendment*, edited by R. E. Barnett. Fairfax, Va.: George Mason University Press, 1989.

Kern, L. J. *An Ordered Love: Sex Roles and Sexuality in Victorian Utopias—The Shakers, the Mormons, and the Oneida Community*. Chapel Hill: University of North Carolina Press, 1981.

Kinsey, A. C., W. B. Pomeroy, and C. E. Martin. *Sexual Behavior in the Human Male*. Philadelphia, Pa.: Saunders, 1948.

Kushner, H. I. "Nineteenth-Century Sexuality and the 'Sexual Revolution' of the Progressive Era." *The Canadian Review of American Studies* 9 (1978): 34-49.

Law, S. A. "Commercial Sex: Beyond Decriminalization." *Southern California Law Review* 73 (2000): 523-610.

Lefler, J. "Shining the Spotlight on Johns: Moving toward Equal Treatment of Male Customers and Female Prostitutes." *Hastings Women's Law Journal* 10 (1999): 11-35.

Lemay, J.A.L., ed. *Reappraising Benjamin Franklin: A Bicentennial Perspective*. Newark: University of Delaware Press, 1993.

Levy, L. W. *Origins of the Bill of Rights*. New Haven, Conn.: Yale University Press, 1999.

Lewis, J. "Lap Dancing: Personal and Legal Implications for Exotic Dancers." In *Prostitution: On Whores, Hustlers, and Johns*, edited by J. E. Elias, V. L. Bullough, V. Elias, and G. Brewer. New York: Prometheus Books, 1998.

Lieberman, J. K. *The Evolving Constitution: How the Supreme Court Has Ruled on Issues from Abortion to Zoning.* New York: Random House, 1992.

Locke, J. *Second Treatise of Government.* Indianapolis: Hackett, 1980.

———*Two Treatises of Government.* Boston: Everyman, 1993.

Lockhart, W. B., and R. C. McClure. "Literature, the Law of Obscenity, and the Constitution." *Minnesota Law Review* 38 (1954): 295-395.

LoPiccolo, J., and W. C. Lobitz. "The Role of Masturbation in the Treatment of Orgasmic Dysfunction." *Archives of Sexual Behavior* 2 (1972): 163-71.

Lyons, C., and R. Fahrner. "HIV in Women in the Sex Industry and/or Injection Drug Users." *NAACOGS Clinical Issues in Perinatal and Women's Health Nursing* 1 (1990): 33-40.

MacKinnon, C. A. *Only Words.* Cambridge: Harvard University Press, 1993.

Madison, J. "Speech to the House Explaining His Proposed Amendments and His Notes for the Amendment Speech." In *The Rights Retained by the People: The History and Meaning of the Ninth Amendment*, edited by R. E. Barnett. Fairfax, Va.: George Mason University Press, 1989.

Mann, E. J. "Telephones, Sex and the First Amendment." *UCLA Law Review* 33 (1986): 1221-46.

Massey, C. R. "Federalism and Fundamental Rights: The Ninth Amendment." In *The Rights Retained by the People: The History and Meaning of the Ninth Amendment*, edited by R. E. Barnett. Fairfax, Va.: George Mason University Press, 1989.

McConaghy, N. "Paedophilia: A Review of the Evidence." *Australia and New Zealand Journal of Psychiatry* 32 (1998): 252-65.

McCorvey, N. *I Am Roe: My Life, Roe v. Wade, and Freedom of Choice.* New York: Harper Collins, 1994.

McIntosh, S.C.R. "On Reading the Ninth Amendment: A Reply to Raoul Berger." In *The Rights Retained by the People: The History and Meaning of the Ninth Amendment*, edited by R. E. Barnett. Fairfax, Va.: George Mason University Press, 1989.

McKeganey, N. P. "Prostitution and HIV: What Do We Know and Where Might Research Be Targeted in the Future?" *AIDS* 8 (1994): 1215-26.

McKeganey, N. P., and M. A. Barnard. *Sex Work on the Streets: Prostitutes and Their Clients.* New York: Open University Press, 1996.

Meyers, M., ed. *The Mind of the Founder: Sources of the Political Thought of James Madison.* Hanover, N.H.: University Press of New England, 1981.

Michael, R. T., J. H. Gagnon, E. O. Laumann, and G. Kolata. *Sex in America: A Definitive Survey.* Boston: Little, Brown and Company, 1994.

Miller, W. L. *The Business of May Next: James Madison and the Founding.* Charlottesville: University Press of Virginia, 1992.

Monto, M. A. "Why Men Seek Out Prostitutes." In *Sex for Sale*, edited by R. Weitzer. New York: Routledge, 2000.

Morris, R. B. *Alexander Hamilton and the Founding of the Nation*. New York: Harper, 1969.

Mumford, K. J. "'Lost Manhood' Found: Male Sexual Impotence and Victorian Culture in the United States." *The Journal of the History of Sexuality* 3 (1992): 33-57.

Niles, M. C. "Ninth Amendment Adjudication: An Alternative to Substantive Due Process Analysis of Personal Autonomy Rights." *UCLA Law Review* 48 (2000): 85-157.

Nussbaum, M. C. "'Whether from Reason or Prejudice': Taking Money for Bodily Services." *The University of Chicago Journal of Legal Studies* 27 (1998): 693-702.

O'Brien, D. M. *Storm Center: The Supreme Court in American Politics*. New York: Norton, 1996.

Paine, T. *The Thomas Paine Reader*. Edited by I. Kramnick. New York: Penguin Books, 1987.

Parker, T., and P. R. Abramson. "The Law Hath Not Been Dead: Protecting Adults with Mental Retardation from Sexual Abuse and Violation of Their Sexual Freedom." *Mental Retardation* 33 (1995): 257-63.

Patterson, B. B. "The Forgotten Ninth Amendment." In *The Rights Retained by the People: The History and Meaning of the Ninth Amendment*, edited by R. E. Barnett. Fairfax, Va.: George Mason University Press, 1989.

Pavelka, M. M. "Sexual Nature: What Can We Learn from a Cross-Species Perspective?" In *Sexual Nature/Sexual Culture*, edited by P. R. Abramson and S. D. Pinkerton. Chicago: University of Chicago Press, 1995.

Pearl, J. "The Highest Paying Customers: America's Cities and the Costs of Prostitution Control." *Hastings Law Journal* 38 (1987): 769-800.

Peplau, L. A., Z. Rubin, and C. T. Hall. "Sexual Intimacy in Dating Relationships." *Journal of Social Issues* 33 (1977): 86-109.

Pinkerton, S. D., and P. R. Abramson. "Condoms and the Prevention of AIDS." *American Scientist* 85 (1997): 364-73.

Pinkerton, S. D., L. M. Bogart, H. Cecil, H., and P. R. Abramson. "Factors Associated with Masturbation in a Collegiate Sample." *Journal of Psychology and Human Sexuality* (2003), forthcoming.

Plachy, S., and J. Ridgeway. *Red Light: Inside the Sex Industry*. New York: PowerHouse, 1996.

Pollak, L. H. "Thomas I. Emerson, Lawyer and Scholar: *Ipse Custodiet Custodes.*" *Yale Law Journal* 84 (1975): 638-55.

Posner, R. A. *Sex and Reason*. Cambridge: Harvard University Press, 1992.

——*Overcoming Law*. Cambridge: Harvard University Press, 1995.

Posner, R. A., and K. B. Silbaugh. *A Guide to America's Sex Laws*. Chicago: University of Chicago Press, 1996.

Redlich, N. "Are There 'Certain Rights . . . Retained by the People'?" In *The*

Rights Retained by the People: The History and Meaning of the Ninth Amendment, edited by R. E. Barnett. Fairfax, Va.: George Mason University Press, 1989.

Reiss, A. J. Jr. "The Social Integration of Queers and Peers." *Social Problems* 9 (1961): 102-21.

Richards, D.A.J. "Free Speech and Obscenity Law: Toward a Moral Theory of the First Amendment." *University of Pennsylvania Law Review* 123 (1974): 45-91.

——"Commercial Sex and the Rights of the Person: A Moral Argument for the Decriminalization of Prostitution." *University of Pennsylvania Law Review* 127 (1979): 1195-1287.

Rind, B., R. Bauserman, and P. Tromovitch. "Interpretation of Research on Sexual Abuse of Boys." *Journal of the American Medical Association* 281 (1999): 2185-86.

Rutland, R. A. *The Ordeal of the Constitution: The Antifederalists and the Ratification Struggle of 1787-1788.* Boston: Northeastern University Press, 1983.

Ryan, A., ed. *John Stuart Mill and Jeremy Bentham: Utilitarianism and Other Essays.* New York: Penguin Books, 1987.

Samar, V. J. *The Right to Privacy: Gays, Lesbians and the Constitution.* Philadelphia: Temple University Press, 1991.

Sanger, W. W. *The History of Prostitution: Its Extent, Causes and Effects Throughout the World.* New York: Eugenics Publishing, 1897.

Savitz, L., and L. Rosen. "The Sexuality of Prostitutes." *The Journal of Sex Research* 24 (1988): 200-208.

Schlesinger, A. M. *The Birth of the Nation.* Boston: Houghton Mifflin, 1968.

Sgalla McClure, C. J. "A Case for Same-Sex Marriage: A Look at Changes around the Globe and in the United States, Including *Baker v. Vermont.*" *Capital University Law Review* 29 (2002): 783-809.

Shade, W. G. "'A Mental Passion': Female Sexuality in Victorian America." *International Journal of Women's Studies* 1 (1978): 13-29.

Shearer, L. "Intelligence Report." *Parade Magazine*, 23 January 1983.

Sherman, R. "Roger Sherman's Draft of the Bill of Rights." In *The Rights Retained by the People: The History and Meaning of the Ninth Amendment*, edited by R. E. Barnett. Fairfax, Va.: George Mason University Press, 1989.

Sprinkle, A. "Forty Reasons Whores Are My Heroines." In *Prostitution: On Whores, Hustlers, and Johns*, edited by J. E. Elias, V. L. Bullough, V. Elias, and G. Brewer. New York: Prometheus Books, 1998.

Stone, L. *The Family, Sex and Marriage in England, 1500-1800.* Abridged edition. New York: Harper and Row, 1979.

Symons, D. *The Evolution of Human Sexuality.* New York: Oxford University Press, 1979.

Taylor, G. R. *Sex in History.* London: Thames and Hudson, 1953.

Tribe, L., and M. C. Dorf. *On Reading the Constitution*. Cambridge: Harvard University Press, 1991.

Van Loan, E. M. "Natural Rights and the Ninth Amendment." In *The Rights Retained by the People: The History and Meaning of the Ninth Amendment*, edited by R. E. Barnett. Fairfax, Va.: George Mason University Press, 1989.

Vaugh, K. I. *John Locke: Economist and Social Scientist*. Chicago: University of Chicago Press, 1980.

Weitzer, R. "The Politics of Prostitution in America." In *Sex for Sale*, edited by R. Weitzer. New York: Routledge, 2000.

West, D. J. "Male Homosexual Prostitution in England." In *Prostitution: On Whores, Hustlers, and Johns*, edited by J. E. Elias, V. L. Bullough, V. Elias, and G. Brewer. New York: Prometheus Books, 1998.

Wills, G. *Inventing America: Jefferson's Declaration of Independence*. New York: Vantage, 1979.

Yolton, J. W. *Locke: An Introduction*. Oxford: Blackwell, 1985.

Zall, P. M. *Ben Franklin Laughing: Anecdotes from Original Sources by and about Ben Franklin*. Berkeley: University of California Press, 1980.

Zemel, C. "Private Pleasures: Fischl's Monotypes." In *Scenes and Sequences: Recent Monotypes by Eric Fischl*. New York: Abrams, 1990.

Index

Abortion: *Roe v. Wade* and, 50–52; sexual literacy and, 178–181
Abramson, Paul, 189, 210
Acquired Immune Deficiency Syndrome (AIDS), 120, 177, 183–184
Acton, William, 116
Adams, John, 112
Adams, Samuel, 8
Adler, Polly, 18
Adolescent sexuality, 202–203
Adult-child sex, 85
Adultery, 134–135
AIDS. *See* Acquired Immune Deficiency Syndrome
Alabama, sex toys and, 102–103
Aldridge, A. Own, 5
American Civil Liberties Union (ACLU), 53, 102
American Society for Sanitary and Moral Prophylaxis, 118, 205
Anal intercourse: as non-reproductive sex, 75, 190; sodomy laws and, 12
Anthony, Susan B., 127
Anti-Federalists, 25, 27, 44
Ashcroft v. Free Speech Coalition, 147, 160
Ashwander v. TVA, 187

Baird, William, 62
Barnett, Randy, 30, 38, 79
Barron v. The Mayor and City Council of Baltimore, 40
Beach Boys No. 2, 147–149
Becker, Carl, 35, 192
Bentham, Jeremy, 72
Berger, Raul, 32–33, 191

Bestiality, 109
Bill of Rights: amendments of, 2; application to the states, 40–41; due process and, 13, 87–88; Lockean ideal and, 81; opposition to, 7, 22; "penumbras" of, 47, 58; set theory and, 169; threats to liberty and, 83. *See also* Fifth Amendment; Fifteenth Amendment; First Amendment; Fourteenth Amendment; Nineteenth Amendment; Thirteenth Amendment; United States Constitution
Black, Charles, 31–32, 40, 77, 79, 198
Black, Justice Hugo, 49; dissent in *Griswold v. Connecticut*, 60
Blackmun, Justice Harry: dissent in *Bowers v. Hardwick*, 55–56, 82, 107, 194, 196
Blackstone, William, 58
Bliley, Thomas J., 99–100
Bork, Robert, 32, 199
Bowers v. Hardwick: consent and, 107; Ninth Amendment and, 175; privacy and, 15, 45, 52–56, 57; sodomy and, 13, 53–56; Supreme Court decision in, 12, 53–56, 89, 108–109
Boyd v. United States, 48
Brandeis, Justice Louis, 73
Brennan, Justice William: on *FCC v. Pacifica Foundation*, 98; in *Eisenstadt v. Baird*, 189
Brothels, 112
Brown v. Board of Education, 108
Buck v. Bell, 59
Burger, Chief Justice Warren, decision in *Bowers v. Hardwick*, 12, 53–54
Butler, Tom, 202

About the Authors

PAUL R. ABRAMSON, Professor of Psychology at UCLA, is one of the world's leading sex researchers. He is the author (or editor) of eight books, including (with Steven Pinkerton) *With Pleasure: Thoughts on the Nature of Human Sexuality; Sexual Nature/Sexual Culture;* and *A House Divided: Suspicions of Mother-Daughter Incest.* He is also the author of more than one hundred scientific publications.

STEVEN D. PINKERTON is a sexuality researcher and a leading expert in HIV/AIDS prevention. He is Associate Professor of Psychiatry and Behavioral Medicine at the Medical College of Wisconsin, where he directs the Cost-Effectiveness Studies Core at the Center for AIDS Intervention Research (CAIR). He has written several books and approximately one hundred scholarly publications on HIV prevention, human sexuality, and other topics.

MARK HUPPIN received his J.D. from Stanford Law School. He has worked as an attorney at Gray, Cary, Ware, and Freidenrich in Palo Alto, California, and is currently pursuing his Ph.D. in psychology at UCLA, specializing in issues of sex and gender. During a stint in Hollywood between his law and psychology careers, he co-wrote and co-directed the feature film *The Idea of Sex* (a.k.a. *Nothing Sacred*). This is his first book.